Christmas 1987

Comfort & Joy

Heritage House INC.

THE SOUTHWESTERN COMPANY

Nashville, Tennessee

Christmas
1987
Comfort & Joy

Copyright © 1987 by Heritage House, Inc.
Publishing division of The Southwestern Company
P.O. Box 820, Nashville, Tennessee 37202

Conceived, edited and published
under the direction of:

Ralph Mosley   Chairman of the Board
Thomas Milam   President and Publisher
Betty Ann Jones   Vice President, Marketing
Ron Hartman   Director of Fulfillment

Christmas 1987
Editor-In-Chief: Mary Jane Blount
Creative Director: Philip Sankey
Art Director: Steve Newman
Contributing Editor: Joan Dew
Crafts Editor: Mary Jo Sherrill
Editors: Georgia Brazil, Mary Cummings,
    Jane Hinshaw, Barbara Peeler, Mary Wilson
Editorial Assistants: Gail Anderson, Paula Cometto,
    Donna Edwards, June Fisher, Julia Harris,
    Jackie Langlois, Debbie Seigenthaler, Paul Stansberry
Test Kitchens: Nancy Lacey, Sam Routh
Illustrator: Barbara Ball
Production: John Moulton, Teresa Fitzgerald
Typographer: William Maul

Library of Congress Catalog Number 87-7478
ISBN: 0-87197-222-0

Manufactured in the United States of America
First Edition. First Printing, 1987.

Contents

Comfort & Joy

Introduction

*we bring you good
" . . . tidings of comfort and joy . . ."*

Christmas 1987 is for all those who cherish everything that is the Christmas season: a time for sharing and giving comfort and joy . . . for bringing and keeping the family closer together . . . for renewing and strengthening friendships.

It is a book for those who take pride and pleasure in making things: presents and stocking stuffers . . . foods for gift-giving and festive occasions . . . holiday decorations and ornaments . . . cards and gift-tags.

It is also for those who want to control the expenses of their Christmas without cutting back on the joy. It is a planning book and a keepsake heirloom.

The Southwestern Company has been dedicated to serving and preserving the traditions and values of the American family for over a century. Our readership has been more than generous with us—buying books from our door-to-door student dealers each summer and our unique books and collectibles through the mail from Heritage House.

Through the publishing of this book, we hope to partially repay our readers' generosity to us. We will feel successful if this annual Christmas volume becomes a part of the Christmas traditions of your family . . . a series of family heirlooms filled with personal Christmas memories.

We hope you will treasure *Comfort & Joy* and then hand it down to your sons and daughters in the well-worn state good books acquire, adding to your family history for future generations.

Christmas 1987 has been an undertaking of great significance for us. Writers, editors, designers, researchers, photographers, and cooks have written and edited, designed and illustrated, stitched and glued, tested and tasted to the limits of their professional skills and abilities.

We have a lot of faith in these results. From test kitchen, sewing room, desk, and typewriter, we would like to say to all of those who have provided, and will continue to provide, comfort and joy to their families and friends, "Merry Christmas!"

Holiday Cheer From The Kitchen

At Christmas the happiest room in the home is the kitchen. It is the center of activity for everyone in the family where some are busily making Christmas gifts, putting together cranberry garlands for the tree, or preparing festive holiday dinners that make this season so special. Others, drawn there by the irresistible aromas, appear only to snatch a freshly baked cookie or to dip a finger in the frosting bowl before the last spoonful goes on the cake.

At our house, the Christmas feast was often three days in the making and another three in the eating! There was always roast turkey with apple or chestnut stuffing and baked ham or roast beef as well. The table was laden with favorite salads, vegetables, and desserts. Leftovers never had a chance to make it to the freezer! Since today there is often less time to spend on preparations, a budget to be considered, or a smaller family, the menus in this chapter include helpful new ideas to meet these special needs. Any Christmas dinner, traditional or not, should be a celebration reflecting the festive and joyous spirit of the holiday season.

In our kitchen there was a big table where we ate most of our family meals. But in the weeks leading up to Christmas, that big table became laden with breads and cakes, tins of cookies and candies, and jars of jellies, preserves, pickles, and relishes.

In those days homemade food gifts were exchanged. It did not matter if you received the same thing you gave—a jar of peach preserves or a loaf of banana-nut bread—because no two cooks made these just alike. It was always fun to compare your recipe to a neighbor's. The reusable containers such as baskets, bowls, and jars were an added benefit.

My grandmother loved giving homemade food gifts because they were also a gift of her talent and love. And in today's fast-paced, high-tech world, where so few of us have the time, homemade gifts and decorations from the kitchen are all the more special.

Decorating for the holidays can be as simple or as elegant as you wish. A centerpiece of shiny red apples can be quite lovely (page 24) in addition to filling the air with a fresh, clean aroma. Or, making a Sugarplum Cookie Tree (pages 2 and 71) can be a fun-filled project the entire family will enjoy.

You do not have to spend hours baking to give a present from the kitchen. This chapter includes gift ideas that require no cooking at all and others that take just a short time. The most important thing is not how many hours you spend preparing a gift from your kitchen but that you care enough to give a little bit of yourself.

Gift Ideas From The Kitchen

HOLLY WREATHS

1 cup shortening
3 ounces cream cheese, softened
½ cup sugar
1 teaspoon vanilla extract
1 cup sifted all-purpose flour
2 drops of green food coloring

- Preheat oven to 375 degrees.
- Cream shortening, cream cheese and sugar in mixer bowl until light and fluffy.
- Blend in vanilla. Add flour gradually, mixing well after each addition. Tint with food coloring.
- Fill cookie press fitted with number-2 star plate. Hold press at 45-degree angle. Pipe dough into circles on ungreased cookie sheet.
- Bake for 8 to 10 minutes or until set. Cool on wire rack. Decorate with frosting leaves and red cinnamon candies if desired.
- Yield: 4 dozen.

HOLIDAY FLORENTINES

½ cup butter or margarine
½ cup sugar
2 tablespoons honey
½ cup sliced almonds
⅓ cup chopped candied cherries
⅓ cup chopped candied orange peel
1 cup all-purpose flour, sifted
⅔ cup semisweet chocolate chips

- Preheat oven to 350 degrees.
- Combine butter, sugar and honey in saucepan. Cook over low heat until butter melts. Remove from heat.
- Stir in almonds, cherries, orange peel and flour. Drop by heaping teaspoonfuls onto parchment-lined cookie sheet.
- Bake for 10 minutes. Cool on cookie sheet.
- Melt chocolate chips in double boiler pan over hot water. Turn cookies over. Spread chocolate on bottoms of cookies. Make wavy pattern in chocolate with fork. Let stand until chocolate is set.
- Yield: 1½ dozen.

CHEERY CHOCOLATE COOKIES

⅔ cup butter or margarine, softened
¾ cup sugar
1 egg
1½ teaspoons vanilla extract
1⅔ cups all-purpose flour
6 tablespoons cocoa
¼ teaspoon baking powder
¼ teaspoon soda
⅛ teaspoon salt
36 candied cherry halves
½ cup semisweet chocolate chips

- Preheat oven to 350 degrees.
- Cream butter, sugar, egg and vanilla in bowl until light and fluffy. Add mixture of flour, cocoa, baking powder, soda and salt; mix well.
- Shape into 1-inch balls. Place 1 inch apart on ungreased cookie sheet. Press cherry half into center of each cookie.
- Bake for 8 minutes.
- Melt chocolate chips in double boiler pan over hot water. Spoon around tops of cookies, leaving cherries unfrosted. Cool on wire rack.
- Yield: 3 dozen.

BUTTER KISSES

½ cup butter or margarine, softened	⅛ teaspoon salt
½ cup sugar	1¼ cups all-purpose flour
1 egg	½ cup finely ground nuts
1 teaspoon vanilla extract	30 milk chocolate kisses
¼ teaspoon soda	

■ Preheat oven to 350 degrees.
■ Cream butter, sugar, egg and vanilla in bowl until light and fluffy. Add mixture of soda, salt and flour; mix well.
■ Shape into 1-inch balls. Roll in nuts. Place on ungreased cookie sheet.
■ Bake for 8 minutes or until almost set. Press chocolate kiss into center of each cookie. Bake for 2 minutes longer. Cool on wire rack.
■ Yield: 3 dozen.

PEANUT BUTTER FOLDOVERS

1 to 1½ cups semisweet miniature chocolate chips	1 cup butter or margarine, softened
¾ cup peanut butter	6 ounces cream cheese, softened
½ cup confectioners' sugar	2½ cups all-purpose flour
½ cup chopped unsalted peanuts	

■ Melt chocolate chips in double boiler pan over hot water. Blend in peanut butter; remove from heat. Stir in confectioners' sugar and peanuts.
■ Cream butter and cream cheese in mixer bowl until light and fluffy. Mix in flour. Divide into 2 portions. Chill, wrapped in plastic wrap, for several minutes.
■ Preheat oven to 350 degrees.
■ Roll chilled dough into two 12½-inch squares on lightly floured surface. Cut each into twenty-five 2½-inch squares. Place 2 teaspoons filling in center of each square. Fold 2 corners to center to partially enclose filling; press corners to seal. Place ½ inch apart on ungreased cookie sheet.
■ Bake for 15 minutes or until light brown. Cool on wire rack.
■ Yield: 4 dozen.

MACAROONS

2 ounces semisweet chocolate	¼ teaspoon salt
2⅔ cups flaked coconut	4 egg whites
⅔ cup sugar	1 teaspoon almond extract
6 tablespoons all-purpose flour	18 whole almonds
	18 maraschino cherries

■ Preheat oven to 325 degrees.
■ Melt chocolate in small double boiler pan over hot water.
■ Combine coconut, sugar, flour and salt in bowl. Add egg whites and almond extract; mix well. Fold in melted chocolate.
■ Drop by teaspoonfuls onto lightly greased cookie sheet. Top each cookie with almond or maraschino cherry.
■ Bake for 20 minutes or until firm. Remove to wire rack to cool completely.
■ Yield: 3 dozen.
■ Note: May omit chocolate and add ⅓ cup mixed candied fruit before baking.

HAZELNUT SHORTBREAD

⅓ cup chopped hazelnuts (filberts)	½ cup sugar
1¼ cups butter or margarine, softened	2 cups all-purpose flour
	1 cup cornstarch

■ Preheat oven to 325 degrees.
■ Process hazelnuts in blender or food processor until finely ground.
■ Cream butter and sugar in mixer bowl until light and fluffy. Add mixture of flour, cornstarch and nuts; mix well. Divide into 6 portions.
■ Roll each portion into 6-inch circle on ungreased cookie sheet. Smooth edges with fingers.
■ Score each circle into 8 wedges with spatula. Press edges with fork.
■ Bake for 35 minutes or until light brown. Cool on cookie sheet on wire rack. Break into wedges. Store in tightly covered container.
■ Yield: 4 dozen wedges.
■ Note: May use pecans, walnuts, almonds or hickory nuts in place of hazelnuts.

NUTTY BUTTERY GEMS

1 cup all-purpose flour	2 tablespoons rum
¼ cup sugar	⅔ cup finely chopped
¼ teaspoon salt	pecans
½ cup butter or	12 whole candied
margarine, softened	cherries
1 egg, separated	12 pecan halves

■ Preheat oven to 350 degrees.
■ Combine flour, sugar and salt in bowl. Cut in butter until crumbly. Add beaten egg yolk and 1 tablespoon rum; mix well.
■ Cover dough tightly. Chill until firm.
■ Beat egg white and remaining 1 tablespoon rum until blended.
■ Shape chilled dough into ¾-inch balls. Dip into egg white mixture; roll in chopped pecans.
■ Place 2 inches apart on ungreased cookie sheet. Press cherry or pecan half into each cookie.
■ Bake for 13 to 15 minutes or until golden. Cool on wire rack.
■ Yield: 2 dozen.

OATMEAL TEA WAFERS

1 egg white	½ cup sugar
½ cup Mazola corn oil	1 cup quick-cooking oats
1 teaspoon vanilla	½ cup sifted all-purpose
extract	flour

■ Preheat oven to 375 degrees.
■ Combine egg white, corn oil, vanilla and sugar in mixer bowl. Beat at medium speed until thick.
■ Add mixture of oats and flour gradually, beating constantly at low speed until well mixed.
■ Drop by level teaspoonfuls 3 inches apart onto foil-lined cookie sheet. Spread into 1½-inch circles with spatula.
■ Bake for 8 minutes or until light brown. Cool on foil on wire rack. Store in airtight container.
■ Yield: 4 dozen.

PEANUTTY BROWNIE BARS

¾ cup melted butter or	½ cup sugar
margarine	½ cup water
½ cup cocoa	2 cups peanut butter
1½ cups sugar	chips
1½ teaspoons vanilla	½ cup semisweet
extract	chocolate chips
3 eggs	1 tablespoon shortening
1¼ cups all-purpose	¼ teaspoon vanilla
flour	extract

■ Preheat oven to 350 degrees. Line 10x15-inch baking pan with greased foil.
■ Combine butter and cocoa in bowl; mix well. Add 1½ cups sugar and 1½ teaspoons vanilla; mix well.
■ Add eggs 1 at a time, beating well after each addition. Stir in flour. Spread in prepared pan.
■ Bake for 12 minutes. Cool for 2 minutes. Invert onto wire rack; peel off foil. Cool completely.
■ Combine ½ cup sugar and water in saucepan. Bring to a boil; remove from heat. Add peanut butter chips; stir until chips melt. Cool slightly.
■ Cut baked layer into two 7½x10-inch layers. Spread peanut butter mixture between and on top of layers.
■ Combine chocolate chips and shortening in double boiler pan. Heat over hot water until melted. Stir in ¼ teaspoon vanilla. Drizzle over brownie layers. Let stand until set. Cut into bars.
■ Yield: 3 dozen.

MINTY GLAZED BROWNIES

2 ounces unsweetened	½ cup butter or
chocolate	margarine, softened
½ cup butter or	3 cups confectioners'
margarine	sugar
2 eggs	5 tablespoons cream
1 cup sugar	½ teaspoon peppermint
1 teaspoon vanilla	extract
extract	½ ounce unsweetened
½ cup all-purpose flour	chocolate
¼ teaspoon salt	½ teaspoon butter or
½ cup chopped nuts	margarine

■ Preheat oven to 350 degrees.
■ Melt 2 ounces chocolate with ½ cup butter in double boiler pan over hot water.
■ Beat eggs in mixer bowl until light. Add sugar gradually, beating constantly. Blend in chocolate and vanilla.
■ Add mixture of flour and salt; mix well. Stir in nuts. Spread in greased 8x8-inch baking pan.
■ Bake for 20 minutes or just until brownies begin to pull from sides of pan. Cool in pan.
■ Cream ½ cup butter and confectioners' sugar in mixer bowl until light and fluffy. Add cream and flavoring. Spread over brownies. Chill until firm.
■ Melt ½ ounce chocolate and ½ teaspoon butter in double boiler pan over hot water. Drizzle over brownies. Chill until set. Cut into squares.
■ Yield: 20 brownies.

MERRY CHERRY BARS

1 cup butter or margarine, softened	¾ cup finely chopped red candied cherries
1 cup sugar	⅓ cup chopped green M and M's plain chocolate candies
1 egg	
½ teaspoon almond extract	
2 cups all-purpose flour	1 cup sifted confectioners' sugar
¼ teaspoon salt	5 teaspoons water

■ Preheat oven to 300 degrees.
■ Cream butter and sugar in bowl until light and fluffy. Add egg and flavoring; mix well.
■ Add mixture of flour and salt; mix well. Add cherries; mix gently.
■ Spread evenly in greased 10 x 15-inch baking pan. Sprinkle candies over top.
■ Bake for 30 minutes or until golden. Cool.
■ Blend confectioners' sugar and water in bowl. Drizzle over baked layer. Cut into bars.
■ Yield: 5 dozen.

MARVEL BARS

½ cup butter or margarine, softened	1 cup quick-cooking oats
	¼ cup chopped nuts
1 cup packed light brown sugar	⅓ cup chopped M and M's plain chocolate candies
1 egg	
2 tablespoons orange juice	¼ cup chopped nuts
1½ cups all-purpose flour	½ cup orange marmalade
1 teaspoon baking powder	¼ cup flaked coconut
	⅓ cup chopped M and M's plain chocolate candies
½ teaspoon salt	
¼ teaspoon soda	

■ Preheat oven to 350 degrees.
■ Cream butter and brown sugar in bowl until light and fluffy. Blend in egg and orange juice.
■ Add mixture of flour, baking powder, salt and soda; mix well. Add oats, ¼ cup nuts and ⅓ cup candies; mix well.
■ Spread half the dough evenly in lightly greased 9 x 13-inch baking pan.
■ Combine remaining ¼ cup nuts, marmalade and coconut in bowl. Spread over dough. Drop remaining dough by rounded teaspoonfuls over marmalade. Sprinkle with ⅓ cup candies.
■ Bake for 25 minutes or until golden brown. Cool on wire rack. Cut into bars.
■ Yield: 4 dozen.

TUTTI-FRUTTI BARS

½ cup butter or margarine, softened	1 tablespoon melted butter or margarine
¾ cup packed light brown sugar	½ teaspoon vanilla extract
1 egg	1 egg
½ teaspoon vanilla extract	⅓ cup all-purpose flour
1¼ cups all-purpose flour	½ teaspoon soda
	¼ teaspoon salt
½ teaspoon soda	1 cup candied fruit
½ teaspoon salt	¾ cup semisweet chocolate chips
2 tablespoons sugar	
2 tablespoons milk	½ cup chopped nuts

■ Preheat oven to 350 degrees.
■ Cream first 4 ingredients in bowl until light and fluffy. Add mixture of 1¼ cups flour, ½ teaspoon soda and ½ teaspoon salt; mix well. Spread in greased 9 x 13-inch baking pan.
■ Bake for 12 minutes or until light brown. Cool.
■ Combine sugar, milk, 1 tablespoon butter, ½ teaspoon vanilla extract and 1 egg in small bowl; mix well. Stir in ⅓ cup flour, ½ teaspoon soda and ¼ teaspoon salt. Spread over baked layer. Sprinkle remaining ingredients over top.
■ Bake for 15 minutes. Cool completely. Cut into 1 x 2-inch bars.
■ Yield: 2 dozen.

SUGAR AND SPICE SNAPS

¾ cup butter or margarine, softened	2 teaspoons soda
	¼ teaspoon salt
1 cup sugar	1 teaspoon cinnamon
1 egg	½ teaspoon nutmeg
¼ cup molasses	1 cup confectioners' sugar
2 cups all-purpose flour	

■ Preheat oven to 350 degrees.
■ Cream butter and sugar in bowl until light and fluffy. Add egg and molasses; mix well.
■ Add mixture of flour, soda, salt and spices; mix well. Chill, covered, for 1 hour.
■ Shape into ¾-inch balls. Place 2 inches apart on greased cookie sheet.
■ Bake for 8 minutes. Remove to wire rack; cool slightly. Sprinkle with confectioners' sugar.
■ Yield: 6½ dozen.

Attach cookie cutter and recipe to wrapped cookies with bow for special gifts.

GERMAN CHOCOLATE CAKE

1 (18-ounce) German chocolate cake mix with pudding	⅓ cup milk
1 cup sour cream	¼ cup butter or margarine
3 eggs	1 (11-ounce) package coconut-pecan frosting mix
1 cup water	

■ Combine cake mix, sour cream, eggs and water in bowl; mix well.
■ Pour into greased microwave tube or bundt pan.
■ Combine milk and butter in glass bowl. Microwave on High (600 to 700 watts) for 1 minute. Stir in coconut-pecan frosting mix.
■ Spoon frosting mixture in circle over top of cake batter. Do not allow frosting to touch side of pan. Cover with waxed paper.
■ Place on inverted saucer in microwave oven. Microwave on Medium-High for 12 minutes or until cake tests almost done.
■ Let stand in pan for 10 minutes. Invert onto cake plate. Frosting will be on top.
■ Yield: 8 to 10 servings.

CANDLELIGHT FRUITCAKE

2½ cups sifted all-purpose flour	2 cups chopped candied pineapple
1 teaspoon salt	2 cups chopped mixed candied fruit
1 teaspoon baking powder	1¼ cups shortening
1 teaspoon cinnamon	1¼ cups honey
½ teaspoon nutmeg	6 eggs
½ teaspoon ginger	½ cup pecan halves
2 cups chopped pecans	½ cup whole candied cherries
2 cups dark seedless raisins	½ cup mixed dark and golden raisins
2 cups golden seedless raisins	½ cup candied pineapple tidbits
1 cup candied cherry halves	½ cup light corn syrup

■ Preheat oven to 250 degrees.
■ Line bottom of greased 10-inch tube pan (not fluted) with 2 layers of greased waxed paper.
■ Sift flour, salt, baking powder and spices into bowl. Combine ½ cup sifted mixture with 2 cups pecans and next 5 fruits in bowl; mix well.
■ Cream shortening and honey in mixer bowl until light and fluffy. Add eggs 1 at a time, beating well after each addition. Add remaining sifted mixture; mix well. Fold in floured fruit. Spoon into tube pan.
■ Place shallow pan of hot water on bottom oven rack. Place tube pan on center rack.

■ Bake for 3 hours and 15 minutes.
■ Combine pecan halves, whole cherries, mixed raisins and candied pineapple tidbits in bowl.
■ Bring corn syrup to a boil in saucepan. Cook for 1½ minutes. Add to fruit mixture, toss to coat fruit. Arrange fruit on partially baked fruitcake.
■ Bake for 45 minutes longer or until fruitcake is firm but not dry. Cool completely in pan. Invert onto cake plate; remove waxed paper. Turn cake decorated side up.
■ Store, tightly covered, in refrigerator.
■ Yield: 20 servings.

ITALIAN CREAM CAKE

½ cup butter or margarine, softened	1 teaspoon soda
½ cup shortening	1 cup buttermilk
2 cups sugar	1 teaspoon vanilla extract
5 eggs, separated	1 cup chopped pecans
2 cups all-purpose flour	2 cups flaked coconut

■ Preheat oven to 350 degrees.
■ Cream butter, shortening and sugar in mixer bowl until light and fluffy.
■ Add egg yolks 1 at a time, beating well after each addition.
■ Add mixture of flour and soda alternately with buttermilk, mixing well after each addition. Blend in vanilla. Fold in pecans and 1 cup coconut.
■ Beat egg whites until stiff peaks form. Fold gently into batter.
■ Pour into 3 greased and floured 8 or 9-inch round cake pans.
■ Bake for 20 to 30 minutes or until layers test done. Cool in pans for 10 minutes. Remove to wire rack to cool completely.
■ Spread frosting between layers and over top and side of cake. Sprinkle with 1 cup coconut.
■ Yield: 12 to 16 servings.

Cream Cheese Frosting

¼ cup butter or margarine, softened	1½ teaspoons vanilla extract
8 ounces cream cheese, softened	2 (16-ounce) packages confectioners' sugar
1 egg, beaten	1 to 2 tablespoons cream

■ Cream butter, cream cheese, egg and vanilla in mixer bowl until light and fluffy.
■ Add confectioners' sugar gradually, beating well after each addition.
■ Add enough cream 1 teaspoon at a time to make of spreading consistency.

OLD-FASHIONED JAM CAKE

2 cups sugar	1 cup pear preserves
4 eggs	1 cup blackberry jam
1 teaspoon allspice	1 cup seedless raisins
1 teaspoon cinnamon	1 cup chopped nuts
1 teaspoon nutmeg	1½ cups sour cream
1 cup peach preserves	1 tablespoon soda
1 cup strawberry	4 cups all-purpose flour
preserves	1 cup buttermilk

- Preheat oven to 325 degrees.
- Line 5 greased 8-inch round cake pans with greased waxed paper.
- Combine sugar, eggs and spices in mixer bowl. Beat until light and fluffy. Add preserves, jam, raisins and nuts; mix well.
- Combine sour cream and soda. Add to jam mixture alternately with flour and buttermilk, mixing well after each addition.
- Pour into prepared cake pans.
- Bake for 35 to 45 minutes or until layers test done. Cover with foil to prevent overbrowning if necessary. Cool in pans for 10 minutes. Invert onto wire rack to cool completely.
- Spread icing between layers and over top and side of cake. Store in freezer if desired.
- Yield: 16 to 20 servings.

Creamy Caramel Icing

2 cups butter	1 cup milk
4 cups packed light	8 cups (about) sifted
brown sugar	confectioners' sugar

- Melt butter in saucepan. Stir in brown sugar.
- Bring to a boil. Cook over low heat for 2 minutes, stirring constantly.
- Stir in milk. Bring to a boil, stirring constantly. Cool to lukewarm.
- Add confectioners' sugar gradually, beating constantly until of spreading consistency.

PRALINE POUND CAKE

1 cup butter or	½ teaspoon baking
margarine, softened	powder
½ cup shortening	¼ teaspoon soda
1 (16-ounce) package	¾ cup milk
light brown sugar	2 cups chopped pecans
5 eggs	½ cup all-purpose flour
2½ cups all-purpose	2 teaspoons vanilla
flour	extract

- Preheat oven to 350 degrees.
- Cream first 3 ingredients in bowl until light and fluffy.

- Add eggs 1 at a time, beating very well after each addition.
- Combine 2½ cups flour, baking powder and soda. Add to creamed mixture alternately with milk, mixing well after each addition.
- Coat pecans with ½ cup flour. Fold floured pecans into batter. Blend in vanilla.
- Pour into greased and floured tube pan.
- Bake for 1 hour and 10 minutes or until cake tests done. Cool in pan for 10 minutes. Invert onto wire rack to cool completely.
- Yield: 12 to 16 servings.

FRESH COCONUT WREATH CAKE

½ cup (about) dry bread	2½ teaspoons baking
crumbs	powder
1¼ cups butter or	¾ cup milk
margarine, softened	¾ cup fresh coconut
2½ cups sugar	milk
5 eggs	⅔ cup sugar
1 tablespoon freshly	⅓ cup fresh lemon juice
grated lemon rind	1¼ cups freshly grated
2 tablespoons freshly	coconut
grated coconut	3 green grape clusters
3¾ cups sifted cake	3 purple grapes
flour	¼ cup sugar
1 teaspoon salt	3 lemon slices

- Preheat oven to 325 degrees.
- Sprinkle greased tube pan with bread crumbs to coat; set aside. Do not use fluted tube pan.
- Combine butter, 2½ cups sugar, eggs, lemon rind and 2 tablespoons coconut in mixer bowl. Beat at high speed for 3 minutes.
- Sift cake flour, salt and baking powder together. Add to creamed mixture alternately with milk and coconut milk, beating well after each addition.
- Pour into prepared tube pan.
- Bake for 1 hour and 45 minutes or until cake tests done. Cool in pan on wire rack for 15 minutes. Invert onto cake plate.
- Combine ⅔ cup sugar and lemon juice in saucepan. Cook over low heat until sugar dissolves, stirring constantly.
- Brush cake with ¾ of the lemon syrup. Sprinkle 1¼ cups coconut over top of cake.
- Dip grape clusters and grapes in remaining syrup; coat with remaining ¼ cup sugar. Arrange on cake.
- Place twisted lemon slices between grapes. Brush side of cake with remaining syrup.
- Yield: 16 servings.

FOUR BREADS OF CHRISTMAS

Basic Sweet Dough

1½ cups milk, scalded	¾ cup sugar
2 packages dry yeast	3 eggs
1 cup all-purpose flour	¾ teaspoon salt
1½ cups butter or margarine, softened	5 to 7 cups all-purpose flour

- Cool milk to 105 to 115 degrees.
- Add yeast. Let stand for 5 minutes. Add 1 cup flour; mix well. Let stand, covered, for 1 hour.
- Cream butter and sugar in mixer bowl until light and fluffy. Add eggs 1 at a time, beating well after each addition. Add salt and 5 cups flour. Stir in enough remaining flour to make stiff dough.
- Knead on floured surface for 8 to 10 minutes or until smooth and elastic. Place in greased bowl, turning to grease surface. Let rise, covered, in warm place for 1 hour or until doubled in bulk.
- Shape into Almond Loaves, Cherry Swirls, Cranberry Braids or Coffee Cake Wreaths as described below. Place on greased baking sheet. Let rise, covered, for 45 minutes.
- Preheat oven to 350 degrees.
- Bake for 30 to 40 minutes or until golden brown. Cool on wire rack. Decorate as desired.

Almond Loaves

¼ teaspoon cardamom	¼ cup chopped citron
½ cup dark seedless raisins	¼ cup chopped candied cherries
¼ cup chopped blanched almonds	1 recipe Basic Sweet Dough

- Add cardamom, raisins, almonds, citron and cherries to Basic Sweet Dough before kneading. Let rise as described in basic recipe.
- Shape into 3 round loaves. Let rise and bake as described in basic recipe.
- Yield: 3 loaves.

Cherry Swirls

16 ounces cream cheese, softened	1 cup chopped candied red cherries
⅓ cup sugar	1 cup chopped pecans
2 egg yolks	1 recipe Basic Sweet Dough
½ teaspoon vanilla extract	

- Combine cream cheese and sugar in bowl; beat until smooth. Add egg yolks and vanilla; mix well. Stir in cherries and pecans. Chill in refrigerator.
- Shape Basic Sweet Dough into 3 portions after first rising. Roll each into 10 x 12-inch rectangle.
- Spread with cream cheese mixture.

- Roll as for jelly roll from long end. Cut into 1-inch slices. Flatten each slice to 2½-inch circle on greased baking sheet. Let rise for 45 minutes.
- Bake for 12 to 15 minutes. Cool on baking sheet for 10 minutes. Remove to wire rack to cool.
- Yield: 3 dozen.

Cranberry Braids

2 cups ground fresh cranberries	1⅓ cups packed dark brown sugar
1 large orange, seeded, ground	1 recipe Basic Sweet Dough

- Combine cranberries, orange and brown sugar in saucepan. Simmer for 10 to 15 minutes or until thickened, stirring constantly. Cool.
- Shape Basic Sweet Dough by dividing into 3 portions after first rising. Roll each portion into 12-inch square. Cut each square into three 4 x 12-inch strips.
- Spoon cooled cranberry filling onto each strip. Fold to enclose filling; seal edges. Braid 3 strips together; seal ends and tuck under. Repeat with remaining strips. Let rise and bake as described in basic recipe.
- Yield: 3 braids.

Coffee Cake Wreaths

2 cups chopped dried figs	1 recipe Basic Sweet Dough
1½ cups water	1 egg yolk, beaten
½ cup chopped pecans	1 tablespoon milk

- Combine figs and water in saucepan. Bring to a boil; reduce heat. Simmer for 3 minutes or until thickened, stirring constantly. Stir in pecans. Cool.
- Shape Basic Sweet Dough by dividing into 2 portions after first rising. Roll each portion into 12 x 16-inch rectangle. Cut each rectangle into four 3 x 16-inch strips.
- Spread fig filling on strips. Roll each strip as for jelly roll from long side; seal seams. Braid 3 strips together; place in circle on baking sheet. Shape 1 strip into bow at seam of circle. Repeat with remaining strips.
- Let rise for 1 hour. Brush with mixture of egg yolk and milk. Bake as described in basic recipe. Cool on wire racks.
- Yield: 2 coffee cakes.

Glue preruffled trim to underside of wicker plate holder. Trim with bow. Line with Christmas paper plate to hold plastic-wrapped breads.

ORANGE AND CRANBERRY BREAD

1 cup sugar	1 teaspoon baking
¼ cup water	powder
½ cup slivered orange	½ teaspoon soda
rind	1 teaspoon salt
¼ cup butter or	½ cup wheat germ
margarine	1 cup coarsely chopped
1 cup orange juice	fresh cranberries
2 eggs, slightly beaten	1 cup confectioners'
2½ cups sifted	sugar
all-purpose flour	4½ teaspoons milk

■ Preheat oven to 350 degrees.
■ Line bottoms of 2 greased 5 x 9-inch loaf pans with greased waxed paper.
■ Combine sugar, water and orange rind in saucepan. Cook over low heat until sugar dissolves, stirring occasionally. Cook for 5 minutes longer, stirring occasionally. Remove from heat.
■ Stir in butter. Cool slightly. Add orange juice and eggs; mix well.
■ Sift flour, baking powder, soda and salt into bowl. Add wheat germ. Add to liquid ingredients, stirring just until moistened.
■ Fold in cranberries. Pour into prepared loaf pans. Let stand for 20 minutes.
■ Bake for 1 hour. Cool in pans for 10 minutes. Remove to wire rack to cool completely. Drizzle with mixture of confectioners' sugar and milk.
■ Yield: 2 loaves.

COCONUT AND BANANA BREAD

1⅓ cups flaked coconut	1 tablespoon grated
2¾ cups all-purpose	orange rind
flour	1 egg, beaten
1 cup sugar	1½ cups mashed
1 tablespoon baking	bananas
powder	⅓ cup milk
1 teaspoon salt	

■ Preheat oven to 350 degrees.
■ Sprinkle coconut into shallow baking pan. Bake for 7 to 10 minutes or until lightly toasted, stirring every 2 minutes.
■ Sift flour, sugar, baking powder and salt into bowl. Add coconut and orange rind.
■ Combine egg, bananas and milk in small bowl; mix well. Add to dry ingredients; stir just until moistened. Pour into well-greased and floured 5 x 9-inch loaf pan.
■ Bake for 1 hour and 10 minutes or until loaf tests done. Cool in pan for 10 minutes. Remove to wire rack to cool completely.

■ Wrap in plastic wrap. Let stand overnight for improved flavor and easier slicing. Slice thinly. Toast if desired.
■ Yield: 1 loaf.

EGGNOG BREAD

¾ cup sugar	1 teaspoon salt
2 eggs	⅛ teaspoon nutmeg
¼ cup melted butter or	1 cup eggnog
margarine	½ cup raisins
2¼ cups all-purpose	½ cup chopped pecans
flour	½ cup chopped candied
2 teaspoons baking	cherries
powder	

■ Preheat oven to 350 degrees.
■ Combine sugar, eggs and butter in mixer bowl. Beat until light.
■ Mix flour, baking powder, salt and nutmeg. Add to sugar mixture alternately with eggnog, mixing well after each addition. Fold in raisins, pecans and cherries. Pour into well-greased and floured 5 x 9-inch loaf pan.
■ Bake for 1 hour and 10 minutes. Cool in pan for 10 minutes. Remove to wire rack to cool completely. Wrap in plastic wrap.
■ Yield: 1 loaf.

WALDORF LOAF

1 egg, beaten	¼ teaspoon salt
¾ cup sugar	¼ cup milk
½ teaspoon vanilla	4 cups chopped
extract	unpeeled Granny
½ cup mayonnaise	Smith apples
1½ cups all-purpose	½ cup chopped walnuts
flour	¼ cup finely chopped
1 teaspoon soda	celery
1 teaspoon cinnamon	

■ Preheat oven to 350 degrees.
■ Combine first 4 ingredients in bowl; mix well.
■ Mix flour, soda, cinnamon and salt. Add to mayonnaise mixture alternately with milk, mixing well after each addition. Fold in apples, walnuts and celery. Pour into well-greased and floured 5 x 9-inch loaf pan.
■ Bake for 1 hour and 5 minutes or until loaf tests done. Cool in pan for 10 minutes. Remove to wire rack to cool completely. Wrap in plastic wrap. Store in refrigerator.
■ Yield: 1 loaf.

GINGERY SPICE LOAF

1 (14-ounce) package gingerbread mix	6 eggs
1 (18-ounce) package lemon cake mix	1 cup water
1 cup water	1½ cups raisins
	1½ cups chopped nuts

■ Preheat oven to 375 degrees.
■ Combine gingerbread mix, cake mix and 1 cup water in mixer bowl. Beat at medium speed for 2 minutes or until smooth.
■ Add eggs and 1 cup water. Beat at low speed for 1 minute. Beat at medium speed for 1 minute. Fold in raisins and nuts. Pour into 2 greased and floured 5 x 9-inch loaf pans.
■ Bake for 20 to 25 minutes or until loaves test done. Cool in pan for 10 minutes. Remove to wire rack to cool completely.
■ Yield: 2 loaves.

ZUCCHINI BREAD

3 cups all-purpose flour	3 eggs
2¼ cups sugar	1 cup oil
1 teaspoon salt	1½ teaspoons vanilla extract
½ teaspoon baking powder	2 cups grated zucchini
1 teaspoon soda	1 cup finely chopped walnuts
1 teaspoon cinnamon	

■ Preheat oven to 350 degrees.
■ Combine flour, sugar, salt, baking powder, soda and cinnamon in bowl.
■ Combine eggs, oil and vanilla in small bowl; mix well. Add to dry ingredients; mix well. Fold in zucchini and walnuts. Pour into 2 greased and floured 5 x 9-inch loaf pans.
■ Bake for 1 hour or until loaves test done. Cool in pans for 10 minutes. Remove to wire rack to cool completely.
■ Yield: 2 loaves.

SUNSHINE BLUEBERRY LOAF

½ cup melted butter or margarine	1 tablespoon baking powder
1 cup sugar	¼ teaspoon soda
3 eggs	1¼ cups orange juice
2 teaspoons lemon rind	½ cup chopped nuts
3 cups all-purpose flour	1 cup fresh blueberries
1 teaspoon salt	

■ Preheat oven to 350 degrees.
■ Combine butter and sugar in bowl. Add eggs and lemon rind; mix well.

■ Combine flour, salt, baking powder and soda. Add to egg mixture alternately with orange juice, mixing well after each addition. Fold in nuts and blueberries. Pour into well-greased and floured 5 x 9-inch loaf pan.
■ Bake for 1¼ hours or until loaf tests done. Cool in pan for 5 minutes. Remove to wire rack to cool completely. Wrap in plastic wrap.
■ Yield: 1 loaf.

STRAWBERRY BREAD

3 cups all-purpose flour	1 cup oil
1 teaspoon soda	3 (10-ounce) packages frozen strawberries
½ teaspoon salt	1 cup unsalted butter or margarine, softened
1 teaspoon cinnamon	½ cup confectioners' sugar
2 cups sugar	
3 eggs, beaten	

■ Preheat oven to 350 degrees.
■ Combine flour, soda, salt, cinnamon and sugar in bowl. Combine eggs, oil and 2 packages thawed strawberries; mix well. Add to dry ingredients; mix well. Pour into 2 greased and floured 5 x 9-inch loaf pans.
■ Bake for 1 hour or until loaves test done. Cool in pans for 10 minutes. Remove to wire rack to cool completely.
■ Combine remaining 1 package thawed strawberries, butter and confectioners' sugar in bowl; mix well. Serve with strawberry bread.
■ Yield: 2 loaves.

PUMPKIN MUFFINS

2 cups all-purpose flour	1 cup canned pumpkin
½ cup packed dark brown sugar	½ cup Mazola corn oil
1 teaspoon soda	2 tablespoons honey
½ teaspoon cinnamon	½ cup water
¼ teaspoon ginger	⅓ cup coarsely chopped walnuts
⅛ teaspoon nutmeg	

■ Preheat oven to 350 degrees.
■ Combine flour, brown sugar, soda and spices in large bowl.
■ Combine pumpkin, oil, honey and water in small bowl; mix well. Add to flour mixture; stir just until moistened. Fold in walnuts. Spoon into greased or paper-lined muffin cups.
■ Bake for 35 minutes or until muffins test done. Remove from pan immediately. Serve warm.
■ Yield: 1 dozen.

FOREVER AMBERS

1 (16-ounce) package
  orange slice candy,
  chopped
1 (14-ounce) can
  sweetened condensed
  milk
1 cup chopped pecans

1 (4-ounce) can flaked
  coconut
1 teaspoon orange
  extract
2 cups confectioners'
  sugar

- Preheat oven to 300 degrees.
- Combine orange candy, sweetened condensed milk, pecans, coconut and orange extract in bowl; mix well. Spoon into baking dish.
- Bake for 20 minutes or until mixture bubbles.
- Stir in confectioners' sugar until smooth. Drop by teaspoonfuls onto waxed paper-lined surface. Let stand until firm.
- Yield: 2 dozen.

IMPOSSIBLE FUDGE

1 cup butter or
  margarine
8 ounces Velveeta
  cheese
½ cup cocoa

2 (16-ounce) packages
  confectioners' sugar
1½ teaspoons vanilla
  extract
1 cup chopped pecans

- Combine butter and cheese in double boiler pan. Cook over hot water until melted.
- Sift cocoa and confectioners' sugar into large bowl. Add cheese mixture and vanilla; mix quickly.
- Spread in buttered 9 x 13-inch dish. Sprinkle pecans on top. Let stand until firm. Cut into squares or diamonds.
- Yield: 3 pounds.

PEPPERMINT CRUNCHIES

½ cup evaporated milk
½ cup sugar
1 tablespoon light
  corn syrup
1 cup semisweet
  chocolate chips

½ cup coarsely chopped
  peppermint stick
  candy
1 cup chopped nuts
¼ teaspoon peppermint
  extract

- Mix evaporated milk, sugar and corn syrup in saucepan. Bring to a boil, stirring constantly.
- Cook for 2 minutes, stirring constantly; remove from heat. Add chocolate chips; stir until chocolate is melted.
- Cool for 10 minutes. Stir in peppermint candy, nuts and flavoring. Drop by teaspoonfuls onto waxed paper-lined surface. Let stand until firm.
- Yield: 2 dozen.

HOLIDAY TOFFEE

½ cup boiling water
1 cup packed light
  brown sugar
1 cup sugar
⅓ cup light corn syrup
⅛ teaspoon salt

⅓ cup butter
1 cup semisweet
  chocolate chips,
  melted
¾ cup chopped toasted
  almonds

- Combine boiling water, brown sugar, sugar, corn syrup and salt in saucepan. Stir until sugars are completely dissolved.
- Cook, covered, over high heat for 2 minutes or until steam washes sugar crystals from side of pan.
- Cook, uncovered, to 240 degrees on candy thermometer, firm-ball stage; do not stir.
- Add butter. Cook to 300 degrees on candy thermometer, hard-crack stage; do not stir.
- Pour into lightly buttered 9 x 13-inch dish. Let stand until firm. Blot with paper towel. Spread half the melted chocolate over top; sprinkle with half the almonds.
- Let stand until chocolate is set. Invert onto waxed paper-lined surface; blot with paper towel. Spread with remaining chocolate; sprinkle with remaining almonds.
- Let stand until chocolate is set. Break into pieces.
- Yield: 2 pounds.

PEANUT BUTTER PINWHEELS

4½ cups sugar
1 (12-ounce) can
  evaporated milk
1 (7-ounce) jar
  marshmallow creme
¼ cup butter or
  margarine

2 cups peanut butter
  chips
¼ cup melted butter or
  margarine
½ cup cocoa
1 teaspoon vanilla
  extract

- Combine sugar, evaporated milk, marshmallow creme and ¼ cup butter in 4-quart saucepan. Bring to a boil over medium heat, stirring constantly. Cook for 5 minutes, stirring constantly.
- Combine half the hot mixture with 1 cup peanut butter chips in bowl. Stir until peanut butter chips melt. Spread in foil-lined 9 x 13-inch dish.
- Combine remaining hot mixture with 1 cup peanut butter chips, ¼ cup melted butter, cocoa and vanilla in bowl. Beat until peanut butter chips melt and mixture is thickened. Spread over peanut butter layer. Let stand until firm.
- Invert onto foil-lined surface. Roll as for jelly roll from long side. Let stand until firm. Cut into slices. Store in airtight container.
- Yield: 4 pounds.

COCONUT GRANOLA SNACK

2⅔ cups flaked coconut	¼ cup chopped prunes
1 cup quick-cooking oats	2 tablespoons sesame
¼ cup packed light	seed
brown sugar	¼ cup oil
¼ cup chopped dried	¼ cup honey
apricots	¼ cup seedless raisins

■ Combine coconut, oats, brown sugar, apricots, prunes and sesame seed in large bowl; mix well.
■ Mix oil and honey in saucepan. Bring to a boil over medium heat. Pour over fruit mixture; mix well. Spread evenly in 10 x 15-inch baking pan.
■ Bake at 325 degrees for 30 minutes, stirring frequently; do not brown. Stir in raisins.
■ Let stand until cool, stirring occasionally to break granola apart. Store in airtight container.
■ Yield: 7 cups.

PECAN CANDY LOGS

1 (7-ounce) jar	1 (14-ounce) package
marshmallow creme	light caramels
1 (16-ounce) package	3 tablespoons
confectioners' sugar	evaporated milk
1 tablespoon vanilla	3 cups finely chopped
extract	pecans

■ Combine marshmallow creme and confectioners' sugar in bowl or plastic bag; mix well. Mixture will be stiff and dry. Add vanilla. Knead until mixture holds together.
■ Shape into four 1½-inch diameter logs. Place in waxed paper-lined dish. Freeze for 1 hour.
■ Combine caramels and evaporated milk in double boiler pan. Cook over hot water until caramels melt; mix well.
■ Dip marshmallow rolls in caramel mixture to coat or spoon caramel over rolls. Coat with pecans.
■ Let stand until caramel is cool. Chill until firm. Store, wrapped in plastic wrap, in refrigerator. Cut into slices.
■ Yield: 3 pounds.

Package wrapped pecan logs in cardboard tubing cut to fit. Wrap and tie ends with ribbon.

PICKLED ASPARAGUS

2 pounds fresh asparagus	2 cloves of garlic
4 sprigs of fresh dillweed	2½ cups white wine vinegar
½ teaspoon cayenne pepper	¼ cup salt
	2½ cups water
	½ cup light corn syrup

■ Wash asparagus; drain. Trim asparagus spears to fit glass jars, removing tough portions of stalks.
■ Pack asparagus spears vertically into hot sterilized jars, leaving 1-inch headspace. Place 2 sprigs of fresh dillweed between asparagus and side of jar. Add ¼ teaspoon cayenne pepper and 1 clove of garlic to each jar.
■ Combine wine vinegar, salt, water and corn syrup in saucepan. Bring to a boil. Pour into jars, leaving ½-inch headspace; seal. Refrigerate for several weeks. Rinse before serving.
■ Yield: 2 (1-quart) jars.

SWEET AND SOUR PINEAPPLE PICKLES

2 medium fresh pineapples	2 cups water
2 cups packed light brown sugar	1 3-inch stick cinnamon
1 cup cider vinegar	2 tablespoons whole cloves

■ Peel pineapple; remove core. Cut into spears.
■ Combine brown sugar, cider vinegar and water in large saucepan. Tie cinnamon stick and cloves in cheesecloth. Add to mixture. Bring to a boil. Cook for 5 minutes. Add pineapple.
■ Simmer, covered, for 5 minutes. Remove spice bag. Pack pineapple into hot sterilized jars, leaving ½-inch headspace; seal with 2-piece lids. Process in boiling water bath for 15 minutes.
■ Yield: 3 (1-pint) jars.

EASY SPICED FRUIT

2 (29-ounce) cans pears	¼ teaspoon salt
2 (29-ounce) cans peach halves	1 teaspoon whole allspice
½ cup cider vinegar	¼ teaspoon whole cloves
⅓ cup packed dark brown sugar	1 cup maraschino cherries
4 2-inch sticks cinnamon	

■ Drain fruit, reserving syrup from 1 can pears and 1 can peaches. Combine reserved syrup with cider vinegar, brown sugar, cinnamon sticks and salt in large saucepan.

■ Tie allspice and cloves in cheesecloth. Add to saucepan. Bring mixture to a boil over high heat. Cook for 5 minutes. Add drained pears, peaches and cherries.
■ Reduce heat to low. Cook for 10 minutes; do not boil. Cool. Remove spice bag.
■ Spoon fruit and cinnamon sticks into sterilized glass jars. Pour syrup over fruit; seal.
■ Refrigerate for 24 hours before serving. May store in refrigerator for several weeks.
■ Yield: 5 (1-pint) jars.

FRESH VEGETABLE JARDINIÈRE

2 carrots	3 tablespoons mixed whole pickling spices
3 turnips	1 bay leaf
3 stalks celery	1 clove of garlic
2 bunches radishes	2¼ cups white vinegar
1 head cauliflower	3 cups water
1 bunch broccoli	1½ cups sugar
1 red onion, thinly sliced	1½ teaspoons salt

■ Peel and slice carrots and turnips. Slice celery diagonally. Trim radishes. Separate cauliflower and broccoli into flowerets.
■ Blanch each vegetable separately in boiling water for 3 minutes; drain. Cover with ice water.
■ Tie pickling spices, bay leaf and garlic in cheese-cloth. Combine with white vinegar, water, sugar and salt in saucepan. Bring to a boil. Cook for 10 minutes. Remove spice bag. Cool.
■ Layer drained vegetables in hot sterilized jars. Add enough liquid to cover; seal. Refrigerate.
■ Yield: 2 (1-quart) jars.

HERBED VINEGAR

3¼ cups (5% acidity) white wine vinegar	¼ cup chopped fresh oregano
½ cup chopped fresh rosemary	4 shallots, thinly sliced
¼ cup chopped chives	12 peppercorns
½ cup chopped fresh thyme	Sprigs of fresh rosemary, oregano and thyme

■ Boil vinegar. Place chopped herbs, shallots and peppercorns in large jar. Add boiling vinegar.
■ Let stand, covered, at room temperature for 2 weeks.
■ Place fresh herbs in decorative bottles. Strain vinegar into bottles. Seal with corks.
■ Yield: 4 (½-pint) bottles.

PEPPER AND CUCUMBER RELISH

2 green peppers, ground	1 cup cider vinegar
2 sweet red peppers, ground	½ cup water
8 cups ground cucumbers	3 cups sugar
4 cups ground onions	2 tablespoons white mustard seed
¼ cup salt	1 teaspoon whole allspice
1 cup cider vinegar	1½ teaspoons peppercorns
2 cups water	

■ Combine ground vegetables and salt in bowl; mix well. Let stand at room temperature overnight. Drain well.
■ Combine 1 cup cider vinegar and 2 cups water in saucepan. Add vegetables. Bring to a boil. Cook for 15 minutes. Drain.
■ Add 1 cup cider vinegar, ½ cup water, sugar and spices. Bring to a boil. Cook for 15 minutes.
■ Spoon into hot sterilized jars, leaving ½-inch headspace; seal with 2-piece lids. Process in boiling water bath for 10 minutes. Cool.
■ Yield: 8 (1-pint) jars.

GOLDEN DELICIOUS CHUTNEY

2 cups cider vinegar	2 cloves of garlic, minced
2¼ cups sugar	
4 cups chopped, peeled Golden Delicious apples	1 cup golden raisins
	1 teaspoon white mustard seed
¾ cup chopped candied gingerroot	½ teaspoon salt

■ Combine cider vinegar and sugar in heavy saucepan. Bring to a boil. Add apples, gingerroot, garlic, raisins, mustard seed and salt.
■ Cook for 10 minutes or until apples are almost tender. Remove fruit with slotted spoon; reserve.
■ Cook syrup over medium heat for 15 minutes or until thickened and reduced by half. Add fruit. Return to a boil.
■ Spoon into hot sterilized jars, leaving ½-inch headspace; seal with 2-piece lids. Process in boiling water bath for 10 minutes. Cool.
■ Yield: 3 (1-pint) jars.

HOT HONEY MUSTARD

¾ cup dry mustard	½ cup honey
¾ cup white wine vinegar	2 egg yolks

■ Combine dry mustard and wine vinegar in small bowl; mix well. Let stand at room temperature for 8 hours.
■ Combine honey, egg yolks and mustard mixture in small heavy saucepan; mix well.
■ Cook over low heat for 7 minutes or until thickened, stirring constantly. Cool. Store in tightly covered container in refrigerator for up to 3 weeks.
■ Yield: 3 (4-ounce) jars.

CINNAMON CANDY JELLY

5½ cups sugar	3 cups water
1 (6½-ounce) package small cinnamon candies	1 (2-envelope) package Certo

■ Combine sugar, candies and water in saucepan. Let stand overnight.
■ Cook over medium heat until sugar and candies are completely dissolved.
■ Bring to a boil. Stir in Certo. Cook for 3 minutes, stirring constantly.
■ Remove from heat. Let stand for several minutes. Skim foam from top. Pour into small sterilized jars, leaving ½-inch headspace; seal. Store in refrigerator.
■ Yield: 8 (4-ounce) jars.

HOLIDAY FRUIT BUTTER

8 large Granny Smith apples	4 cups sugar
5 large Bartlett pears	⅓ cup fresh orange juice
½ cup water	1 teaspoon grated orange rind
2 bananas, sliced	

■ Cut apples and pears into quarters. Combine with water in 5-quart saucepan.
■ Cook over medium heat until fruit is tender, stirring occasionally. Add bananas.
■ Put fruit through sieve. Add sugar, orange juice and orange rind; mix well.
■ Cook over medium heat for 1 hour or until thick, stirring frequently.
■ Pour into hot sterilized jars, leaving ½-inch headspace; seal with 2-piece lids. Process in boiling water bath for 10 minutes. Cool.
■ Yield: 8 (½-pint) jars.

JALAPEÑO JAM

1 cup chopped green pepper	1 teaspoon cayenne pepper
1 cup chopped jalapeño peppers	½ (6-ounce) bottle of pectin
1½ cups cider vinegar	Several drops of green food coloring
6 cups sugar	
½ teaspoon salt	

■ Combine green pepper, jalapeño peppers and cider vinegar ½ at a time in blender container. Purée until smooth.
■ Combine purée, sugar, salt and cayenne pepper in saucepan. Bring to a boil. Cook for 2 minutes.
■ Remove from heat. Add pectin. Let stand for 5 minutes, stirring constantly. Add food coloring; mix well.
■ Pour into hot sterilized jars, leaving ½-inch headspace; seal. Store in refrigerator.
■ Yield: 4 (½-pint) jars.

LEMON CURD

Grated rind of 3 lemons	1 stick butter or margarine
Juice of 2 lemons	2 eggs, well beaten
1 cup sugar	

■ Combine lemon rind, juice, sugar and butter in double boiler pan.
■ Cook over hot water until butter melts and sugar dissolves, stirring frequently.
■ Add eggs. Cook until mixture coats wooden spoon, stirring frequently.
■ Pour into hot sterilized jars, leaving ½-inch headspace; seal. Store in refrigerator.
■ Yield: 2 (½-pint) jars.

GINGERED BLUEBERRY SAUCE

1 cup apple juice	1 2-inch stick cinnamon
1 cup sugar	2 (12-ounce) packages frozen blueberries
1 tablespoon cornstarch	
1 teaspoon ginger	

■ Combine apple juice and mixture of sugar, cornstarch and ginger in saucepan. Stir until sugar dissolves. Add cinnamon stick.
■ Bring to a boil. Add blueberries. Reduce heat to medium. Cook for 12 to 15 minutes or just until mixture returns to a boil and thickens, stirring occasionally. Remove cinnamon stick.
■ Pour into hot sterilized jars, leaving ½-inch headspace; seal. Cool. Store in refrigerator. Serve with cake, ice cream or pancakes.
■ Yield: 4 (½-pint) jars.

FANCY PARTY MIX

1 (12-ounce) package rice Chex	1 (16-ounce) jar Spanish peanuts
1 (12-ounce) package corn Chex	1 (16-ounce) jar mixed nuts
1 (12-ounce) package wheat Chex	2 cups melted butter or margarine
1 (14-ounce) package honey-nut oat cereal	1 teaspoon chili powder
1 (12-ounce) package miniature pretzels	1 tablespoon Tabasco sauce
1 (14-ounce) package cheese crackers	1 tablespoon Worcestershire sauce
1 (11-ounce) package corn chips	1 teaspoon garlic powder
2 cups pecan halves	Special Seasoning Salt to taste

■ Preheat oven to 250 degrees.
■ Combine cereals, pretzels, crackers, corn chips and nuts in large bowl; mix lightly. Spread in 2 large roasting pans.
■ Mix butter and seasonings in bowl. Pour over cereal mixture; mix lightly.
■ Bake for 1 hour, stirring frequently. Cool. Store in airtight containers.
■ Yield: Approximately 50 cups.

HOLIDAY NUTS

2 cups mixed nuts	1 teaspoon Special Seasoning Salt
½ cup melted butter or margarine	

■ Preheat oven to 250 degrees.
■ Combine nuts and butter in shallow baking pan; mix well. Sprinkle with Special Seasoning Salt.
■ Bake for 1 hour, stirring occasionally. Cool on paper towels. Store in airtight container.
■ Yield: 2 cups.

SPECIAL SEASONING SALT

1 (26-ounce) box table salt	2 tablespoons paprika
1 tablespoon onion salt	¼ cup black pepper
1 tablespoon garlic salt	¼ cup white pepper
2 tablespoons celery salt	1 tablespoon dillweed
	¼ cup sugar

■ Combine salt, onion salt, garlic salt, celery salt, paprika, black pepper, white pepper, dillweed and sugar in bowl; mix well. Let stand, covered, in dark place for 24 hours.
■ Package in salt shakers or spice jars.
■ Yield: 3 cups.

SESAME WHEAT CRACKERS

    1 cup all-purpose flour   **½ cup skim milk**
    1 cup whole wheat flour   **⅓ cup Mazola corn oil**
    ⅓ cup sesame seed   **1 tablespoon grated**
    1 teaspoon baking   **onion**
      powder   **Salt to taste**

■ Preheat oven to 400 degrees.
■ Combine flours, sesame seed and baking powder in bowl. Mix skim milk, oil and onion in small bowl. Add to flour mixture; mix well.
■ Knead on lightly floured surface until smooth. Divide into 2 portions. Let rest for 10 minutes.
■ Roll ¹⁄₁₆ inch thick; cut into squares. Place on ungreased baking sheet. Sprinkle with salt.
■ Bake for 8 to 10 minutes or until light brown. Cool on wire rack. Store in airtight container. Crackers may be frozen.
■ Yield: 4 dozen.

SUGAR PRETZELS

    3 cups all-purpose flour   **1 teaspoon lemon**
    1 cup butter or   **extract**
      margarine, softened   **1 egg**
    ½ cup sugar   **1 egg yolk**
    1 teaspoon grated   **1 egg white**
      lemon rind   **¼ cup (or more)**
    ¼ teaspoon salt   **rainbow sugar crystals**

■ Preheat oven to 400 degrees.
■ Combine flour, butter, ½ cup sugar, lemon rind, salt, lemon extract, egg and 1 egg yolk in mixer bowl. Beat at low speed until blended. Chill for 15 minutes.
■ Roll 2 tablespoonfuls at a time into ½ x 10-inch long ropes. Shape into pretzels.
■ Place 1 inch apart on ungreased cookie sheet. Brush with egg white; sprinkle with sugar crystals.
■ Bake for 10 to 12 minutes or until golden. Cool on wire rack. Store in airtight container.
■ Yield: 1½ dozen.

FRENCH MARKET SOUP MIX

1 pound dried black-eyed peas	1 pound dried kidney beans
1 pound dried split peas	1 pound dried Great Northern beans
1 pound dried lentils	
1 pound dried black beans	1 pound dried navy beans
1 pound dried baby lima beans	1 (16-ounce) package pearl barley

■ Layer ¼ cup each ingredient in glass jars; seal.
■ Include soup recipe with each gift, or assemble baskets with soup mix, soup ingredients and copy of recipe.
■ Yield: 8 (1-pint) jars.

French Market Bean Soup Recipe

1 jar French Market Soup Mix	1 bay leaf
6 cups water	½ teaspoon oregano
8 cups water	8 ounces kielbasa, sliced
1 pound cooked ham, chopped	1 (16-ounce) can tomatoes
1 onion, chopped	
2 cloves of garlic, minced	1 (10-ounce) can Ro-Tel tomatoes and green chilies

■ Soak Soup Mix in 6 cups water in saucepan overnight; drain.
■ Add 8 cups water, ham, onion, garlic, bay leaf and oregano. Simmer, covered, for 1½ hours or until beans are tender. Remove bay leaf.
■ Add sausage and undrained tomatoes. Simmer for 30 minutes longer. Ladle into soup bowls.

FRUITED CURRIED RICE MIX

4 cups long grain rice	8 teaspoons curry powder
2 cups chopped dried fruit	
2 cups slivered almonds	8 teaspoons instant beef bouillon granules
1 cup golden raisins	2 teaspoons salt
¼ cup dried minced onion	Butter or margarine

■ Combine 1 cup rice, ½ cup fruit, ½ cup almonds, ¼ cup raisins, 1 tablespoon onion, 2 teaspoons each curry powder and bouillon and ½ teaspoon salt in 4 containers. Seal.
■ Include the following directions with each gift: Combine rice mix with 2½ cups water and 2 tablespoons butter in covered saucepan. Bring to a boil; reduce heat. Simmer for 20 minutes.
■ Yield: 4 (1-pint) containers.

FRIENDSHIP TEA MIX

1 (18-ounce) jar orange-flavored breakfast drink mix	½ cup unsweetened instant tea powder
1 cup sugar	1 (3-ounce) package apricot gelatin
1½ (3-ounce) packages sweetened lemonade mix	2½ teaspoons cinnamon
	1 teaspoon ground cloves

■ Combine all ingredients in bowl, mix well.
■ Store in airtight container. Add 1½ tablespoons Friendship Tea Mix to each tea cup boiling water.
■ Yield: 7 (1-cup) containers.

HOT BUTTERED RUM MIX

4 sticks butter or margarine, softened	2 quarts French vanilla ice cream, softened
1 (16-ounce) package confectioners' sugar	Rum extract to taste
1 (16-ounce) package light brown sugar	2 teaspoons vanilla extract

■ Combine all ingredients in bowl; mix well.
■ Spoon into freezer containers; seal. Store in freezer for up to 4 weeks.
■ Add 3 tablespoons mix to 6 ounces boiling water.
■ Yield: 6 (1-pint) containers.

HOMEMADE DOG BISCUITS

1 package dry yeast	½ cup yellow cornmeal
¼ cup (110 to 115-degree) warm water	½ cup nonfat dry milk powder
1 cup warm chicken broth	2 tablespoons salt
2 tablespoons molasses	2 teaspoons garlic powder
1 cup all-purpose flour	¾ to 1 cup all-purpose flour
1½ cups whole wheat flour	
1 cup bran cereal	1 egg, beaten
	1 tablespoon milk

■ Preheat oven to 300 degrees.
■ Dissolve yeast in warm water in large bowl. Add broth, molasses, 1 cup all-purpose flour, whole wheat flour, bran cereal, cornmeal, dry milk powder and seasonings; mix well.
■ Knead in enough remaining flour to make stiff dough. Roll ½ at a time to ⅜-inch thickness. Cut with bone-shaped cookie cutter.
■ Place on ungreased baking sheet. Brush with mixture of egg and milk. Bake for 45 minutes.
■ Turn off oven. Let stand in closed oven overnight. Store in airtight container.
■ Yield: 3½ dozen.

Dress A Christmas Window

COOKIE CUTTER WINDOW TREATMENT

Cut ribbon into different lengths. Tie bow in one end. Attach ribbons to top of window frame. Hang cookie cutters from bow ends with large ornament hooks.

Light Up Holiday Tables

APPLE CENTERPIECE

Choose large, shiny red apples. Remove core from top of each apple to within 2 inches of bottom. Enlarge hole to fit votive or other candle. Insert candle. Fill center of vine wreath with whole apples and intersperse with apple candleholders.

GINGERBREAD STARBURST

1 (14-ounce) package gingerbread mix	4 green candied cherries
⅓ cup lukewarm water	4 walnut halves
1 egg white	6 to 7 dozen whole
5 red candied cherries	blanched almonds

■ Combine gingerbread mix and water in bowl; mix well. Chill for 1 hour.
■ Preheat oven to 300 degrees.
■ Roll dough into 12-inch square on foil-lined cookie sheet. Cut into 8-point star. Cut 2-inch circle from center of star. Remove excess dough.
■ Brush star with egg white. Cut red cherries into quarters. Arrange cherry pieces on star to resemble petals; center with whole green cherries. Place walnut halves between cherries. Outline star and center cut-out with almonds.
■ Bake for 18 to 20 minutes or until firm. Cool on wire rack. Remove foil.
■ Loop ribbon through center. Hang from window or door.

POMANDER CENTERPIECE

Arrange greenery around candle in glass chimney. Decorate with cinnamon sticks, clove-studded oranges, and pine cones.

BREAD CENTERPIECE

Place coffee cake ring on tray in center of table. Stand fat white candle in center. Our Coffee Cake Wreath (page 12) may be used for this centerpiece.

Trim A Comfort Tree

A tabletop tree for any room in the house, fragrant with spices and herbs, decorated with favorite things from the heart of the home.

Tie on any or all of the following:

- Spices, vanilla beans, or coffee beans tied in tiny cheesecloth bags
- Dried herbs in miniature shopping bags or tied in clusters
- Small wooden mixing or measuring spoons
- Cookie cutters, pizza or pastry cutters, or nutmeg graters
- Small wire whisks or tea balls or strainers
- Gingerbread men or any kind of cookie
- Macaroni or popcorn chains
- Cinnamon ornaments (recipe below)

CINNAMON ORNAMENTS

¾ cup ground cinnamon	1 tablespoon ground nutmeg
1 tablespoon ground allspice	1 cup applesauce
2 tablespoons ground cloves	

- Combine spices in glass bowl or plastic bag. Add applesauce; mix well. Mixture will be stiff.
- Roll to ¼-inch thickness on ungreased cookie sheet, marble slab or other flat surface. Do not roll on waxed paper. Cut with cookie cutters.
- Remove excess dough. Make holes for hanging in each ornament with metal skewer. Let dry, uncovered, at room temperature for 4 to 5 days.
- Hang ornaments from Christmas tree, tie onto wreath or packages or pile into basket.
- Yield: 25 small or 18 medium ornaments.

CANDLES EVERYWHERE

- Place fluted tartlet tins on tray. Stand votive candles in each tin.
- Arrange long tapers as for bouquet in tall canning jars.
- Add enough sand to mason jars to fill ⅓ full. Place large votive candles in sand.

HEARTS FOR THE HOLIDAY

Enlist the aid of all the children for this charming heart wreath. Children love the process of mixing, rolling, and shaping the dough into spicy hearts. These hearts are pretty enough to top with a bow and to use as individual tree ornaments. We chose a heart-shaped cookie cutter, but you could choose to make a wreath of Christmas trees or Santa Clauses. Dough may be tinted with food coloring.

Materials: Wreath

Play clay	16 paper clips
Rolling pin	3 yards (1-inch wide)
2-inch heart-shaped	plaid ribbon
cookie cutter	1 yard (¼-inch wide)
1 plastic straw	red ribbon
Waxed paper	Foam wreath form
Wire rack	9 cinnamon sticks

Play Clay

1 cup cornstarch	3 tablespoons ground
2 cups (1 pound) soda	ginger
1½ cups cold water	Ground cinnamon

Directions: Play Clay

■ Stir together cornstarch and soda in medium saucepan. Mix water and ginger in measuring cup.

■ Add water and ginger to cornstarch mixture; stir until smooth. Cook over medium heat until mixture reaches the consistency of slightly dry mashed potatoes, stirring constantly. (Mixture will come to a boil, start to thicken in lumps then form a thick mass which holds its shape.)

■ Turn dough onto a plate; cover with a damp cloth. Let cool.

■ Divide dough in half. Always keep dough that is not being worked covered with a damp cloth. Knead ground cinnamon into one half until deep brown, smooth and pliable on a cornstarch-dusted surface. Cover with a damp cloth. Knead remaining half dough without the cinnamon.

■ Store cooled clay in a tightly closed plastic bag or airtight container. Clay may be kept in a cool place up to 2 weeks.

Directions: Hearts

■ Roll out each half separately to ½-inch thickness. Place halves one on top of the other. Roll as for jelly roll starting at short end.

■ Cut into 1½-inch slices. Remember to keep dough covered with a damp cloth whenever possible. Roll each slice ¼ inch thick.

■ Cut each slice of dough with a 2-inch heart-shaped cookie cutter.

■ Punch a hole in the top of each heart using a plastic straw.

■ Place hearts on waxed paper on a wire rack. Clay will dry and harden at room temperature. When fronts of hearts are dry (several hours to overnight), turn over and continue drying, turning occasionally.

Directions: Assembling Wreath

■ Straighten paper clips; bend in half to form a V. Cut plaid ribbon into 6-inch lengths. Cut red ribbon into 12-inch lengths.

■ Lace a 6-inch length of plaid ribbon through the hole in the heart. Tie a knot so that the knot is on the back of the heart. Insert paper clip into knot with the base of the V at the knot.

■ Insert paper clip ends into foam wreath. If ends of clips appear on back side of wreath, bend ends to secure.

■ Tie a V-shaped paper clip in the middle of the 12-inch lengths of red ribbon. Tie the ribbon around 3 cinnamon sticks with clip in back and bow in front. Attach to wreath.

HOLIDAY GREEK BREAD WREATH

Holiday breads are so pretty we had to use them as a Christmas decoration. Any hard-crust bread or roll can be used for the center of this special design. We have hung our wreath on the wall, but it would be equally effective as a table centerpiece.

Materials:

Loaf of Greek bread	Straw
8 large florist picks	30 magnolia leaves
6 x 8-inch styrofoam base	30 holly leaves
	Red berry sprigs
Shellac and brush	Florist wire

Directions:

- Dry bread loaf in 200-degree oven for 2 hours.
- Insert florist picks evenly across 6 x 8-inch surface of styrofoam base.
- Force bread onto upright florist picks.
- Apply 2 coats shellac to top and sides of bread.
- Insert straw into upper left corner of base; repeat straw placement at lower right of base.
- Insert stems of magnolia leaves into base around the bread loaf, overlapping leaves slightly.
- Add holly leaves and red berries to wreath. Overlap holly so stems are hidden.
- Attach wire loop to back of wreath for hanging.

NEW MEXICO PEPPER WREATH

We chose dried New Mexico chili pepper pods that are sold in food specialty shops. You could buy pepper pods at a farmers' market, which would make your wreath less expensive to construct. Dry pepper pods by placing pods on a cookie sheet in a 200-degree oven for 3 hours.

Materials:

Wire coat hanger	String
80 pepper pods	

Directions:

- Straighten coat hanger and reshape into circle. Bend last 2 inches of hanger into right angle.
- Thread each pepper pod through center onto wire. Push pepper pod to end of wreath.
- Thread first pepper pod with stem toward center of wreath; turn second pepper pod in opposite direction.
- Alternate direction of pepper pods around entire wreath.
- Thread pepper pods as tightly as possible around wreath.
- Leave 2 inches of wire at end of wreath; bend at a right angle. Twist 2 ends of wire together.
- Tie a loop of string to wire to hang wreath.

Traditional Family Dinner

Menu

Special Shrimp Cocktail
Cranberry Aspic–Endive Salad
Easy Cranberry Relish
Glazed Ham or Rib Eye Roast
Turkey with Apple Stuffing
Festive Green Bean Bundles or
Zucchini and Rice Casserole
Cranberry Yams or Creamed Potatoes
Monterey Corn Bake
Whole Wheat Crescents or Savarin Buns
Praline Pumpkin Pie or Cherry Pie
Pecan Fruitcake
Holiday Ambrosia
Hot Mulled Cider
Marzipan Candy Fruit

SPECIAL SHRIMP COCKTAIL

¾ cup chili sauce	¼ cup lemon juice
2 teaspoons Worcestershire sauce	4 drops of Tabasco sauce
1 teaspoon minced onion	Lettuce leaves
2 tablespoons horseradish	1 pound large cooked shrimp

■ Combine chili sauce, Worcestershire sauce, onion, horseradish, lemon juice and Tabasco sauce in bowl; mix well. Chill until serving time.
■ Line cocktail glasses with lettuce leaves. Arrange shrimp around edge. Spoon sauce into center.
■ Yield: 6 servings.

CRANBERRY ASPIC

2 envelopes unflavored gelatin	½ teaspoon whole allspice
½ cup cold water	1 (6-ounce) package raspberry gelatin
2 cups cranberry juice	
1 cup dry red wine	1 cup chilled cranberry juice
1 2-inch stick cinnamon	1 cup ice water
½ teaspoon whole cloves	1 (8-ounce) can jellied cranberry sauce

■ Soften unflavored gelatin in mixture of next 3 ingredients in saucepan. Add spices. Simmer for several minutes; strain. Stir in raspberry gelatin. Add chilled cranberry juice and ice water; mix well.
■ Pour ½ cup into fluted 6-cup mold. Chill until firm. Place sliced cranberry sauce on congealed layer. Add remaining gelatin. Chill until firm. Unmold onto serving plate.
■ Yield: 8 to 12 servings.

ENDIVE SALAD

8 (6-inch long) heads Belgian endive
4 cups torn spinach
1 cup sliced radishes
2 cups fresh tangerine segments
½ cup wine vinegar
1 tablespoon Dijon-style mustard
⅛ teaspoon pepper
½ cup walnut oil
½ cup salad oil
1 tablespoon minced onion

■ Separate endive into individual leaves. Arrange on serving plate. Layer spinach, radishes and tangerine segments in center.
■ Combine wine vinegar, mustard, pepper, oils and onion in covered jar; shake to mix well. Serve dressing with salad. Store any remaining dressing in refrigerator.
■ Yield: 10 servings.

EASY CRANBERRY RELISH

¼ cup orange juice
2 teaspoons lemon juice
1 (12-ounce) package cranberries
1½ cups sugar
2 (1-inch) strips orange rind
½ cup chopped nuts
1 lemon slice

■ Combine orange juice, lemon juice, cranberries, sugar and orange rind in saucepan or microwave-safe glass bowl.
■ Simmer for 15 minutes or Microwave, covered, on High (600 to 700 Watts) for 7 minutes or until cranberries burst, stirring frequently. Remove orange rind. Stir in nuts.
■ Pour relish into serving dish. Garnish with lemon twist. Serve warm or chilled.
■ Yield: 2 cups.

GLAZED HAM

1 (10-pound) whole cured ham	½ cup cider vinegar
Whole cloves	1 cup honey
2 (16-ounce) jars pickled peaches	1 cup packed light brown sugar

- Preheat oven to 300 degrees.
- Remove rind from ham; score fat. Stud with cloves. Place ham in roaster.
- Drain peaches, reserving juice. Combine juice and cider vinegar in bowl; mix well. Spoon over ham. Cover with foil.
- Bake for 2½ hours or until ham is almost tender, basting frequently with pan juices.
- Spread honey over ham; sprinkle with brown sugar. Arrange peaches around ham. Bake, uncovered, for 30 minutes or until ham is glazed and tender.
- Yield: 16 servings.

TURKEY WITH APPLE STUFFING

2 cups chopped onions	1 tablespoon sage
2 cups chopped celery	1 teaspoon poultry seasoning
1 cup melted butter or margarine	Salt and pepper to taste
4 cups chopped unpeeled Granny Smith apples	1 (12 to 15-pound) oven-ready turkey
12 cups day-old bread cubes	½ cup melted butter or margarine

- Preheat oven to 325 degrees.
- Sauté onions and celery in 1 cup butter in skillet for 3 minutes. Add apples, bread cubes and seasonings; mix well.
- Spoon stuffing into turkey cavity; truss turkey. Spoon remaining stuffing into deep baking dish.
- Place turkey breast side up in roasting pan. Brush with ½ cup melted butter. Cover with foil tent. Make hole in foil; insert meat thermometer. Foil should not touch thermometer.
- Bake for 4 hours or to 175 degrees on meat thermometer, basting with butter occasionally. Remove foil.
- Bake for 30 minutes longer or to 185 degrees. Remove turkey from oven.
- Bake stuffing casserole for 30 minutes.
- Yield: 12 to 15 servings.
- Note: Stuffing may be prepared ahead and stored in refrigerator. Do not stuff turkey until just before baking. Turkey should stand for 15 to 30 minutes before carving.

RIB EYE ROAST

1 (6-pound) boneless rib eye roast	1 teaspoon paprika
⅓ cup cracked pepper	1 cup sour cream
½ teaspoon cardamom	1 tablespoon cider vinegar
¾ cup red wine vinegar	2 tablespoons Dijon-style mustard
1 cup soy sauce	½ cup whipping cream
1 tablespoon tomato paste	½ cup mayonnaise
½ teaspoon garlic powder	2 tablespoons horseradish

- Trim any excess fat from roast. Rub mixture of pepper and cardamom on roast.
- Combine wine vinegar, soy sauce, tomato paste, garlic powder and paprika in large glass dish. Place roast in dish.
- Marinate roast in refrigerator for 8 hours, turning roast occasionally. Drain.
- Prepare Yorkshire Pudding batter. Refrigerate.
- Preheat oven to 325 degrees.
- Place roast in foil-lined roasting pan; insert meat thermometer. Seal foil tightly; foil should not touch thermometer.
- Bake for 2 hours or to 140 degrees on meat thermometer for rare or to 160 degrees on meat thermometer for medium.
- Blend sour cream, cider vinegar and mustard in small serving bowl. Chill until serving time.
- Whip cream until stiff. Fold in mayonnaise and horseradish. Spoon into serving bowl. Chill until serving time.
- Bake Yorkshire Pudding.
- Place roast on heated serving platter. Serve with mustard sauce and horseradish sauce.
- Yield: 16 servings.

Yorkshire Pudding

4 eggs	¼ cup roast beef drippings or melted butter
1 teaspoon salt	
2 cups all-purpose flour	
1 cup milk	

- Combine eggs, salt, flour and milk in blender container. Process at high speed for 30 seconds. Scrape sides of container. Process for 10 seconds.
- Chill for 1 hour or longer.
- Preheat oven to 400 degrees.
- Pour hot drippings or butter into 10x15-inch baking pan. Pour in batter.
- Bake for 15 minutes. Decrease temperature to 375 degrees. Bake for 15 minutes longer. Cut into squares. Serve immediately.
- Yield: 16 servings.

FESTIVE GREEN BEAN BUNDLES

1½ pounds tender
  fresh (3-inch long)
  green beans
	2 tablespoons butter or
	  margarine

1 clove of garlic, minced	Salt and pepper to taste 1 (2-ounce) jar pimento

■ Trim ends from green beans.
■ Cook, covered, in boiling water in large sauce-pan for 3 to 5 minutes or just until tender; drain.
■ Cover with ice water; drain and set aside.
■ Sauté garlic in butter in saucepan for 1 minute. Add green beans; toss to coat. Cook until heated through. Season with salt and pepper.
■ Drain pimento; cut into long thin strips. Arrange green beans in bundles on serving plate. Garnish with pimento strips to resemble bows.
■ Yield: 6 servings.

ZUCCHINI AND RICE CASSEROLE

1 cup chopped onion	1 tablespoon flour
3 tablespoons melted butter or margarine	2½ cups half and half

2 teaspoons minced
  garlic
	½ cup uncooked long
	  grain white rice

5 cups shredded zucchini	¾ cup Parmesan cheese Salt and pepper to taste ¼ cup Parmesan cheese

■ Preheat oven to 425 degrees.
■ Sauté onion in butter in skillet until tender.
■ Add garlic and zucchini. Stir-fry for 5 minutes. Sprinkle with flour. Stir-fry for 1 minute longer.
■ Add half and half, rice, ¾ cup Parmesan cheese and salt and pepper; mix well. Pour into greased 9 x 13-inch baking dish. Sprinkle with ¼ cup Parmesan cheese.
■ Bake for 30 minutes or until golden and rice is tender. Let stand for 10 minutes before serving.
■ Yield: 12 servings.

CRANBERRY YAMS

2 (28-ounce) cans yams,
  drained
	2 tablespoons
	  cornstarch

1 (10-ounce) can apricots	½ teaspoon cinnamon
1 cup fresh cranberries	½ cup golden raisins

3 tablespoons light
  brown sugar
	½ teaspoon grated
	  orange rind

■ Preheat oven to 350 degrees.
■ Arrange yams in 6 x 10-inch baking dish. Drain apricots, reserving syrup. Arrange apricots between sweet potatoes. Add cranberries.

■ Add enough water to reserved syrup to measure 1 cup. Combine brown sugar, cornstarch and cinnamon in saucepan. Stir in syrup and raisins.
■ Bring to a boil over high heat. Add orange rind; mix well. Pour over sweet potatoes.
■ Bake for 20 minutes or until heated through.
■ Yield: 10 to 12 servings.

MONTEREY CORN BAKE

2 cups fresh or frozen corn	2 cups sour cream
¼ cup chopped onion	½ cup cornmeal

2 tablespoons chopped
  pimento
	½ cup melted butter or
	  margarine

1 (4-ounce) can
  chopped green chilies
	1 cup grated Monterey
	  Jack cheese

2 eggs, beaten	Parsley sprigs Cherry tomatoes

■ Preheat oven to 350 degrees.
■ Combine corn, onion, pimento and green chilies in bowl. Add eggs, sour cream, cornmeal, butter and cheese; mix well.
■ Pour into greased 9 x 13-inch baking dish.
■ Bake for 1 hour or until set. Cover with foil to prevent overbrowning if necessary. Garnish with parsley and tomatoes.
■ Yield: 8 servings.

CREAMED POTATOES

5 pounds russet
  potatoes
	¼ cup butter or
	  margarine, softened

6 ounces cream cheese, softened	2 teaspoons onion salt
1 cup sour cream	¼ teaspoon pepper ½ cup Parmesan cheese

■ Scrub and peel potatoes. Cut into quarters. Cook in water to cover in saucepan for 30 minutes or until tender. Drain. Mash with potato masher or put through ricer.
■ Combine potatoes, cream cheese, sour cream, margarine, onion salt and pepper in large bowl; mix well. Spoon into casserole. Sprinkle with Parmesan cheese.
■ Chill, covered, in refrigerator for several hours.
■ Preheat oven to 350 degrees.
■ Bake casserole for 30 minutes or until brown.
■ Yield: 12 servings.
■ Note: Potato mixture may be stored in tightly covered container in refrigerator for up to 2 weeks and baked in smaller portions as desired.

WHOLE WHEAT CRESCENTS

2 packages dry yeast	½ cup yogurt
½ cup sugar	4 cups sifted all-purpose
½ cup (110 to 115-	flour
degree) warm water	2 cups whole wheat
¾ cup milk, scalded	flour
2 eggs, beaten	¾ cup melted butter or
2 teaspoons salt	margarine

■ Dissolve yeast and sugar in warm water in large bowl. Stir in milk, eggs, salt, yogurt, 2 cups all-purpose flour and 1 cup whole wheat flour.
■ Stir in butter and remaining flour; mix well. Do not knead. Chill, covered, for 4 to 8 hours.
■ Divide dough into 3 portions. Roll each portion into 12-inch circle on floured surface. Cut each into 16 wedges. Roll up from wide end.
■ Shape into crescents on greased baking sheet. Let rise for 3 hours or until doubled in bulk.
■ Preheat oven to 400 degrees. Bake rolls for 15 minutes or until golden brown.
■ Yield: 4 dozen.

SAVARIN BUNS

¾ cup chopped walnuts	⅓ cup milk, scalded
1 (16-ounce) package	3 eggs
hot roll mix	¼ cup sugar
⅔ cup (110 to 115-	1 teaspoon grated
degree) warm water	lemon rind
3 tablespoons butter or	½ cup honey
margarine	¾ cup apricot nectar

■ Preheat oven to 350 degrees.
■ Blanch walnuts in boiling water in saucepan for 3 minutes; drain. Place in shallow baking pan. Toast for 12 minutes. Set aside.
■ Dissolve yeast packet from roll mix in warm water. Add butter to hot milk. Cool to lukewarm.
■ Combine eggs and sugar in mixer bowl. Beat until light and lemon-colored. Add yeast, milk mixture and lemon rind; mix well.
■ Add flour from roll mix gradually, beating well after each addition. Stir in toasted walnuts. Fill greased miniature bundt pans ½ full. Let rise for 1 hour or until doubled in bulk.
■ Preheat oven to 350 degrees. Bake savarin buns for 20 minutes or until brown. Let stand for 5 minutes. Invert onto plate. Prick with fork.
■ Heat honey and apricot nectar in saucepan. Spoon over hot buns until liquid is absorbed.
■ Yield: 1 dozen.
■ Note: If roll mix contains mixture of yeast and flour, add mixture of water, milk and butter according to package directions.

PRALINE PUMPKIN PIE

½ cup packed light	1 cup evaporated milk
brown sugar	2 teaspoons vanilla
1 tablespoon all-purpose	extract
flour	1 unbaked (9-inch)
1 teaspoon cinnamon	pie shell
½ teaspoon ginger	2 tablespoons packed
½ teaspoon nutmeg	light brown sugar
½ teaspoon salt	2 tablespoons butter or
1 (16-ounce) can	margarine, softened
pumpkin	½ cup finely chopped
2 eggs	pecans

■ Preheat oven to 425 degrees.
■ Combine ½ cup brown sugar, flour, spices and salt in bowl; mix well.
■ Add pumpkin, eggs, evaporated milk and vanilla; mix well. Pour into pie shell.
■ Bake for 15 minutes. Reduce temperature to 350 degrees.
■ Combine 2 tablespoons brown sugar, butter and pecans in bowl; mix well. Sprinkle on top of pie.
■ Bake for 30 minutes longer or until set. Cool.
■ Yield: 8 servings.

CHERRY PIE

¼ cup sugar	1 tablespoon butter or
3 tablespoons	margarine
cornstarch	3 cups drained tart
¼ teaspoon salt	cherries
¾ cup cherry juice	1 recipe 2-crust pie
¾ cup sugar	pastry or 2
1½ teaspoons lemon	refrigerator
juice	pie shells
¼ teaspoon almond	2 tablespoons milk
extract	1 tablespoon sugar

■ Preheat oven to 450 degrees.
■ Combine ¼ cup sugar, cornstarch, salt and cherry juice in saucepan. Cook over low heat until thickened, stirring constantly.
■ Add ¾ cup sugar. Cook until glossy, stirring constantly. Stir in lemon juice, flavoring and butter. Fold in cherries gently. Cool.
■ Line 9-inch pie plate with half the pastry. Spoon in cherry mixture. Cut remaining pastry into strips; weave into lattice on top of pie. Seal and flute edge.
■ Cover edge of pie with foil. Brush lattice top with milk; sprinkle with 1 tablespoon sugar.
■ Bake for 15 minutes. Reduce temperature to 350 degrees. Remove foil. Bake for 25 minutes or until golden brown.
■ Yield: 6 servings.

PECAN FRUITCAKE

¾ cup cake flour	½ cup packed light
12 ounces candied	brown sugar
cherries	5 eggs
8 ounces candied citron,	1 teaspoon vanilla
chopped	extract
8 ounces candied	1 cup cake flour
pineapple	¼ teaspoon baking
4 cups chopped pecans	powder
1 cup butter or	1 teaspoon soda
margarine, softened	1 cup pecan halves
½ cup sugar	

■ Line bottom of greased tube pan with greased waxed paper. Do not use fluted tube pan.
■ Combine ¾ cup cake flour, candied fruits and chopped pecans in bowl; mix well.
■ Cream butter and sugars in mixer bowl until light and fluffy. Add eggs 1 at a time, beating well after each addition. Blend in vanilla.
■ Combine 1 cup cake flour, baking powder and soda. Add to creamed mixture; mix well. Fold in floured fruit mixture.
■ Spoon into prepared tube pan. Decorate top with pecan halves. Place in cold oven. Turn oven to 250 degrees. Bake for 2 hours or until cake tests done. Cool in pan on wire rack. Invert onto cake plate; remove waxed paper. Turn cake over.
■ Yield: 16 to 20 servings.

HOLIDAY AMBROSIA

2 large pineapples	¼ cup green maraschino
12 large navel oranges	cherries
2 cups grated coconut	2 cups pineapple yogurt
¼ cup red maraschino	1 cup grated coconut
cherries	

■ Peel and core pineapples. Cut into large chunks. Peel oranges; remove any seeds. Slice thinly. Layer pineapple, oranges, 2 cups coconut and cherries in large glass serving bowl.
■ Combine yogurt and 1 cup coconut in bowl. Spoon into serving dish. Chill yogurt mixture and fruit for 4 hours or longer.
■ Serve ambrosia with yogurt sauce.
■ Yield: 12 servings.

HOT MULLED CIDER

16 cups apple cider	24 whole cloves
1 cup sugar	2 teaspoons allspice
2 3-inch sticks	¼ cup lemon juice
cinnamon	

■ Combine cider, sugar, cinnamon sticks, cloves, allspice and lemon juice in saucepan.
■ Simmer for 5 minutes; strain. Serve hot.
■ Yield: 16 servings.

MARZIPAN CANDY FRUIT

1 recipe Marzipan	Whole cloves
Paste or liquid food	Candied angelica
coloring	Gum arabic

■ Divide marzipan into 5 portions. Tint each portion with a small amount of red, yellow, green, orange or purple food coloring. Knead until coloring is evenly distributed.
■ Shape red marzipan into strawberries. Roll gently on nutmeg grater for texture. Insert cloves for stems and small slices of angelica for leaves.
■ Shape yellow marzipan into 1½-inch long bananas. Paint markings with brown food coloring using toothpick or fine paint brush.
■ Shape green marzipan into pears. Paint brown dot on large end with brown food coloring. Insert cloves for stems.
■ Shape orange marzipan into small oranges. Roll gently on nutmeg grater for texture. Insert cloves for stems.
■ Shape purple marzipan into tiny grapes. Arrange in cluster.
■ Glaze candies with gum arabic if desired.
■ Store in airtight container in refrigerator.

Marzipan

1 cup blanched almonds	2 cups sifted
1 teaspoon almond	confectioners' sugar
extract	2 egg whites

■ Grind almonds in blender or food processor until extremely fine.
■ Combine almonds, flavoring and confectioners' sugar in bowl; mix well. Add egg whites 1 teaspoon at a time until mixture is moist, mixing well after each addition.
■ Knead until smooth and pliable on a surface sprinkled with confectioners' sugar.
■ Store in airtight container in refrigerator for several weeks.
■ Yield: 1¼ cups.
■ Note: For easy Marzipan, combine 1 egg white, 1 cup almond paste, 1½ cups confectioners' sugar and 1 teaspoon lemon juice in mixer bowl, beating until smooth.

Christmas Dinner In-A-Minute

Menu

Vegeberry Cocktail
Crab Meat Chowder
Boston Lettuce and Beet Salad
Roast Filet of Beef or
Turkey Divan Rolls
Holiday Potato Casserole
Green Beans with Red Peppers
Triflets

VEGEBERRY COCKTAIL

1 (48-ounce) can vegetable juice cocktail	1 cup cranberry juice
	1 cup orange juice
	8 lime slices

■ Combine juices in pitcher. Chill in refrigerator.
■ Serve over ice. Garnish with lime slice.
■ Yield: 8 servings.

CRAB MEAT CHOWDER

1½ cups chicken broth	1 tablespoon Sherry
1 (11-ounce) can whole kernel corn, drained	1 tablespoon cornstarch
	2 tablespoons water
1 (6½-ounce) can crab meat	2 egg whites
3 ounces chopped cooked ham	2 tablespoons chopped fresh parsley

■ Combine broth and corn in saucepan. Bring to a boil. Add crab meat, ham and Sherry.
■ Stir in mixture of cornstarch and water. Cook until thick, stirring constantly. Stir in egg whites. Cook for 2 minutes longer, stirring frequently.
■ Ladle into soup bowls. Garnish with parsley.
■ Yield: 6 servings.

BOSTON LETTUCE AND BEET SALAD

1 cup olive oil	Salt and freshly ground pepper to taste
2 tablespoons lemon juice	1 (16-ounce) can sliced beets, drained
¼ cup wine vinegar	1 large head Boston lettuce
2 tablespoons Dijon-style mustard	

■ Combine olive oil, lemon juice, vinegar, mustard and seasonings in covered jar. Shake to mix well.
■ Place beets in shallow dish. Pour half the dressing over beets. Chill for 1 hour.
■ Remove core from bottom of lettuce. Rinse, keeping head intact; drain. Chill in sealed plastic bag in refrigerator.
■ Place lettuce on serving plate. Spread leaves apart. Drain beets. Arrange slices between leaves and on serving plate. Drizzle remaining dressing over salad.
■ Yield: 8 servings.

ROAST FILET OF BEEF

1 (5-pound) filet of beef	½ cup oil
4 cloves of garlic, slivered	1 cup red wine vinegar
	1 teaspoon thyme
1 teaspoon pepper	1 bay leaf
½ teaspoon hot sauce	3 slices bacon
1 cup soy sauce	

■ Make 1-inch slits in roast; insert garlic. Rub roast with pepper and hot sauce.
■ Combine soy sauce, oil, wine vinegar and herbs in plastic bag. Add roast. Seal; place in shallow dish. Marinate at room temperature for 15 minutes or in refrigerator for several hours.
■ Preheat oven to 425 degrees. Drain roast, reserving marinade. Place on rack in roasting pan. Arrange bacon over top.
■ Insert meat thermometer. Bake for 45 minutes or to 125 degrees on meat thermometer for rare, or to 145 degrees for medium, basting occasionally. Place on serving plate. Slice thinly.
■ Yield: 12 to 15 servings.
■ Note: Marinated the night before, roast requires less than 1 hour to bake.

TURKEY DIVAN ROLLS

2 (16-ounce) packages individually frozen broccoli spears
1 can cream of chicken soup
½ cup mayonnaise
½ teaspoon curry powder
⅓ cup cream
2 teaspoons lemon juice
12 very thin slices deli turkey breast
1 cup shredded Cheddar cheese
1 cup stuffing mix
2 tablespoons melted butter

- Preheat oven to 350 degrees.
- Cook broccoli in a small amount of water until tender; drain. Cover with ice water; drain.
- Combine soup, mayonnaise, curry powder, cream and lemon juice in bowl; mix well. Spread a small amount in 9 x 13-inch baking dish.
- Wrap turkey slices around broccoli spears. Arrange in prepared dish. Spoon remaining sauce over turkey. Sprinkle with cheese and mixture of dry stuffing mix and butter.
- Bake for 20 minutes or until brown and bubbly.
- Yield: 6 servings.

HOLIDAY POTATO CASSEROLE

½ cup chopped celery
1 green pepper, chopped
¼ cup chopped pimento
½ cup melted butter or margarine
1 teaspoon salt
¼ teaspoon pepper
1 can cream of celery soup
2 cups sour cream with chives
1 (16-ounce) can small whole onions, drained
2 pounds frozen shredded hashed-brown potatoes
2 cups shredded Cheddar cheese
1 cup fresh bread crumbs
¼ cup melted butter or margarine

- Preheat oven to 350 degrees.
- Combine celery, green pepper, pimento, ½ cup butter, salt and pepper in bowl. Add soup and sour cream; mix well.
- Add onions, potatoes and 1 cup cheese; mix well.
- Spoon into greased 2-quart casserole. Layer remaining 1 cup cheese and bread crumbs over top. Drizzle with ¼ cup butter.
- Bake for 45 minutes.
- Yield: 8 servings.

GREEN BEANS WITH RED PEPPERS

3 pounds (3 inch long) green beans
3 sweet red peppers
2 tablespoons chopped onion
6 tablespoons butter or margarine
1 tablespoon lemon juice
Salt and pepper to taste

- Trim green beans. Cook in a small amount of water in saucepan for 8 to 10 minutes or until tender-crisp; drain. Cover with ice water; drain.
- Slice red peppers. Sauté with onion in butter in skillet for 2 minutes. Reduce heat to low. Add lemon juice and green beans.
- Cook, covered, for 3 to 4 minutes or until green beans are heated through. Season to taste. Spoon into serving dish.
- Yield: 8 servings.

TRIFLETS

1 (10 to 12-inch) bakery jelly roll
¼ cup orange juice
2 (3-ounce) packages vanilla instant pudding mix
3½ cups milk
1 teaspoon almond extract
1 cup whipping cream or 8 ounces whipped topping
1 cup sour cream
1 (16-ounce) can sliced peaches, drained
½ cup sliced almonds

- Cut jelly roll into 1-inch slices. Place in bottom of glass sherbet dishes. Sprinkle with orange juice.
- Prepare pudding mix according to package directions using 3½ cups milk and almond extract. Whip cream until stiff. Fold whipped cream and sour cream gently into pudding.
- Spoon half the pudding over jelly roll slices. Layer peaches and remaining pudding on top. Sprinkle with almonds.
- Chill until serving time.
- Yield: 10 to 12 servings.
- Note: May assemble trifle in glass serving bowl.

Make an instant centerpiece by arranging candles of varying heights on mirror.

Make-Ahead Holiday Dinner

Menu

Shrimp Mousse Wreath—Cranberry Star Salad
Dijon Ham or Smoked Turkey
Broccoli Casserole Parmesan—Braised Baby Carrots
Candied Apple Rings
Bubble Brioche
Tutti-Frutti Ice Cream Cake or
Strawberry Glacé Pie or Pumpkin Cheesecake
Café au Lait

SHRIMP MOUSSE WREATH

1 cup sour cream	⅓ cup cold water
1 cup mayonnaise	2 teaspoons instant
2 pounds cooked	vegetable bouillon
shrimp, ground	1 cup boiling water
⅔ cup finely chopped	8 ounces cream cheese,
onion	softened
1 cup finely chopped	3 tablespoons sour
celery	cream
2 teaspoons	1 bunch parsley,
Worcestershire sauce	chopped
2 teaspoons salt	3 whole pimento halves
⅛ teaspoon pepper	1 pint cherry tomatoes
2 envelopes unflavored	
gelatin	

■ Blend 1 cup sour cream and mayonnaise in large bowl. Add shrimp, onion, celery, Worcestershire sauce, salt and pepper; mix well.
■ Soften gelatin in cold water. Dissolve bouillon in boiling water. Add softened gelatin. Stir until gelatin is dissolved. Stir into shrimp mixture.
■ Pour into shallow 8-cup ring mold. Chill for 8 hours or until firm.
■ Unmold onto serving plate. Combine cream cheese and 3 tablespoons sour cream in bowl; mix well. Spread over mold. Sprinkle parsley around mold to resemble wreath. Chill for 30 minutes.
■ Pat pimento halves dry. Place 2 pimento halves, narrow ends together, at top of wreath. Open and flatten wide ends carefully; trim. Cut remaining pimento in half lengthwise. Trim outer edges to resemble ribbon. Place on wreath to complete bow.
■ Fill center of mold with whole cherry tomatoes. Serve with crackers.
■ Yield: 20 servings.

CRANBERRY STAR SALAD

1 envelope unflavored	1 (16-ounce) can whole
gelatin	cranberry sauce
2 tablespoons cold water	1 (8-ounce) can
½ cup dry red wine	crushed pineapple
2 cups water	⅓ cup chopped walnuts
1 (6-ounce) package	1 bunch parsley
raspberry gelatin	

■ Soften unflavored gelatin in 2 tablespoons cold water. Combine wine and 2 cups water in saucepan. Bring to a boil. Add softened gelatin and raspberry gelatin. Stir until gelatin is dissolved.
■ Add cranberry sauce and undrained pineapple; mix well. Chill until partially set.
■ Stir in walnuts. Pour into 5 to 6-cup star mold. Chill for 4 hours or until set.

■ Unmold onto serving plate. Garnish with parsley if desired.
■ Yield: 10 servings.

DIJON HAM

1 (3-pound) canned	¼ cup maple syrup
ham	2 tablespoons cider
¼ cup Dijon-style	vinegar
mustard	1 cup red wine
Whole cloves	⅓ cup cola
⅓ cup orange	
marmalade	

■ Preheat oven to 350 degrees.
■ Place ham in shallow baking dish. Spread with mustard. Stud with cloves. Spoon marmalade over ham. Drizzle with maple syrup and mixture of cider vinegar, wine and cola.
■ Bake for 1 hour, basting every 15 minutes. Let stand for 15 minutes before slicing.
■ Yield: 8 servings.

SMOKED TURKEY

1 bag hickory chips	1 cup Worcestershire
3 foil loaf pans	sauce
1 (10 to 13-pound)	1 tablespoon salt
oven-ready turkey	¼ teaspoon cayenne
1 foil roasting pan	pepper
½ cup dry white wine	1 teaspoon Tabasco
or apple juice	sauce
2 cups oil	1 tablespoon paprika
1 cup lemon juice	

■ Soak hickory chips in water using package directions. Punch holes in bottoms of 2 foil loaf pans. Place chips in pans. Fill third foil loaf pan half full of water.
■ Preheat grill with hood to 325 degrees.
■ Place turkey breast side up in foil roasting pan. Place in deeper heavy metal roasting pan. Pour wine into turkey cavity.
■ Baste turkey with mixture of oil, lemon juice, Worcestershire sauce, salt, cayenne pepper, Tabasco sauce and paprika. Cover drumsticks and breast with foil. Insert meat thermometer.
■ Place loaf pans with hickory chips on coals. Place water-filled loaf pan on grill. Place turkey roaster beside water pan. Close hood.
■ Roast turkey for 4 hours or to 185 degrees on meat thermometer, basting with oil mixture frequently. Cool. Store, covered, in refrigerator.
■ Yield: 12 servings.

BROCCOLI CASSEROLE PARMESAN

1 onion, finely chopped	⅛ teaspoon pepper
¼ cup butter or margarine	2½ pounds fresh or 2 (16-ounce) packages frozen broccoli
¼ cup all-purpose flour	
2 cups milk	
1 egg yolk, beaten	2 tablespoons melted butter or margarine
1 cup Parmesan cheese	
½ teaspoon salt	½ cup bread crumbs

- Preheat oven to 400 degrees.
- Sauté onion in ¼ cup butter in saucepan. Stir in flour. Add milk gradually, stirring constantly. Cook until thickened, stirring constantly.
- Stir a small amount of hot mixture into egg yolk; stir egg yolk into hot mixture. Add cheese, salt and pepper; mix well. Remove from heat.
- Cook broccoli in a small amount of water in covered saucepan for 7 to 10 minutes or just until tender; drain. Arrange stalks toward center in 9 x 13-inch baking dish.
- Pour sauce over broccoli. Sprinkle mixture of butter and crumbs over top.
- Bake for 20 minutes or until brown and bubbly.
- Yield: 8 servings.

CANDIED APPLE RINGS

12 Winesap apples	1 stick butter or margarine, sliced
2 (6-ounce) packages small cinnamon candies	Several drops of red food coloring
3 cups sugar	1 tablespoon water

- Peel apples; remove cores. Cut into rings.
- Layer apple rings, candies, sugar and butter in large electric skillet. Drizzle with mixture of food coloring and water.
- Cook, covered, at 275 degrees for 15 to 30 minutes until apple rings are tender and syrup is thickened. Serve hot or cold.
- Yield: 12 servings.
- Note: May be stored in refrigerator and reheated at 350 degrees for 20 minutes.

Fashion napkins into festive Christmas roses for holiday table settings. Unfold each napkin completely. Fold all 4 corners to center. Repeat process 2 additional times. Turn napkin over. Fold 4 points to center once more. Hold points together firmly in center of napkin with finger. Pull 1 petal out and up from underneath each corner. Pull 1 petal out and up from between each of first 4 petals. Pull remaining 4 petals out and up.

BRAISED BABY CARROTS

40 baby carrots	⅛ teaspoon nutmeg
¼ cup melted butter	Salt and pepper to taste

- Peel and trim carrots. Cook in a small amount of water in large saucepan for 5 minutes or just until tender; drain.
- Add butter, nutmeg and salt and pepper to taste; toss gently.
- Place in serving dish or arrange on platter around turkey.
- Yield: 8 servings.

BUBBLE BRIOCHE

1 package dry yeast	1 cup all-purpose flour
¼ cup (105 to 115-degree) warm water	3 eggs
½ cup milk, scalded	1 egg yolk
½ cup butter or margarine, softened	2¼ cups all-purpose flour
⅓ cup sugar	1 egg white
½ teaspoon salt	1 tablespoon sugar

- Dissolve yeast in warm water. Cool milk.
- Cream butter, ⅓ cup sugar and salt in mixer bowl until light and fluffy. Add milk and 1 cup flour; mix well.
- Add yeast, eggs and egg yolk; mix well. Add remaining 2¼ cups flour. Beat for 5 to 8 minutes or until very smooth.
- Let rise, covered, for 2 hours or until doubled in bulk. Stir dough down; beat well. Chill, tightly covered, for 8 hours.
- Stir dough down. Spoon into greased tube pan in 6 portions. Let rise, covered, for 1 to 2 hours or until doubled in bulk.
- Preheat oven to 375 degrees.
- Brush dough with mixture of egg white and 1 tablespoon sugar. Bake for 35 to 45 minutes or until brown. Remove to wire rack to cool.
- Yield: 12 servings.

CAFÉ AU LAIT

1 (6-ounce) jar instant nondairy creamer	¼ cup instant coffee powder
¼ cup packed light brown sugar	Dash of salt

- Combine all ingredients in bowl; mix well. Store in airtight container.
- Combine ¼ cup mix and ⅔ cup boiling water in cup for each serving or 2 cups mix and 5⅓ cups boiling water in coffeepot for 8 servings.
- Yield: 2 cups mix or 8 servings.

TUTTI-FRUTTI ICE CREAM CAKE

20 ladyfingers, split	1 quart vanilla ice cream
1 quart vanilla ice cream	1 teaspoon rum extract
1 (6-ounce) can frozen	1 teaspoon almond
orange juice	extract
concentrate, thawed	⅓ cup chopped
2 (10-ounce) packages	maraschino cherries
frozen raspberries,	¼ cup chopped
thawed	pistachio nuts
2 cups drained	½ cup whipped cream
crushed pineapple	8 whole maraschino
1 tablespoon frozen	cherries
lemonade concentrate	

■ Line bottom of 9-inch springform pan with ladyfingers. Arrange ladyfingers vertically around side of pan. Cut any remaining ladyfingers to fill in spaces on bottom.
■ Soften 1 quart ice cream in mixer bowl for several minutes. Add orange juice concentrate, mix well. Spoon into prepared springform pan. Freeze for several hours or until firm.
■ Combine raspberries, pineapple and lemonade concentrate in blender container. Purée until smooth; strain.
■ Pour into shallow pan. Freeze for 1 hour or until partially frozen. Beat slightly. Pour over ice cream layer. Freeze for several hours or until firm.
■ Soften 1 quart ice cream in mixer bowl for several minutes. Add flavoring, chopped cherries and pistachio nuts; mix well. Spoon over raspberry layer. Freeze, covered, for 8 hours or longer.
■ Place on serving plate; remove side of pan. Thaw in refrigerator for several minutes. Garnish with whipped cream and whole cherries.
■ Yield: 12 to 16 servings.

STRAWBERRY GLACÉ PIE

⅓ cup butter or	8 ounces cream cheese,
margarine, softened	softened
3 tablespoons sugar	1 quart strawberries
1 egg yolk	1 cup sugar
1 cup all-purpose flour	3 tablespoons
1 cup flaked coconut	cornstarch
½ cup sugar	1 cup whipped cream
1 teaspoon lemon juice	

■ Preheat oven to 325 degrees.
■ Cream butter and 3 tablespoons sugar in mixer bowl until light and fluffy. Blend in egg yolk. Stir in flour and coconut.
■ Press over bottom and side of 9-inch pie plate; flute edge. Prick with fork.
■ Bake for 25 minutes or until light brown. Cool on wire rack.
■ Cream ½ cup sugar, lemon juice and cream cheese in bowl until light and fluffy. Spread in cooled pie shell.
■ Arrange enough whole strawberries stem side down in pie shell to cover filling. Refrigerate.
■ Mash and strain remaining strawberries to extract juice. Add enough water to strawberry juice to measure 1½ cups.
■ Bring strawberry juice to a boil in saucepan. Add mixture of 1 cup sugar and cornstarch gradually, stirring constantly. Cook for 1 minute, stirring constantly. Cool.
■ Spoon glaze over strawberries. Chill for several hours. Top with whipped cream.
■ Yield: 6 servings.

PUMPKIN CHEESECAKE

2½ cups graham cracker	3 eggs, beaten
crumbs	1 teaspoon cinnamon
½ cup melted butter or	½ teaspoon ginger
margarine	16 ounces cream cheese,
2 tablespoons sugar	softened
½ teaspoon cinnamon	1 tablespoon vanilla
1 envelope unflavored	extract
gelatin	1 cup whipping cream
¾ cup pineapple juice	1 (20-ounce) can
1 (16-ounce) can	crushed pineapple,
pumpkin	drained
1 cup packed light	½ cup miniature
brown sugar	marshmallows

■ Preheat oven to 350 degrees.
■ Combine graham cracker crumbs, butter, sugar and ½ teaspoon cinnamon in bowl; mix well.
■ Press mixture over bottom and 1½ inches up side of springform pan.
■ Bake for 10 minutes. Cool on wire rack.
■ Soften gelatin in pineapple juice in saucepan. Add pumpkin, brown sugar, eggs, cinnamon and ginger; mix well. Simmer, covered, for 30 minutes, stirring occasionally.
■ Beat cream cheese with vanilla in mixer bowl until fluffy. Add to warm pumpkin mixture, stirring just until blended.
■ Pour into prepared springform pan. Chill, covered, for 8 hours.
■ Whip cream until stiff. Fold in pineapple and marshmallows gently. Spoon over cheesecake. Chill until serving time. Remove side of pan.
■ Yield: 16 servings.

Christmas à Bon Marché

Menu

Golden Cheese Wheel or Pumpkin Bisque
Granny Smith Apple Salad
Chicken Cordon Bleu en Croûte or
Blanquette of Pork Roast or Steak Roulades
Pasta Nests with Vegetables or
Carrot Ring or
Christmas Cabbage
Sour Cream and Chive Buns
Holiday Strawberry Squares or
Chocolate Angel Tarts or
Steamed Cranberry Pudding
Cranberry Spritzers

GOLDEN CHEESE WHEEL

1 package dry yeast	1 egg, beaten
⅔ cup (110 to 115-degree) warm water	3 cups shredded Monterey Jack cheese
1 cup all-purpose flour	½ cup chopped parsley
2 tablespoons oil	½ teaspoon garlic salt
½ teaspoon sugar	⅛ teaspoon pepper
½ teaspoon salt	1 egg, beaten
1 cup all-purpose flour	1 tablespoon water

■ Dissolve yeast in ⅔ cup warm water in large bowl. Add 1 cup flour, oil, sugar and salt; mix well. Add remaining 1 cup flour; mix well.
■ Knead on floured surface for 5 to 8 minutes or until smooth and elastic. Place in greased bowl, turning to grease surface. Let rise, covered, for about 1 hour or until doubled in bulk.
■ Preheat oven to 400 degrees.
■ Divide dough in half. Let rest, covered, for 10 minutes. Roll into 13-inch circles on floured surface. Fit 1 circle into greased 12-inch pizza pan.
■ Combine 1 egg, cheese, parsley, garlic salt and pepper in bowl; mix well. Spread over dough. Top with remaining circle; flute edge.

■ Bake for 20 minutes. Brush with mixture of 1 egg and 1 tablespoon water. Bake for 12 to 15 minutes longer or until brown. Cut into small wedges. Serve hot.
■ Yield: 16 servings.

PUMPKIN BISQUE

1 tablespoon chopped green onion	⅛ teaspoon white pepper
2 tablespoons butter or margarine	⅛ teaspoon cinnamon
1 (16-ounce) can pumpkin	2 teaspoons instant chicken bouillon
1 cup water	2 cups half and half
1 tablespoon light brown sugar	1 lemon, thinly sliced
½ teaspoon salt	2 tablespoons chopped fresh parsley

■ Sauté green onion in butter in 2-quart saucepan until tender. Add pumpkin, water, brown sugar, salt, pepper, cinnamon and bouillon; mix well.
■ Simmer for 5 minutes.
■ Stir in half and half. Heat just to serving temperature. Ladle into soup cups. Garnish each serving with lemon slice and parsley.
■ Yield: 10 first-course servings.

GRANNY SMITH APPLE SALAD

6 large Granny Smith apples, thinly sliced	1⅓ cups yogurt
¼ cup lemon juice	½ cup mayonnaise
2 cups chopped celery	4 teaspoons lemon juice
2 cups diced Gruyère cheese	2 teaspoons chopped parsley
1 cup chopped walnuts	Celery leaves

■ Sprinkle apple slices with ¼ cup lemon juice.
■ Combine celery, cheese, walnuts and ⅔ of the apples in bowl.
■ Combine yogurt and next 3 ingredients in small bowl. Add to apple mixture; mix well.
■ Arrange remaining apple slices around edge of serving dish. Spoon salad into center. Garnish with celery leaves.
■ Yield: 8 servings.

CHICKEN CORDON BLEU EN CROÛTE

1 package dry yeast	1½ cups all-purpose
¼ cup (110 to 115-	flour
degree) warm water	6 chicken breast filets
¼ cup butter or	2 tablespoons oil
margarine, softened	6 (½-ounce) strips
3 tablespoons sugar	Brie cheese
¼ teaspoon salt	6 (1-ounce) slices
1 egg	boiled ham
1 egg yolk	1 tablespoon water
¾ cup all-purpose flour	1 egg white
2 tablespoons milk	

■ Dissolve yeast in warm water.
■ Cream butter, sugar and salt in mixer bowl until light and fluffy. Add egg, egg yolk, ¾ cup flour, milk and yeast.
■ Beat at low speed for 1 minute. Beat at high speed for 2 minutes. Stir in remaining 1½ cups flour. Chill for 2 hours or longer.
■ Preheat oven to 375 degrees.
■ Brown chicken filets in oil in skillet for 1 minute on each side. Drain on paper towel. Place 1 strip cheese on each filet; wrap each with 1 slice ham.
■ Roll dough into 14x21-inch rectangle on floured surface. Cut into six 7-inch squares. Place 1 filet on each square. Wrap dough around filet; seal edges.
■ Place seam side down on baking sheet. Decorate with scraps of dough. Brush with mixture of water and egg white. Make 2 steam vents in each.
■ Bake for 20 minutes or until golden.
■ Yield: 6 servings.

BLANQUETTE OF PORK ROAST

1 (4 to 4½-pound)	1 pound medium
rolled boneless pork	mushrooms
shoulder roast or	1 (16-ounce) can small
boneless loin	onions, drained
2 teaspoons salt	2 tablespoons
½ teaspoon white	all-purpose flour
pepper	2 tablespoons water
¼ teaspoon rosemary	2 egg yolks, beaten
2 cups water	2 cups cooked peas
1 pound baby carrots,	
peeled	

■ Brown roast on all sides in Dutch oven. Sprinkle with salt, pepper and rosemary. Add 2 cups water.
■ Simmer, tightly covered, or bake at 350 degrees for 1 hour and 15 minutes.
■ Add carrots. Cook for 30 minutes longer . Add mushrooms and onions. Cook for 15 minutes or until roast and vegetables are tender.

■ Arrange roast and vegetables on heated serving plate. Remove string from roast.
■ Skim pan juices. Stir in mixture of flour and 2 tablespoons water. Cook until thickened, stirring constantly. Stir a small amount of hot mixture into egg yolks; stir egg yolks into hot mixture. Cook until thickened, stirring constantly; do not boil.
■ Add peas. Spoon ½ cup gravy over roast. Serve remaining gravy with roast.
■ Yield: 12 servings.
■ Note: To bone shoulder roast, cut in from 1 side to expose arm bone. Remove bone; trim fat. Roll firmly and tie at 1-inch intervals.

PASTA NESTS WITH VEGETABLES

3 tablespoons butter or	1 cup sour cream
margarine	1 (16-ounce) package
2 tablespoons	frozen vegetables
all-purpose flour	1 (8-ounce) package
1 teaspoon grated	fettucini
lemon rind	1 egg, beaten
Salt and pepper to taste	¼ cup Parmesan cheese
1 cup milk	

■ Preheat oven to 350 degrees.
■ Melt butter in saucepan. Stir in flour, lemon rind and salt and pepper. Add milk. Cook until thickened, stirring constantly. Fold in sour cream. Set aside.
■ Cook vegetables in a small amount of water in saucepan until tender; drain. Cover with ice water; drain and set aside.
■ Cook fettucini using package directions; drain. Stir in egg and cheese. Divide into 8 portions.
■ Spoon half the sauce into greased 7x12-inch baking dish. Twirl fettucini 1 portion at a time around long-tined fork. Remove to prepared baking dish to form nests.
■ Spoon vegetables into and between nests. Pour remaining sauce over top.
■ Bake for 20 minutes or until bubbly.
■ Yield: 8 servings.

CRANBERRY SPRITZERS

1 (32-ounce) bottle of	2 cups white grape
cranberry-apple juice	juice
1 cup club soda	Lemon slices

■ Chill cranberry-apple juice, club soda and grape juice. Combine in pitcher.
■ Serve in chilled glasses. Garnish with lemon slices.
■ Yield: 10 servings.

STEAK ROULADES

12 (3 x 5 x ¼-inch thick) pieces round steak	⅔ cup chopped celery
Salt and pepper to taste	½ cup sliced mushrooms
1 cup (about) flour	2 cups beef broth
¼ cup butter or margarine	1 cup sour cream

■ Prepare Mushroom or Sausage Stuffing.
■ Pound round steak very thin with meat mallet. Sprinkle with salt and pepper. Place 2 tablespoons stuffing on each piece.
■ Roll as for jelly roll; tie with butcher's string. Coat with flour. Brown several at a time on all sides in butter in Dutch oven for 5 to 7 minutes. Drain on paper towel.
■ Add celery and mushrooms to Dutch oven. Stir-fry for 2 minutes. Add steak rolls and broth; cover tightly. Simmer or bake at 350 degrees for 1½ hours or until tender.
■ Place roulades on heated serving plate; remove butcher's string.
■ Stir sour cream into pan juices. Heat to serving temperature; do not boil. Spoon gravy over steak rolls. Serve with remaining gravy.
■ Yield: 12 servings.

Mushroom Stuffing

1 cup chopped onion	½ cup water
2 tablespoons butter or margarine	1 egg, beaten
	½ teaspoon salt
½ cup chopped mushrooms	⅛ teaspoon pepper
2 cups soft bread crumbs	2 tablespoons minced parsley

■ Sauté onion in butter in skillet until golden. Add mushrooms. Sauté for 1 minute. Remove from heat.
■ Add remaining ingredients; mix well.
■ Yield: Enough stuffing for 12 roulades.

Sausage Stuffing

½ cup minced onion	½ teaspoon salt
8 ounces Italian sausage	⅛ teaspoon pepper
2 tablespoons oil	1 egg, beaten
1 cup soft bread crumbs	½ teaspoon oregano

■ Sauté onion and sausage in oil in skillet until brown, stirring frequently; drain.
■ Add remaining ingredients; mix well.
■ Yield: Enough stuffing for 12 roulades.

CARROT RING

1 cup butter or margarine, softened	3 cups finely grated carrots
1 cup packed light brown sugar	2 teaspoons lemon juice
2 eggs	2 teaspoons water
2½ cups sifted cake flour	1 (16-ounce) package frozen peas
2 teaspoons baking powder	1 tablespoon melted butter or margarine
1 teaspoon soda	

■ Preheat oven to 350 degrees.
■ Cream 1 cup butter and brown sugar in mixer bowl until light and fluffy. Add eggs 1 at a time, beating well after each addition.
■ Add sifted cake flour, baking powder and soda to creamed mixture; mix well. Stir in carrots, lemon juice and water. Spoon into lightly greased ring mold.
■ Bake for 50 minutes or until set. Cook peas in a small amount of water in saucepan until tender; drain. Add butter.
■ Unmold carrot ring onto serving plate. Fill center with peas.
■ Yield: 8 servings.

CHRISTMAS CABBAGE

1 medium head red cabbage	1 (10-ounce) package frozen peas
1 medium head green cabbage	1 medium onion, chopped
2 tablespoons red wine vinegar	½ teaspoon caraway seed
1 teaspoon sugar	1 teaspoon salt
1 teaspoon salt	3 tablespoons oil
3 tablespoons oil	1 bunch watercress

■ Slice each head cabbage coarsely.
■ Combine red cabbage, wine vinegar, sugar, 1 teaspoon salt and 3 tablespoons oil in saucepan. Cook for 20 minutes, stirring occasionally. Add peas. Cook for 5 minutes longer.
■ Combine green cabbage, onion, caraway seed, 1 teaspoon salt and 3 tablespoons oil in saucepan. Cook for 20 minutes, stirring occasionally.
■ Spoon red and green cabbage onto opposite sides of serving platter. Arrange watercress down center of platter.
■ Yield: 10 to 12 servings.

SOUR CREAM AND CHIVE BUNS

¾ cup sour cream	¼ cup (110 to 115-
2 tablespoons sugar	degree) warm water
1 teaspoon salt	2¼ cups flour
2 tablespoons	1 egg
shortening	1½ tablespoons
1 package dry yeast	chopped chives

■ Combine sour cream, sugar, salt and shortening in saucepan. Bring to a boil. Cool to lukewarm.
■ Dissolve yeast in ¼ cup warm water in mixer bowl. Add sour cream mixture and half the flour. Beat until smooth.
■ Add remaining flour, egg and chives; mix well. Let rise, covered, in warm place for 30 minutes or until doubled in bulk.
■ Stir dough down. Fill greased muffin cups ½ full. Let rise in warm place for 20 to 30 minutes or until doubled in bulk.
■ Preheat oven to 400 degrees.
■ Bake for 15 to 20 minutes or until brown.
■ Yield: 1 dozen.

HOLIDAY STRAWBERRY SQUARES

1 (10-ounce) package	⅔ cup sugar
frozen strawberries	2 tablespoons lemon
1 cup all-purpose flour	juice
¼ cup packed light	1 cup whipping cream
brown sugar	or 8 ounces whipped
¼ cup chopped pecans	topping
½ cup melted butter or	12 whole fresh
margarine	strawberries
2 egg whites	

■ Let strawberries stand at room temperature until partially thawed.
■ Preheat oven to 350 degrees.
■ Combine flour, brown sugar, pecans and butter in bowl. Spread in 9 x 13-inch baking dish.
■ Bake for 20 minutes, stirring frequently. Cool. Stir to crumble. Reserve ⅓ of the crumbs.
■ Combine partially thawed strawberries, egg whites, sugar and lemon juice in mixer bowl. Beat at high speed for 15 minutes or until very stiff peaks form; do not underbeat.
■ Whip cream until stiff. Fold into strawberry mixture gently. Spoon into prepared dish. Sprinkle with reserved crumbs.
■ Freeze, covered, for 8 hours or until firm. Cut into squares. Place on dessert plates. Garnish with fresh strawberries.
■ Yield: 12 servings.

CHOCOLATE ANGEL TARTS

4 egg whites	1 cup semisweet
¼ teaspoon cream of	chocolate chips
tartar	6 tablespoons water
1 cup sugar	2 teaspoons vanilla
1 cup chopped pecans	extract
1 teaspoon vanilla	2 cups whipping cream
extract	

■ Preheat oven to 300 degrees.
■ Let egg whites stand in mixer bowl until at room temperature. Add cream of tartar. Beat until foamy. Add sugar 2 tablespoons at a time, beating constantly at high speed until stiff peaks form.
■ Fold in pecans and 1 teaspoon vanilla. Spoon into 8 portions on foil-lined baking sheet. Shape into 5-inch diameter shells with back of spoon.
■ Bake for 30 to 40 minutes or until firm and dry. Cool. Peel off foil. Place on tray.
■ Melt chocolate with water in double boiler pan over hot water. Cool. Blend in 2 teaspoons vanilla.
■ Whip cream until stiff. Fold in melted chocolate gently. Spoon into meringue shells. Chill for 2 hours or longer.
■ Yield: 8 servings.

STEAMED CRANBERRY PUDDING

6 tablespoons butter or	½ cup milk
margarine, softened	2 cups fresh cranberries
¾ cup sugar	½ cup chopped pecans
2 eggs	1 cup butter or
2¼ cups all-purpose	margarine
flour	1½ cups sugar
2½ teaspoons baking	1 cup eggnog
powder	2 teaspoons rum extract
¼ teaspoon salt	

■ Cream 6 tablespoons butter and ¾ cup sugar in mixer bowl until light and fluffy. Add eggs 1 at a time, mixing well after each addition.
■ Add sifted flour, baking powder and salt to creamed mixture alternately with milk, mixing well after each addition. Fold in cranberries and pecans.
■ Pour into greased bundt pan. Cover tightly with heavy duty foil. Place on rack in large stockpot. Add enough water to cover half the bundt pan.
■ Steam, tightly covered, over low heat for 2 to 2½ hours or until pudding tests done. Uncover. Invert onto serving plate.
■ Combine 1 cup butter, 1½ cups sugar, eggnog and flavoring in saucepan. Heat until butter melts and sugar dissolves. Serve over pudding.
■ Yield: 16 servings.

Christmas Eve Dinner For Two

Menu

Poinsettia Spread
Snappy Cheese Sticks
Spinach and Strawberry Salad
Cornish Hens for Two or
Steak Diane
Festive Baked Acorn Squash
Sesame Asparagus
Sour Cream Muffins
Christmas Alaskas
Harvest Iced Tea

POINSETTIA SPREAD

1 (8-ounce) Gouda cheese	¾ cup sour cream
¼ cup white Worcestershire sauce	1 teaspoon prepared mustard
	2 to 3 tablespoons milk

■ Bring cheese to room temperature. If red shell is cracked, dip in hot water; press to seal. Make 4 to 8 intersecting cuts 2½ inches long across top.
■ Pull each section back carefully to make petals. Scoop out cheese. Chill shell in refrigerator.
■ Combine cheese, white Worcestershire sauce, sour cream, and mustard in food processor or blender container. Process until smooth, adding enough milk to make light and smooth.
■ Spoon into Gouda shell. Chill for several hours. Bring to room temperature. Serve with crackers.
■ Yield: Enough dip to fill and refill shell.

SNAPPY CHEESE STICKS

½ stick pie crust mix	⅛ teaspoon dry mustard
½ cup shredded sharp Cheddar cheese	½ teaspoon paprika

■ Preheat oven to 425 degrees.
■ Prepare pie crust mix using package directions. Add cheese, dry mustard and paprika.

■ Roll into 8 x 12-inch rectangle on lightly floured surface. Cut into ½ x 4-inch sticks.
■ Bake on baking sheet for 10 to 12 minutes or until golden brown. Store in airtight container.
■ Yield: 4 dozen.

SPINACH AND STRAWBERRY SALAD

2 tablespoons sugar	Pinch of paprika
1½ teaspoons sesame seed	2 tablespoons oil
¾ teaspoon poppy seed	1 tablespoon cider vinegar
½ teaspoon minced onion	8 ounces fresh spinach
Dash of Worcestershire sauce	½ cup sliced strawberries

■ Combine first 8 ingredients in small covered jar; shake well. Chill in refrigerator.
■ Wash spinach; dry with paper towels. Store in sealed plastic bag in refrigerator.
■ Arrange spinach and strawberries on salad plates. Drizzle with dressing.
■ Yield: 2 servings.

CORNISH HENS FOR TWO

½ (1¼-ounce) envelope dry onion soup mix	2 oven-ready Cornish game hens
6 tablespoons water	1 tablespoon melted butter or margarine
1 cup unseasoned stuffing mix cubes	½ cup water
¼ cup chopped peanuts	1 (1-serving) envelope instant cream of chicken soup mix
3 tablespoons raisins	
Pinch of ginger	

■ Preheat oven to 375 degrees.
■ Combine onion soup mix and 6 tablespoons water in bowl. Add next 4 ingredients.
■ Spoon stuffing into game hens. Place in shallow baking dish. Brush with butter.
■ Bake for 45 minutes or until tender. Place on heated serving plate.
■ Combine 3 tablespoons pan drippings, ½ cup water and chicken soup mix in saucepan. Heat to serving temperature. Serve with game hens.
■ Yield: 2 servings.

STEAK DIANE

2 (4-ounce) ½-inch thick tenderloin steaks	1½ teaspoons lemon juice
Salt and pepper to taste	¾ teaspoon Worcestershire sauce
1 tablespoon butter or margarine	1½ teaspoons chopped chives
½ teaspoon dry mustard	1½ teaspoons chopped parsley
1 tablespoon butter or margarine	

■ Sprinkle steaks with salt and pepper.
■ Combine 1 tablespoon butter and dry mustard in skillet. Heat until sizzling. Add steaks.
■ Cook for 1 minute on each side. Place on heated serving plate. Add 1 tablespoon butter, lemon juice and Worcestershire sauce to skillet.
■ Cook over high heat until thickened. Stir in chives and parsley. Spoon over steaks.
■ Yield: 2 servings.

FESTIVE BAKED ACORN SQUASH

1 acorn squash	1 (8-ounce) can crushed pineapple, drained
1½ tablespoons melted butter or margarine	
¼ cup packed light brown sugar	2 tablespoons chopped walnuts

■ Preheat oven to 400 degrees.
■ Cut squash in half lengthwise. Discard seed and fibers. Place cut side down in greased baking dish.
■ Bake for 35 minutes or until squash is tender. Turn squash over.
■ Combine butter, brown sugar, pineapple and walnuts in bowl. Spoon into squash halves.
■ Bake for 10 minutes longer.
■ Yield: 2 servings.

SESAME ASPARAGUS

8 ounces fresh asparagus	1 tablespoon lemon juice
2 tablespoons unsalted butter	1 tablespoon sesame seed
1 teaspoon oil	Salt and pepper to taste

■ Trim asparagus. Cook in a small amount of water in skillet for 3 to 4 minutes or until tender-crisp; drain. Cover with ice water; drain.
■ Melt butter in skillet. Add oil, lemon juice, sesame seed and seasonings; mix well. Add asparagus. Heat to serving temperature, shaking skillet constantly. Arrange on serving plate.
■ Yield: 2 servings.

SOUR CREAM MUFFINS

¼ cup butter or margarine, softened	½ cup buttermilk baking mix or self-rising flour
¼ cup sour cream	

■ Preheat oven to 425 degrees.
■ Combine butter and sour cream in bowl; mix well. Stir in baking mix. Spoon into greased miniature muffin cups.
■ Bake for 12 to 15 minutes or until golden brown. Serve hot.
■ Yield: 1 dozen.

CHRISTMAS ALASKAS

2 egg whites	2 individual sponge cake cups
⅛ teaspoon cream of tartar	2 chocolate-coated peppermint ice cream patties
¼ teaspoon vanilla extract	
Pinch of salt	2 tablespoons crushed peppermint stick
¼ cup sugar	

■ Preheat oven to 500 degrees.
■ Combine egg whites, cream of tartar, vanilla and salt in mixer bowl. Beat until soft peaks form. Add sugar gradually, beating constantly until stiff peaks form.
■ Place sponge cake cups on foil-lined wooden cutting board. Place ice cream patty in each cup.
■ Cover each with meringue, sealing meringue to bottom of sponge cups. Sprinkle with candy.
■ Bake for 2 to 3 minutes or until light brown. Serve immediately.
■ Yield: 2 servings.

HARVEST ICED TEA

1 cup water	1 (6-ounce) can frozen orange juice concentrate
2 tea bags	
¼ (12-ounce) can frozen cranberry juice concentrate	½ cup pear nectar

■ Bring water to a boil in saucepan. Add tea bags; remove from heat. Let stand, covered, for 5 minutes. Remove tea bags.
■ Add juice concentrates and pear nectar. Stir until concentrates melt. Serve over ice.
■ Yield: 2½ cups.

Frosted cranberries make a beautiful garnish. Dip in egg white. Coat with sugar. Dry on waxed paper-lined surface.

Comfort & Joy

Christmas Parties

*H*oliday parties are the most joyous celebrations of the year. They can also be the easiest.

The house is decorated. Much of the baking—from breads to desserts—is finished and the guests are in a party mood before they even arrive.

The best parties are those where everyone, including the host and hostess, can relax and enjoy himself. The decor, the surroundings, even the menu are not nearly as important as the mood created by bringing together a special group of friends. If the group is family and friends and the time is Christmas, you cannot fail.

A famous hostess once told me that the secret of her party success was knowing how to have more fun than her guests. She did this by planning ahead, staying organized, and making everything look spontaneous.

Being well-organized simply means making lists and planning ahead beginning with the guest list. A time schedule is essential. Calls to florists or rental services (for tables, chairs, etc.) should be made a month or more in advance because the holidays are their busiest season.

Select a menu that allows most of the items to be prepared ahead and frozen or refrigerated. This is not the time to serve soufflés or dishes that require last-minute preparation. It is also best not to try a new recipe. I feel more comfortable testing new recipes first for my family. Then, we vote to decide whether it is good enough for the party file.

On the actual day of the party, you should have no more than two or three items to prepare. Do not spend all day in the kitchen. You will feel frazzled and worn-out by the time your guests arrive.

I enjoy informal parties— salad and casserole buffets or brunch buffets—just for the pleasure of seeing my family and friends. But, there is also much to be said for the elegant suppers we all enjoy. You may want to be different and try the special Chocolate Dessert Buffet. Whichever you prefer, each is perfect for a Christmas open house, for it allows you to "open" your home and your heart to your friends. It is the best way to say, "Merry Christmas."

Whether you choose a casual or dressy affair, be sure to add those small touches that can make such a big difference in setting the mood. I love candlelight and Christmas greenery, beautiful table settings, lots of flowers, and exquisitely prepared foods. I love to see guests decked out in their holiday finery and to hear Christmas music as background to their lively chatter. I love the comfort of being with good friends at Christmas and the joy of celebration.

Twelfth Night Buffet Supper

Menu

Sparkling Fruit Compote
Festive Cheese Tray
Seafood Lasagna
Double Dippers
Buried Treasure
Spinach on Artichoke Bottoms
Twelfth Night Cake
Wassail

SPARKLING FRUIT COMPOTE

4 pears	4 cups orange sections
4 kiwifruit	4 cups sliced
2 cups seedless green	Winesap apples
grapes	¼ cup sugar
2 cups purple grapes	1 (32-ounce) bottle
4 cups fresh	of sparkling white
pineapple chunks	grape juice

■ Peel and slice pears and kiwifruit. Cut grapes into halves. Combine all fruit in large serving bowl. Sprinkle with sugar; mix lightly.
■ Chill for several hours. Add grape juice just before serving.
■ Yield: 18 cups.

FESTIVE CHEESE TRAY

1 (16-ounce) package	Creamy Cheddar Wheel
gingersnaps	2 (16-ounce) packages
1 (16-ounce) package	whole grain crackers
baby Brie cheese	2 loaves French bread,
Camembert with	thinly sliced
Pistachios	Lemon leaves
Aegean Cream Cheese	

■ Arrange gingersnaps, cheeses, crackers and bread on tray lined with lemon leaves. Let stand at room temperature for 30 minutes before serving.
■ Yield: 24 servings.
■ Note: Purchase lemon leaves from florist.

Camembert with Pistachios

3 (8-ounce) packages	½ cup chopped
Camembert cheese,	pistachio nuts
softened	6 tablespoons dry
1¼ cups finely	bread crumbs
shredded Swiss	2 tablespoons butter or
cheese	margarine

■ Combine cheeses in bowl; mix well. Shape into two 6-inch discs. Press pistachio nuts on top of 1 disc; cover with remaining disc.
■ Sauté crumbs in butter in saucepan until golden brown. Cool. Pat crumbs over cheese.
■ Chill until serving time.
■ Yield: 1 (2-pound) wheel.

Aegean Cream Cheese

16 ounces cream cheese,	¼ teaspoon garlic
softened	powder
2 tablespoons minced	1 jar of brine-pack
dill	grape leaves
¼ cup minced green	
onions	

■ Combine cream cheese, dill, green onions and garlic powder in bowl; mix well. Shape into 6-inch disc; wrap with plastic wrap. Chill for 1 hour.
■ Cross two 12-inch lengths of string on flat surface. Rinse grape leaves. Arrange overlapping grape leaves to make 8-inch circle on string.
■ Place cheese disc in center; fold leaves over cheese. Add 1 leaf on top to enclose completely. Tie with string over all. Chill until serving time.
■ Remove string and open leaves before serving.
■ Yield: 1 (16-ounce) disc.

Creamy Cheddar Wheel

1½ pounds sharp	2 drops of
Cheddar cheese,	Tabasco sauce
finely shredded	1½ cups chopped
8 ounces cream cheese,	parsley
softened	

■ Combine cheeses and Tabasco sauce in bowl; mix well. Shape into wheel on surface lined with plastic wrap. Coat with parsley.
■ Chill, tightly wrapped, for several hours.
■ Yield: 1 (2-pound) wheel.

SEAFOOD LASAGNA

10 to 12 lasagna noodles	2 (10-ounce) cans
1 cup chopped onion	cream of mushroom
2 tablespoons butter or	soup
margarine	⅓ cup dry white wine
8 ounces cream cheese	1 pound cooked shrimp
1½ cups cottage cheese	8 ounces crab meat
1 egg, beaten	¼ cup Parmesan cheese
2 teaspoons basil	1 cup shredded
Salt and pepper to taste	Cheddar cheese
⅓ cup milk	8 tomato wedges

■ Preheat oven to 350 degrees.
■ Cook lasagna noodles using package directions; drain. Rinse with cold water; drain.
■ Sauté onion in butter in saucepan until tender. Cut cream cheese into small pieces. Combine sautéed onion, cream cheese, cottage cheese, egg and seasonings in bowl; mix well.
■ Combine milk, soup and wine in bowl. Reserve several shrimp for garnish. Add remaining shrimp and crab meat to soup mixture; mix well.
■ Alternate layers of noodles, cheese mixture and shrimp mixture ⅓ at a time in greased 9x13-inch baking dish. Sprinkle with Parmesan cheese.
■ Bake for 45 minutes or until bubbly. Top with Cheddar cheese. Bake for 2 minutes longer or until cheese melts.
■ Let stand for 15 minutes before serving. Garnish with tomato wedges and reserved shrimp.
■ Yield: 12 servings.

DOUBLE DIPPERS

½ cup melted butter or	¼ cup finely chopped
margarine	onion
4 dozen chicken	1½ teaspoons salt
drumettes	2 pounds lean ground
1½ cups all-purpose	beef
flour	2 cups catsup
1 teaspoon salt	1 cup whole cranberry
1 tablespoon paprika	sauce
½ teaspoon pepper	⅓ cup lemon juice
1½ cups soft bread	2 tablespoons prepared
crumbs	horseradish
½ cup milk	2 teaspoons
2 eggs	Worcestershire sauce

■ Preheat oven to 375 degrees. Pour butter into 10x15-inch baking pan.
■ Coat chicken with mixture of flour, 1 teaspoon salt, paprika and pepper. Dip chicken in butter; arrange in pan.
■ Bake for 1 hour or until brown and tender. Drain on paper towel.

■ Combine bread crumbs, milk, eggs, onion and 1½ teaspoons salt in bowl. Add ground beef; mix well. Shape into 1-inch balls.
■ Place in 10x15-inch baking pan. Bake for 30 minutes or until brown. Drain on paper towel.
■ Combine catsup, cranberry sauce, lemon juice, horseradish and Worcestershire sauce in saucepan. Bring to a boil; mix well. Pour into serving bowl.
■ Place sauce in center of serving platter. Arrange chicken and meatballs around sauce. Serve hot.
■ Yield: 24 servings.

BURIED TREASURE

2 cups mayonnaise	2 (8-ounce) cans water
½ cup sour cream	chestnuts
1 (5-ounce) jar	1 (16-ounce) can
horseradish	artichoke heart
2 teaspoons lemon juice	quarters
½ teaspoon salt	1 (16-ounce) can hearts
2 teaspoons dry mustard	of palm
1 head cauliflower	2 cucumbers
1 bunch broccoli	2 green peppers
2 (16-ounce) cans	1 basket cherry tomatoes
ripe olives	

■ Combine first 6 ingredients in bowl; mix well.
■ Separate cauliflower and broccoli into flowerets. Drain and rinse olives, water chestnuts, artichoke hearts and hearts of palm. Slice hearts of palm.
■ Peel and slice cucumbers. Cut green peppers into bite-sized pieces.
■ Combine vegetables and sauce in large serving bowl; mix well. Serve with cocktail forks.
■ Yield: 24 servings.

SPINACH ON ARTICHOKE BOTTOMS

2 (16-ounce) cans	2 tablespoons melted
artichoke bottoms,	butter
drained	8 ounces cream cheese,
2 (10-ounce) packages	softened
frozen spinach	5 tablespoons Parmesan
¼ cup milk	cheese

■ Preheat oven to 350 degrees.
■ Cook spinach using package directions; drain.
■ Arrange artichoke bottoms in shallow greased casserole. Spoon spinach onto each.
■ Blend milk, butter and cream cheese in bowl. Beat until light and fluffy. Spoon onto spinach; swirl with knife. Sprinkle with cheese.
■ Bake for 20 minutes.
■ Yield: 12 servings.

■ Preheat oven to 350 degrees.
■ Sift first 4 ingredients together; set aside.
■ Cream butter and 1½ cups sugar in bowl until light and fluffy. Add ½ cup orange juice, milk, eggs, orange rind and vanilla; mix well.
■ Add sifted ingredients ¼ at a time, beating well after each addition. Fold in walnuts, raisins, currants, chopped almonds and whole almond. Pour into well-greased 8-inch bundt pan.
■ Bake for 55 minutes or until cake tests done. Cool in pan on wire rack for 15 minutes.
■ Combine remaining ¼ cup sugar and ¼ cup orange juice in saucepan. Bring to a boil. Cool for several minutes.
■ Prick top of cake with fork. Spoon orange juice mixture over cake until liquid is completely absorbed. Cool cake completely.
■ Remove to cake plate. Wrap in plastic wrap. Let stand for 12 hours before slicing.
■ Yield: 16 servings.
■ Note: Whoever has the whole almond in his serving is king or queen for the night and will have good luck for the new year.

TWELFTH NIGHT CAKE

2½ cups all-purpose flour	1 tablespoon grated orange rind
1 teaspoon soda	1 teaspoon vanilla extract
1 teaspoon salt	½ cup chopped walnuts
½ teaspoon cinnamon	½ cup golden raisins
¾ cup butter or margarine, softened	¼ cup currants
1½ cups sugar	1 cup chopped almonds
½ cup Florida orange juice	1 whole almond
½ cup milk	¼ cup sugar
2 eggs	¼ cup Florida orange juice

WASSAIL

2 cups sugar	4 cups Florida grapefruit juice
1 cup packed light brown sugar	4 cups Florida orange juice
8 cups apple cider	7 orange slices
2 3-inch sticks cinnamon	7 maraschino cherry halves
12 whole cloves	Whole cloves
1 cup pineapple juice	

■ Combine sugars and cider in large saucepan. Cook over low heat until sugar dissolves, stirring constantly. Add cinnamon sticks and 12 cloves. Simmer for 5 minutes.
■ Add pineapple juice, grapefruit juice and orange juice. Heat just to serving temperature; do not boil.
■ Strain wassail into heatproof punch bowl; discard spices. Insert cloves around edges of orange slices. Place cherry half on each. Float orange slices in wassail.
■ Yield: 16 cups.

Christmas Brunch Buffet

Menu

Strawberries and Cream Toast
Festive Scrambled Eggs
Crispy Cooked Bacon
Golden Winter Fruit Casserole
Citrus Eggnog

STRAWBERRIES AND CREAM TOAST

½ cup chopped fresh strawberries	¾ cup half and half
8 ounces cream cheese, softened	3 tablespoons strawberry preserves
3 tablespoons frozen orange juice concentrate	2 tablespoons butter or margarine
12 (1-inch) slices French bread	1½ tablespoons oil
3 eggs, beaten	⅓ cup strawberry preserves
	¼ cup butter or margarine, softened

■ Combine first 3 ingredients in bowl; mix well. Cut pocket in each bread slice.
■ Spoon cream cheese mixture into each pocket. Arrange bread in large shallow dish. Pour mixture of eggs, half and half and 3 tablespoons preserves over bread. Chill, covered, overnight.
■ Melt 2 tablespoons butter with oil in skillet. Brown bread on both sides. Arrange on serving plate. Spoon mixture of ⅓ cup preserves and ¼ cup butter over toast.
■ Yield: 12 servings.

FESTIVE SCRAMBLED EGGS

1 medium zucchini, sliced	½ teaspoon salt
4 cups fresh mushrooms	8 eggs, beaten
2 medium sweet red peppers, sliced	¼ cup milk
2 large onions, sliced	2 tablespoons melted butter or margarine
¼ cup melted butter or margarine	½ cup shredded Cheddar cheese

■ Cut zucchini slices and mushrooms in half. Sauté peppers and onions in ¼ cup butter in skillet for 5 minutes. Add zucchini, mushrooms and salt. Cook until tender, stirring occasionally. Remove vegetables; keep warm.
■ Beat eggs and milk in bowl. Add 2 tablespoons butter to skillet. Add eggs. Cook until eggs are almost set, stirring frequently. Stir in cheese.
■ Spoon eggs and vegetables onto serving platter.
■ Yield: 8 servings.

GOLDEN WINTER FRUIT CASSEROLE

3 winter pears, chopped	1 (6-ounce) package dried peaches
2 Golden Delicious apples, chopped	½ cup maraschino cherries
2 teaspoons lemon juice	½ cup white wine
2 cups pineapple chunks, drained	½ cup sugar
1 (6-ounce) package dried apricots	¼ cup melted butter
	3 tablespoons all-purpose flour

■ Combine first 7 ingredients in 2-quart casserole.
■ Mix wine, sugar, butter and flour in saucepan. Cook until thickened, stirring constantly. Pour over fruit; mix gently. Marinate for 12 to 24 hours.
■ Preheat oven to 350 degrees.
■ Bake casserole for 45 minutes or until bubbly.
■ Yield: 10 servings.

CITRUS EGGNOG

3 eggs	3 cups orange juice
2 tablespoons sugar	2 tablespoons lemon juice
¼ teaspoon cinnamon	2 cups chilled ginger ale
⅛ teaspoon ground cloves	¼ teaspoon nutmeg
1 pint vanilla ice cream	

■ Combine first 4 ingredients in mixer bowl. Beat at medium speed until very light.
■ Add ice cream and juices. Beat at low speed until blended. Chill, covered, until serving time.
■ Stir in ginger ale gradually. Pour into glasses. Sprinkle with nutmeg.
■ Yield: 10 cups.

Chocolate Dessert Buffet

Menu

Tasse de Chocolat
Bûche de Noël
Chocolate Cream Puffs
Milk Chocolate Fondue
Chocolate Cheesecake
Pecan and Chocolate Pie
Mocha Cake
Holiday Secret Cake
Hot Fudge Sauce
Chocolate Truffles
Chocolate Mousse Parfaits
Café Brûlot

TASSE DE CHOCOLAT

2 (8-ounce) packages semisweet chocolate	2 tablespoons all-purpose flour
5 egg yolks	⅔ cup butter or margarine, softened
1 tablespoon sugar	5 egg whites
1 teaspoon vanilla extract	¼ cup confectioners' sugar
¼ teaspoon salt	

■ Preheat oven to 400 degrees.
■ Break chocolate into pieces. Melt in double boiler pan over hot water; remove from heat.
■ Beat egg yolks until very thick. Add sugar, vanilla, salt, flour and butter; mix well. Blend in melted chocolate.
■ Beat egg whites until stiff peaks form. Fold gently into chocolate mixture. Spoon into paper-lined foil baking cups.
■ Bake for 10 minutes or just until firm in center. Cool on wire rack. Garnish with sprinkle of confectioners' sugar or frost with favorite icing.
■ Yield: 16 servings.

BÛCHE DE NOËL

4 egg whites	¼ teaspoon salt
¼ cup sugar	½ cup confectioners' sugar
4 egg yolks	1 cup whipping cream
½ cup sugar	3 tablespoons sugar
½ cup all-purpose flour	1 tablespoon cocoa
¾ teaspoon baking powder	¼ cup semisweet chocolate chips
⅓ cup cocoa	1 teaspoon shortening

■ Preheat oven to 375 degrees. Line bottom of greased 10 x 15-inch jelly roll pan with greased waxed paper.
■ Beat egg whites until soft peaks form. Add ¼ cup sugar 1 tablespoon at a time, beating until very stiff peaks form.
■ Beat egg yolks and ½ cup sugar until very thick. Add flour, baking powder, ⅓ cup cocoa and salt. Beat at low speed until blended.
■ Fold stiffly beaten egg whites gently into batter. Spread batter evenly in prepared pan.
■ Bake for 12 minutes or just until cake springs back when lightly touched.
■ Sprinkle clean towel with confectioners' sugar. Invert cake onto towel; remove waxed paper. Roll cake and towel from narrow end as for jelly roll. Cool on wire rack for 30 minutes.
■ Prepare Vanilla Buttercream Frosting.
■ Whip cream with 3 tablespoons sugar and 1 tablespoon cocoa until stiff. Unroll cake; remove towel. Spread whipped cream over cake; reroll. Frost with Vanilla Buttercream Frosting. Draw lines and rings with fork to resemble bark.
■ Melt chocolate chips with shortening in double boiler pan over hot water. Drizzle over cake. Chill until serving time. Cut into slices.
■ Yield: 16 servings.

Vanilla Buttercream Frosting

1 cup butter or margarine, softened	1 tablespoon milk
2 cups confectioners' sugar	1½ teaspoons vanilla extract
1 egg yolk	2 teaspoons cocoa

■ Combine all ingredients in mixer bowl. Beat until light and fluffy.
■ Yield: 1½ cups.

CHOCOLATE CREAM PUFFS

½ cup butter or margarine	1½ cups milk
¼ teaspoon salt	2 squares unsweetened chocolate, grated
1 cup water	
1 cup all-purpose flour	2 tablespoons butter
4 eggs	2 teaspoons vanilla extract
¼ cup all-purpose flour	1 cup whipping cream
¾ cup sugar	1 cup chopped walnuts

- Preheat oven to 400 degrees.
- Combine ½ cup butter, salt and water in saucepan. Bring to a full rolling boil. Reduce heat. Stir in 1 cup flour. Cook until mixture forms ball, stirring constantly. Remove from heat.
- Add eggs 1 at a time, beating well after each addition. Drop by tablespoonfuls 3 inches apart onto greased baking sheet.
- Bake for 10 minutes. Reduce temperature to 350 degrees. Bake for 25 minutes longer or until golden brown and firm.
- Slit tops; remove soft dough. Cool on wire rack.
- Combine ¼ cup flour and sugar in double boiler pan. Add milk and chocolate. Cook over hot water until thickened, stirring constantly.
- Add 2 tablespoons butter and vanilla. Cool. Whip cream until stiff. Fold into chocolate mixture with walnuts.
- Spoon into cream puffs. Place on serving plate.
- Yield: 16 servings.

MILK CHOCOLATE FONDUE

1 (16-ounce) pound cake	2 teaspoons vanilla extract
1 (8-ounce) angel food cake	¼ teaspoon cinnamon
2 pounds milk chocolate, grated	2 cups apple slices
	2 cups pear slices
1 cup whipping cream	2 pints fresh strawberries
2 tablespoons instant coffee powder	2 cups fresh pineapple cubes
¼ cup hot water	

- Cut pound cake and angel food cake into 1½-inch cubes. Arrange fruit and cake cubes on serving tray. Serve with fondue for dipping.
- Combine chocolate and cream in fondue pot.
- Cook over very low heat until chocolate melts, stirring constantly.
- Dissolve coffee in hot water. Add to chocolate mixture with vanilla and cinnamon; mix well. Keep warm over fondue flame.
- Yield: 16 servings.

CHOCOLATE CHEESECAKE

1 (8½-ounce) package chocolate wafers	2 cups semisweet chocolate chips
⅓ cup melted butter or margarine	1 teaspoon vanilla extract
2 tablespoons sugar	⅛ teaspoon salt
¼ teaspoon nutmeg	1 cup sour cream
3 eggs	1 cup whipping cream
1 cup sugar	2 tablespoons confectioners' sugar
24 ounces cream cheese, softened	

- Preheat oven to 350 degrees.
- Process wafers in blender container to make fine crumbs. Combine with butter, 2 tablespoons sugar and nutmeg; mix well.
- Press evenly over bottom and side of 9-inch springform pan. Chill in refrigerator.
- Combine eggs and 1 cup sugar in mixer bowl. Beat at high speed until very thick and light. Add cream cheese. Beat until smooth.
- Melt chocolate chips in double boiler pan over hot water. Cool.
- Blend melted chocolate, vanilla, salt and sour cream into cream cheese mixture. Pour into prepared pan.
- Bake for 1 hour or just until firm. Cool in pan on wire rack. Chill, covered, overnight.
- Place on serving plate. Remove side of pan. Whip cream with confectioners' sugar until stiff. Serve with cheesecake.
- Yield: 16 servings.

PECAN AND CHOCOLATE PIE

1 stick pie crust mix	½ cup dark corn syrup
2 tablespoons chopped pecans	½ teaspoon salt
	¼ cup Brandy
3 eggs, beaten	1 cup pecan halves
1 cup sugar	½ cup semisweet chocolate chips
2 tablespoons melted butter or margarine	1 teaspoon vanilla extract
½ cup whipping cream	

- Preheat oven to 375 degrees.
- Crumble pie crust mix into bowl. Add chopped pecans. Prepare pastry according to package directions. Fit into 9-inch pie plate.
- Combine eggs, sugar, butter, whipping cream, corn syrup and salt in bowl; mix well. Stir in Brandy, pecan halves, chocolate chips and vanilla. Pour into prepared pie plate.
- Bake for 40 to 50 minutes or until filling is set. Cool on wire rack.
- Yield: 8 servings.

MOCHA CAKE

2 cups sugar	½ cup buttermilk
½ cup shortening	2 eggs
½ cup cocoa	2 cups sifted
1 teaspoon vanilla	all-purpose flour
extract	¼ teaspoon salt
1 cup boiling water	1¼ teaspoons soda

■ Preheat oven to 350 degrees.
■ Cream sugar, shortening, cocoa and vanilla in mixer bowl until light and fluffy. Add water gradually, mixing well after each addition.
■ Stir in buttermilk and eggs. Sift remaining ingredients together. Add to batter gradually, mixing well after each addition. Pour into 2 greased and floured 8-inch round cake pans.
■ Bake for 30 minutes or until cake tests done. Cool in pan for 10 minutes. Remove to wire rack to cool completely.
■ Spread Mocha Frosting between layers and over top and side of cake. Decorate top of cake with Chocolate Leaves.
■ Yield: 12 servings.

Mocha Frosting

⅓ cup semisweet	¼ cup strong black
chocolate chips	coffee
1 cup butter or	6 cups sifted
margarine, softened	confectioners' sugar
3 egg yolks	

■ Melt chocolate chips in double boiler pan over hot water.
■ Cream butter in mixer bowl until light. Add egg yolks and coffee. Beat until blended.
■ Add confectioners' sugar gradually, beating well after each addition. Add chocolate; mix well.
■ Yield: 3 cups.

Chocolate Leaves

1 cup semisweet	1 cup rose leaves
chocolate chips	

■ Melt chocolate chips in double boiler pan over hot water. Wash rose leaves; pat dry.
■ Brush chocolate over back of each leaf. Place on waxed paper-lined dish. Chill until firm. Peel off leaves. Store in refrigerator.

HOLIDAY SECRET CAKE

1 (18-ounce) package	4 eggs
white cake mix	¾ cup oil
1 (3¾-ounce) package	1 cup water
vanilla instant	1 cup chocolate syrup
pudding mix	

■ Preheat oven to 350 degrees.
■ Beat cake mix, pudding mix, eggs, oil and water in mixer bowl at medium speed for 2 minutes.
■ Pour half the batter into greased and floured bundt pan. Stir chocolate syrup into remaining batter. Pour over white cake batter.
■ Bake for 45 to 55 minutes or until cake tests done. Cool in pan for 10 minutes. Invert onto wire rack to cool completely.
■ Yield: 16 servings.

CHOCOLATE TRUFFLES

½ cup whipping cream
½ cup sugar
6 tablespoons butter or
  margarine
2 cups semisweet
  chocolate chips

1 teaspoon vanilla
  extract
½ cup cocoa

■ Combine cream, sugar and butter in saucepan. Bring to a boil; remove from heat. Add chocolate chips; stir until chocolate melts. Stir in vanilla. Cool to room temperature, stirring occasionally.
■ Chill, covered, for 12 hours or longer. Mixture will be soft. Drop by teaspoonfuls into cocoa; shape into balls.
■ Place in paper bonbon cups. Store, tightly covered, in refrigerator.
■ Yield: 1½ dozen.

CHOCOLATE MOUSSE PARFAITS

1 envelope unflavored
  gelatin
¼ cup cold milk
1 cup semisweet
  chocolate chips
¾ cup milk, scalded
1 egg
¼ cup sugar

⅓ cup nonalcoholic
  Crème de Menthe
  syrup
⅛ teaspoon salt
1 cup whipping cream
2 large ice cubes
6 peppermint candy
  sticks

■ Soften gelatin in cold milk in blender container. Process for 10 seconds. Add chocolate chips and hot milk. Process until smooth.
■ Add egg, sugar, Crème de Menthe and salt. Process until blended. Add cream and ice cubes. Process until smooth.
■ Pour into tall slender glasses. Chill until set. Garnish each parfait with peppermint candy stick.
■ Yield: 6 servings.

HOT FUDGE SAUCE

⅔ cup semisweet
  chocolate chips
2 tablespoons butter or
  margarine
⅛ teaspoon salt

1 (14-ounce) can
  sweetened condensed
  milk
1 teaspoon vanilla
  extract

■ Melt chocolate and butter in heavy saucepan over low heat, stirring constantly. Stir in salt and sweetened condensed milk.
■ Cook for 5 minutes or until slightly thickened, stirring constantly. Blend in vanilla. Serve warm or cold over ice cream.
■ Yield: 1½ cups.

CAFÉ BRÛLOT

1 1-inch stick cinnamon
6 whole cloves
1 large piece orange
  rind
2 tablespoons sugar

1 teaspoon rum extract
4 cups hot coffee
2 tablespoons semisweet
  chocolate chips
½ cup whipped cream

■ Combine spices, orange rind, sugar, rum extract and coffee in saucepan. Heat just to serving temperature. Strain.
■ Place 1 teaspoon chocolate chips in each coffee cup. Add hot coffee.
■ Serve with whipped cream.
■ Yield: 6 servings.

VERY CHEESY DIP

8 ounces cream cheese, softened	1 cup sour cream
1 cup cottage cheese	2 tablespoons minced onion
1 cup shredded mozzarella cheese	Garlic salt to taste
2½ cups shredded sharp Cheddar cheese	1 teaspoon white Worcestershire sauce
1 cup yogurt	2 heads Bibb lettuce

■ Combine cheeses, yogurt, sour cream, onion, garlic salt and Worcestershire sauce in food processor container. Pulse 8 to 10 times or until well mixed. Chill for several hours.
■ Remove centers from heads of lettuce. Place on serving plates. Fill centers with dip. Serve with fresh vegetables and crackers.
■ Yield: 5 cups.

SHRIMP TWISTS

2 (4½-ounce) cans shrimp, drained	¼ cup finely chopped pimento
2 (4-ounce) containers whipped cream cheese with chives	1 (17¼-ounce) package frozen puff pastry, thawed

■ Preheat oven to 450 degrees.
■ Combine shrimp, cream cheese and pimento in food processor. Pulse until blended.
■ Roll each sheet puff pastry into 10x15-inch rectangle on cookie sheet. Spread with shrimp mixture. Fold in half lengthwise. Cut into thirty 1x5-inch strips.
■ Twist into spirals. Place 1 inch apart on baking sheet; press ends down.
■ Bake for 10 minutes or until golden brown.
■ Yield: 2½ dozen.

MINIATURE CHICKEN PUFFS

½ cup butter or margarine	⅔ cup shredded carrots
1 cup water	1 (8-ounce) can crushed pineapple, drained
1 cup flour	
¼ teaspoon salt	½ cup yogurt
4 eggs	2 (6-ounce) cans chunky chicken, drained
½ cup small-curd cottage cheese	

■ Preheat oven to 400 degrees.
■ Melt butter in saucepan. Add water. Bring to a boil. Add flour and salt; mix vigorously. Cook until mixture forms ball, stirring constantly. Remove from heat.

■ Add eggs 1 at a time, beating well after each addition. Drop by teaspoonfuls into miniature muffin cups or onto greased baking sheet.
■ Bake for 25 minutes or until golden brown. Remove to wire rack. Slit puffs; remove soft centers. Let stand until cool.
■ Combine cottage cheese, carrots, pineapple, yogurt and chicken in bowl; mix well. Chill until serving time. Spoon into puffs. Arrange on serving plate.
■ Yield: 4 dozen.

NACHO CHEESECAKE

1¼ cups finely crushed tortilla chips	1½ cups shredded Cheddar cheese
⅓ cup shredded Cheddar cheese	½ cup shredded Monterey Jack cheese with jalapeños
¼ cup melted butter or margarine	¼ cup sour cream
32 ounces cream cheese, softened	¼ cup beer
6 eggs	1 tablespoon cornstarch
¼ cup minced onion	1 cup sour cream
1 teaspoon Tabasco sauce	1 tablespoon taco sauce
½ teaspoon garlic salt	½ cup sliced pimento-stuffed green olives
1 teaspoon Worcestershire sauce	½ cup chopped green onion tops

■ Preheat oven to 325 degrees.
■ Combine crushed chips, ⅓ cup Cheddar cheese and butter in bowl; mix well. Press over bottom of 10-inch springform pan.
■ Beat cream cheese and eggs in bowl until light and fluffy. Add onion, Tabasco sauce, garlic salt and Worcestershire sauce; mix well.
■ Add cheeses, ¼ cup sour cream, beer and cornstarch; mix well. Pour into prepared pan.
■ Bake for 1 hour. Turn off oven; open door. Let stand with door ajar until completely cool.
■ Place on serving tray; remove side of pan.
■ Spread mixture of 1 cup sour cream and taco sauce over cheesecake. Sprinkle olives and green onions over top. Cut into very thin slices. Serve with large tortilla chips.
■ Yield: 16 servings.

To make an hors d'oeuvre wreath, attach fresh cauliflowerets, broccoli flowerets, radish roses and carrot strips to lettuce-covered 14-inch styrofoam ring with toothpicks. Place bowl of dip in center.

CRAB MEAT IN PATTY SHELLS

12 ounces fresh mushrooms	2 cups sour cream
½ cup water	Salt and pepper to taste
5 tablespoons butter or margarine	⅛ teaspoon nutmeg
2 tablespoons chopped chives	1½ cups flaked crab meat
3 tablespoons all-purpose flour	3 tablespoons Sherry
	1 dozen baked patty shells

■ Remove stems from mushrooms. Combine stems with water in saucepan. Cook until tender. Drain, reserving liquid. Discard stems.
■ Slice mushroom caps. Melt butter in chafing dish or double boiler pan over hot water. Add sliced mushrooms and chives. Sauté for 3 minutes.
■ Stir in flour. Add mixture of sour cream and reserved mushroom liquid. Cook until thickened, stirring constantly. Add seasonings, crab meat and Sherry; mix well. Cook, covered, for 5 minutes.
■ Lower flame. Keep mixture warm. Serve in patty shells.
■ Yield: 1 dozen.

HOT MUSHROOM TURNOVERS

8 ounces cream cheese, softened	3 tablespoons butter or margarine
1½ cups all-purpose flour	¼ cup sour cream
½ cup butter or margarine, softened	1 teaspoon salt
8 ounces mushrooms, minced	¼ teaspoon thyme
1 large onion, minced	2 tablespoons all-purpose flour
	1 egg, beaten

■ Combine cream cheese, 1½ cups flour and ½ cup butter in bowl; mix well. Shape into ball. Chill for 1 hour.
■ Sauté mushrooms and onion in 3 tablespoons butter in skillet until tender, stirring frequently; drain. Stir in sour cream, seasonings and 2 tablespoons flour.
■ Preheat oven to 450 degrees.
■ Roll dough, ½ at a time, ⅛ inch thick on floured surface. Cut into 2¾-inch circles. Brush edges with egg.
■ Place 1 teaspoon mushroom mixture on each circle. Fold over; seal edges with fork. Pierce tops. Brush with egg. Place on ungreased baking sheet.
■ Bake for 12 to 14 minutes or until golden.
■ Yield: 3½ dozen.

PARTY HAM AND CHEESE ROLLS

2 (20-count) packages Pepperidge Farm brown and serve party rolls	2 tablespoons Worcestershire sauce
8 ounces boiled ham, thinly sliced	2 tablespoons prepared mustard
8 ounces Swiss cheese, thinly sliced	2 tablespoons poppy seed
1 cup melted butter or margarine	¼ cup packed light brown sugar

■ Split rolls. Cut ham and cheese into 40 roll-sized pieces. Place 1 piece ham and 1 piece cheese on each roll. Replace tops; return to baking pan.
■ Combine remaining ingredients in saucepan. Bring to a boil. Spoon over rolls. Let stand, tightly covered, for 2 hours.
■ Preheat oven to 350 degrees.
■ Bake for 5 to 10 minutes or until cheese melts.
■ Yield: 40 servings.

BLEU CHEESE GRAPES

3 cups chopped almonds	1 pound large seedless grapes
8 ounces cream cheese, softened	3 small clusters green grapes
2 ounces bleu cheese, softened	2 lemons, sliced
¼ cup whipping cream	

■ Preheat oven to 275 degrees.
■ Spread almonds in shallow baking dish. Bake for 5 minutes or until lightly toasted. Chop in food processor. Place in plastic bag.
■ Combine cream cheese, bleu cheese and cream in mixer bowl; beat until smooth. Add seedless grapes; stir until coated.
■ Add grapes several at a time to almonds. Shake to coat grapes. Place grapes on serving plate.
■ Garnish with grape clusters and lemon slices. Chill until serving time.
■ Yield: 3 pounds.

To serve large groups easily, use such pastry-based foods as quiche or pizza. Recipes can be doubled, baked on cookie sheets, and cut into bite-sized pieces. Or, roll 2 sheets thawed puff pastry to fit baking sheet. Layer 1 sheet pastry, Dijon mustard, boiled ham, Swiss cheese and remaining pastry on baking sheet. Cut steam vents. Bake in 450-degree oven for about 15 minutes or until golden brown.

CHOCOLATE AND CHERRY DROPS

1¼ cups butter or margarine, softened	1 teaspoon soda
2 cups sugar	1 teaspoon salt
2 eggs	2 cups chopped maraschino cherries, drained
2 teaspoons vanilla extract	1 cup chopped nuts
2½ cups all-purpose flour	36 whole maraschino cherries
¾ cup cocoa	

■ Preheat oven to 350 degrees.
■ Cream butter and sugar in mixer bowl until light and fluffy. Add eggs and vanilla; mix well. Stir in mixture of flour, cocoa, soda and salt. Fold in chopped cherries and nuts.
■ Chill, covered, in refrigerator for 30 minutes. Drop by teaspoonfuls onto ungreased cookie sheet. Cut cherries into halves. Place one cherry half on each cookie.
■ Bake for 10 minutes or until crisp around edges. Remove to wire rack to cool.
■ Yield: 6 dozen.

FRUIT AND NUT BARS

½ cup butter or margarine, softened	½ teaspoon salt
1 cup packed light brown sugar	¼ teaspoon cinnamon
1 egg	½ cup golden raisins
1 teaspoon vanilla extract	½ cup chopped dried apricots
1½ cups all-purpose flour	½ cup chopped prunes
½ teaspoon baking powder	½ cup chopped pecans
	2 cups semisweet chocolate chips
	4½ teaspoons shortening

■ Preheat oven to 350 degrees.
■ Cream butter and brown sugar in mixer bowl until light and fluffy. Add egg and vanilla; mix well. Stir in mixture of flour, baking powder, salt and cinnamon.
■ Add raisins, apricots, prunes, pecans and ½ cup chocolate chips; mix well. Spread in greased 9 x 13-inch baking pan.
■ Bake for 20 minutes. Cool in pan.
■ Melt 1½ cups chocolate chips and shortening in double boiler pan over hot water, stirring frequently. Spread over baked layer. Let stand until set. Cut into bars.
■ Yield: 3 dozen.

HOLIDAY FRUIT BARS

½ cup butter or margarine, softened	1 egg
¾ cup packed light brown sugar	⅓ cup all-purpose flour
1 egg	½ teaspoon soda
1 teaspoon vanilla extract	½ teaspoon cinnamon
1¼ cups all-purpose flour	¼ teaspoon salt
½ teaspoon soda	¾ cup semisweet miniature chocolate chips
½ teaspoon salt	½ cup raisins
2 tablespoons light brown sugar	½ cup chopped dried apricots
2 tablespoons milk	½ cup chopped mixed candied red and green cherries
1 tablespoon melted butter or margarine	½ cup chopped nuts

■ Preheat oven to 350 degrees.
■ Cream first 4 ingredients in bowl until light and fluffy. Add mixture of 1¼ cups flour, ½ teaspoon soda and ½ teaspoon salt; mix well. Spread in greased 9 x 13-inch baking dish.
■ Bake for 12 to 15 minutes or until light brown.
■ Blend 2 tablespoons brown sugar, milk, melted butter and 1 egg in bowl. Add mixture of ⅓ cup flour, ½ teaspoon soda, cinnamon and ¼ teaspoon salt; mix well. Spread over baked layer. Sprinkle remaining ingredients over top.
■ Bake for 15 minutes or until set. Let stand until cool. Cut into bars.
■ Yield: 3 dozen.

OATMEAL CHIPPERS

½ cup butter or margarine, softened	½ teaspoon soda
½ cup packed light brown sugar	½ teaspoon salt
⅓ cup sugar	¼ cup milk
1 egg	1 cup semisweet miniature chocolate chips
½ teaspoon vanilla extract	1¼ cups oats
1 cup all-purpose flour	½ cup chopped nuts

■ Preheat oven to 375 degrees.
■ Cream butter, brown sugar and sugar in bowl. Add egg and vanilla; mix well. Add mixture of flour, soda and salt alternately with milk, mixing well after each addition.
■ Stir in chocolate chips, oats and nuts. Drop by teaspoonfuls onto lightly greased cookie sheet.
■ Bake for 10 to 12 minutes or until brown and crisp. Remove to wire rack to cool.
■ Yield: 4 dozen.

CHOCOLATE NUTTERS

1 cup butter or margarine, softened	6 ounces cream cheese, softened
1 cup confectioners' sugar	1 egg yolk
¼ cup cocoa	1 teaspoon vanilla extract
1¾ cups all-purpose flour	2 tablespoons cocoa
1 cup confectioners' sugar	1 egg white
	1 cup chopped pecans
	18 candied cherries

■ Preheat oven to 350 degrees.
■ Cream butter and 1 cup confectioners' sugar in mixer bowl until light and fluffy. Add ¼ cup cocoa and flour; mix well. Chill for 30 minutes.
■ Cream 1 cup confectioners' sugar, cream cheese, egg yolk and vanilla in mixer bowl until light and fluffy. Divide into 2 portions. Blend 2 tablespoons cocoa into 1 portion.
■ Shape chilled cookie dough into 1-inch balls. Dip in egg white; coat with pecans. Place on ungreased cookie sheet. Make indentation in each; fill with chocolate or vanilla mixture.
■ Bake for 12 minutes or until filling is set. Cut cherries into halves. Place cherry half on each cookie. Remove to wire rack to cool completely. Store, tightly covered, in refrigerator.
■ Yield: 3 dozen.

MACAROON KISSES

⅓ cup butter or margarine, softened	1¼ cups all-purpose flour
3 ounces cream cheese, softened	2 teaspoons baking powder
¾ cup sugar	¼ teaspoon salt
1 egg yolk	1 (14-ounce) package flaked coconut
2 teaspoons almond extract	1 (9-ounce) package chocolate kisses
2 teaspoons orange juice	

■ Preheat oven to 350 degrees.
■ Cream butter, cream cheese and sugar in bowl until light and fluffy. Add egg yolk, almond extract and orange juice; mix well.
■ Add mixture of flour, baking powder and salt; mix well. Stir in 3 cups coconut. Chill, covered, for 1 hour. Shape into balls. Roll in remaining coconut. Place on ungreased cookie sheet.
■ Bake for 10 minutes or until light brown on bottom. Press chocolate kiss into center of each cookie. Cool for 1 minute. Remove to wire rack to cool completely.
■ Yield: 4½ dozen.

CHOCOLATE TOFFEE BARS

1 cup butter or margarine, softened	2 cups all-purpose flour
½ cup sugar	1 egg white
½ cup packed light brown sugar	1½ cups semisweet miniature chocolate chips
1 egg yolk	¾ cup chopped nuts
1 teaspoon vanilla extract	

■ Preheat oven to 350 degrees.
■ Cream butter, sugar and brown sugar in mixer bowl until light and fluffy. Add egg yolk and vanilla; mix well. Stir in flour. Pat into ungreased 9 x 13-inch baking pan. Brush with egg white.
■ Bake for 25 minutes or until light brown. Cool for 5 minutes. Sprinkle with chocolate chips. Let stand until chocolate melts. Spread over top. Sprinkle with nuts. Chill until set. Cut into bars.
■ Yield: 3 dozen.

SPIRITED FRUITCAKE

2½ cups golden raisins	4 cups all-purpose flour
1¾ cups chopped dried apricots	½ teaspoon salt
1¾ cups chopped candied pineapple	¾ cup milk
¼ cup Brandy	3 cups coarsely chopped blanched almonds, lightly toasted
1½ cups butter or margarine, softened	½ cup Brandy
2 cups sugar	¼ cup water
6 eggs	1 cup sifted confectioners' sugar
1 teaspoon vanilla extract	2 teaspoons Brandy

■ Combine raisins, apricots, pineapple and ¼ cup Brandy in bowl. Let stand for 30 minutes.
■ Cream butter and sugar in mixer bowl until light and fluffy. Add eggs 1 at a time, beating well after each addition. Add vanilla.
■ Add mixture of flour and salt alternately with milk, beating well after each addition. Add almonds and Brandied fruit; mix well.
■ Preheat oven to 275 degrees. Spoon batter into greased tube pan. Do not use fluted pan.
■ Bake for 3 hours. Cool in pan on wire rack. Remove from pan.
■ Moisten cheesecloth with ½ cup Brandy. Wrap fruitcake in cheesecloth. Store in tightly covered container in refrigerator for 2 weeks.
■ Unwrap cake. Place on cake plate. Mix water, confectioners' sugar and 2 teaspoons Brandy in bowl. Drizzle over fruitcake.
■ Yield: 20 servings.

RASPBERRY CHARLOTTE RUSSE

18 to 20 ladyfingers, split	1½ cups whipping cream
2 envelopes unflavored gelatin	2 (10-ounce) packages frozen raspberries
2 cups milk	¼ cup sugar
3 eggs	1½ tablespoons cornstarch
⅔ cup confectioners' sugar	1 teaspoon butter or margarine
2 tablespoons grated lemon rind	2 tablespoons lemon juice
1½ teaspoons almond extract	½ cup whipping cream
1 teaspoon vanilla extract	

■ Line 2-quart Charlotte mold or bowl with plastic wrap or grease with butter. Line bottom and side of prepared mold with ladyfingers.
■ Soften gelatin in ½ cup cold milk.
■ Heat remaining 1½ cups milk in saucepan until scalded; do not boil.
■ Beat eggs and confectioners' sugar in mixer bowl until thick. Stir a small amount of hot milk into eggs; stir eggs into hot milk. Cook over low heat until slightly thickened, stirring constantly; do not boil.
■ Add gelatin; stir until gelatin dissolves. Add lemon rind and flavorings. Chill, covered, for 1 hour or until slightly thickened.
■ Whip 1½ cups whipping cream until stiff. Fold in custard mixture gently. Pour into prepared mold. Chill for 12 hours or longer.
■ Thaw raspberries. Drain, reserving ¼ cup juice. Combine raspberries, reserved juice, sugar and cornstarch in saucepan. Cook over medium heat for 3 minutes or until thickened, stirring constantly. Cook for 2 minutes longer. Stir in butter and lemon juice; strain. Chill for 1 hour.
■ Unmold Charlotte onto serving plate. Spoon sauce over top. Whip ½ cup whipping cream until stiff. Spoon onto center of Charlotte.
■ Yield: 12 servings.

CHOCOLATE SPRITZ COOKIES

1 cup butter or margarine, softened	1 egg
⅔ cup sugar	2¼ cups all-purpose flour
1 teaspoon vanilla extract	⅓ cup cocoa
	½ teaspoon salt

■ Preheat oven to 350 degrees.
■ Cream butter, sugar, vanilla and egg in mixer bowl until light and fluffy.

■ Add flour, cocoa and salt gradually, mixing well after each addition.
■ Fill cookie press fitted with snowflake plate. Press dough onto cool ungreased cookie sheet.
■ Bake for 5 minutes or just until set. Remove to wire rack to cool completely.
■ Yield: 4½ dozen.

CHRISTMAS CHEESECAKE

1 cup sifted all-purpose flour	1½ teaspoons grated orange rind
1 teaspoon grated lemon rind	3 tablespoons all-purpose flour
¼ cup sugar	¼ teaspoon vanilla extract
¾ teaspoon vanilla extract	5 eggs
1 egg yolk	2 egg yolks
¼ cup butter or margarine, softened	¼ cup whipping cream
1¾ cups sugar	1 cup sugar
5 (8-ounce) packages cream cheese, softened	1 tablespoon cornstarch
	½ cup water
1½ teaspoons grated lemon rind	1½ cups cranberries

■ Preheat oven to 400 degrees.
■ Combine 1 cup flour, 1 teaspoon lemon rind and ¼ cup sugar in bowl. Add ¾ teaspoon vanilla, 1 egg yolk and butter; mix well. Shape into ball; wrap in plastic wrap. Chill for 1 hour.
■ Press ⅓ of the dough over bottom of 10-inch springform pan. Remove side of pan.
■ Bake for 8 minutes. Cool. Attach side of pan. Press remaining dough over side of pan to within 1 inch of top. Chill in refrigerator.
■ Preheat oven to 500 degrees.
■ Cream 1¾ cups sugar and cream cheese in mixer bowl until light and fluffy. Add next 4 ingredients; mix well. Add eggs and 2 egg yolks 1 at a time, beating well after each addition. Add cream; mix well. Pour into prepared pan.
■ Bake for 10 minutes. Reduce temperature to 250 degrees. Bake for 1 hour longer. Cool in pan on wire rack.
■ Combine 1 cup sugar and cornstarch in sauce-pan. Add water and cranberries. Cook over low heat until thickened, stirring constantly. Simmer for 2 minutes. Cool. Spread over cheesecake. Chill, covered, for 3 hours or longer. Place on serving plate; remove side of pan.
■ Yield: 16 to 20 servings.

A Dickens Family Gathering

Mrs. Cratchit made the gravy (ready beforehand in a little saucepan) hissing hot; Master Peter mashed the potatoes with incredible vigor; Miss Belinda sweetened up the apple-sauce; Martha dusted the hot plates. . . . At last the dishes were set on, and grace was said. It was succeeded by a breathless pause, as Mrs. Cratchit, looking slowly all along the carving-knife, prepared to plunge it in the breast; but when she did, and when the long-expected gush of stuffing issued forth, one murmur of delight arose all round the board, and even Tiny Tim, excited by the two young Cratchits, beat on the table with the handle of his knife and feebly cried, Hurrah!

There never was such a goose. Bob said he didn't believe there ever was such a goose cooked. Its tenderness and flavor, size and cheapness, were the themes of universal admiration. Eked out by apple-sauce and mashed potatoes, it was a sufficient dinner for the whole family; indeed, as Mrs. Cratchit said with great delight (surveying one small atom of a bone upon the dish), they hadn't ate it all at last! Yet every one had had enough, and the youngest Cratchits, in particular, were steeped in sage and onion to the eyebrows! But now, the plates being changed by Miss Belinda, Mrs. Cratchit left the room alone—too nervous to bear witnesses—to take the pudding up and bring it in. . . .

. . . In half a minute Mrs. Cratchit entered—flushed but smiling proudly—with the pudding, like a speckled cannon-ball, so hard and firm, blazing in half of half-a-quartern of ignited brandy, and bedight with Christmas holly stuck into the top.

Oh, a wonderful pudding! Bob Cratchit said, and calmly too, that he regarded it as the greatest success achieved by Mrs. Cratchit since their marriage . . . they were happy, grateful, pleased with one another, and contented with the time. . . .

—A Christmas Carol

The Cratchits' Christmas Menu

Menu

Christmas Goose
Chestnut Stuffing or Savory Stuffing
Cherry Sauce
Brussels Sprouts
Glazed Onions
Mashed Potato Rosettes
Spicy Applesauce
Holiday Bread
Mincefruit Pastries and Custard Sauce
Plum Pudding with Fluffy Hard Sauce
Grogg

CHRISTMAS GOOSE

1 (10 to 12-pound) oven-ready goose	1½ cups maple syrup
2 tablespoons lemon juice	10 spiced crab apples
	1 bunch parsley

■ Prepare Chestnut Stuffing or Savory Stuffing.
■ Preheat oven to 350 degrees. Line roasting pan with large sheet of heavy foil.
■ Place goose in prepared pan. Combine lemon juice and maple syrup in bowl; mix well. Brush goose cavity with half the maple syrup.
■ Spoon stuffing into goose cavity; truss as for turkey. Brush goose with remaining maple syrup. Seal foil. Make hole in foil; insert meat thermometer. Foil should not touch thermometer.
■ Bake for 2½ hours. Open foil. Bake for 15 minutes or to 190 degrees on meat thermometer. Let stand for 20 minutes before serving. Place on serving platter. Garnish with crab apples and sprigs of parsley.
■ Yield: 8 to 10 servings.

"There never was such a goose."

CHESTNUT STUFFING

1 pound chestnuts	¾ teaspoon pepper
1 cup melted butter	⅓ cup chopped parsley
1 cup minced onion	¾ cup chopped celery
1 teaspoon thyme	8 cups soft bread
1 teaspoon sage	crumbs
1½ teaspoons salt	

■ Slash flat side of chestnuts. Place in saucepan. Add enough water to cover. Bring to a boil. Cook for 1 minute. Remove outer shells and inner skins.
■ Cook in boiling water to cover for 35 minutes or until tender. Drain and chop.
■ Combine chestnuts with remaining ingredients in large bowl; mix lightly.
■ Yield: Enough stuffing for one 12-pound goose.

"the youngest Cratchits . . . were steeped in sage and onion to the eyebrows!"

SAVORY STUFFING

3 cups coarsely chopped celery	9 cups day-old bread cubes
1½ cups chopped onions	¾ cup chopped parsley
¾ cup butter	1½ teaspoons salt
	½ teaspoon savory

■ Sauté celery and onions in butter in skillet until tender. Combine with bread cubes, parsley, salt and savory; mix lightly.
■ Spoon stuffing into goose cavity. Spoon any remaining stuffing into greased casserole. Bake stuffing casserole at 350 degrees for 30 minutes.
■ Yield: Enough stuffing for one 12-pound goose.

CHERRY SAUCE

1 (12-ounce) jar whole cherry preserves	¼ cup wine vinegar
2 tablespoons light corn syrup	½ teaspoon cinnamon
	¼ teaspoon nutmeg
	¼ teaspoon cloves

■ Combine preserves, corn syrup, vinegar and spices in saucepan; mix well. Bring to a boil over medium heat, stirring frequently.
■ Simmer for 5 minutes, stirring frequently. Pour into serving dish. Serve warm as sauce for goose.
■ Yield: 2 cups.

BRUSSELS SPROUTS

2 pounds fresh Brussels sprouts	1 tablespoon sugar
4 slices bacon, chopped	¾ teaspoon salt
½ cup minced onion	¼ teaspoon dry mustard
2 tablespoons cider vinegar	⅛ teaspoon pepper

■ Wash Brussels sprouts; pat dry. Remove outer leaves; trim stems. Make crisscross cut in stem ends with sharp knife.
■ Brown bacon in saucepan, stirring frequently. Remove bacon with slotted spoon. Add Brussels sprouts, onion, vinegar, sugar and seasonings.
■ Cook for 10 minutes or until Brussels sprouts are tender-crisp. Stir in bacon. Spoon into heated serving dish.
■ Yield: 8 servings.

GLAZED ONIONS

2 (10-ounce) packages frozen small onions	½ teaspoon cornstarch
¼ cup packed light brown sugar	2 tablespoons melted butter
2 to 4 tablespoons Sherry	2 teaspoons lemon juice

■ Cook onions using package directions; drain.
■ Add mixture of brown sugar, Sherry and cornstarch. Cook for 5 minutes, stirring constantly.
■ Add butter and lemon juice. Spoon into heated serving dish.
■ Yield: 6 servings.

MASHED POTATO ROSETTES

6 large russet potatoes, peeled	½ teaspoon pepper
6 tablespoons butter	Pinch of nutmeg
1½ teaspoons salt	3 whole eggs, beaten
	2 egg yolks, beaten

■ Preheat oven to 450 degrees.
■ Cook potatoes in boiling water to cover for 30 minutes or until tender. Drain. Add butter and seasonings. Whip until light and fluffy. Add eggs and egg yolks; beat well.
■ Spoon into 8 mounds on greased baking sheet, swirling tops, or spoon into pastry tube fitted with large rosette tip and pipe into 8 rosettes.
■ Bake for 5 minutes. Arrange on serving platter.
■ Yield: 8 servings.

"Master Peter mashed the potatoes with incredible vigor. . . ."

SPICY APPLESAUCE

1 pound Winesap apples, peeled	⅛ teaspoon cinnamon
⅓ cup water	1 tablespoon sugar
3 whole cloves	2 tablespoons butter
	1 teaspoon lemon juice

■ Slice apples thinly. Combine apples, water, cloves, cinnamon and sugar in saucepan. Simmer until apples are tender, stirring frequently.
■ Remove cloves. Stir in butter and lemon juice.
■ Yield: 3 cups.

"Miss Belinda sweetened up the apple-sauce. . . ."

HOLIDAY BREAD

1 cup oats	2½ teaspoons salt
2 cups boiling water	½ cup molasses
2 packages dry yeast	2 tablespoons butter, softened
⅓ cup (110 to 115-degree) warm water	6 cups all-purpose flour

■ Combine oats and boiling water in bowl; mix well. Let stand for 30 minutes.
■ Dissolve yeast in warm water.
■ Add salt, molasses and butter to oats; mix well. Stir in yeast. Add flour 2 cups at a time, mixing well after each addition.
■ Knead on floured surface for 5 to 10 minutes or until smooth and elastic. Place in greased bowl, turning to grease surface. Let rise, covered, for 2 hours or until doubled in bulk.
■ Punch dough down. Shape into 2 loaves. Place in greased 5x9-inch loaf pans. Let rise, covered, for 1 hour or until doubled in bulk.
■ Preheat oven to 325 degrees.
■ Place loaf pans on rack 4 inches from bottom of oven. Bake for 50 minutes. Remove from pans. Cool on wire rack.
■ Yield: 2 loaves.

Fruit Bread

¼ cup chopped candied citron	¼ cup chopped candied fruit peel
¼ cup chopped dried fruit	1 recipe Holiday Bread

■ Add fruits to Holiday Bread dough before adding yeast.

Herb Bread

2 teaspoons sage	1 teaspoon marjoram
½ teaspoon caraway seed	1 recipe Holiday Bread

■ Add herbs to Holiday Bread dough before adding yeast.

MINCEFRUIT PASTRIES

1 pound pears	1 tablespoon sugar
¾ pound Winesap apples	1 teaspoon salt
1 orange	1 cup butter
1 cup raisins	1 egg yolk
1¼ cups sugar	7 tablespoons (about) milk
¼ teaspoon salt	1 egg white
1 teaspoon cinnamon	2 tablespoons lemon juice
1 teaspoon cloves	1 cup confectioners' sugar
2½ cups all-purpose flour	

■ Cut pears, apples and orange into quarters; remove seed. Put through medium blade of food grinder. Combine fruit, raisins, 1¼ cups sugar, ¼ teaspoon salt and spices in saucepan. Cook over low heat for 1 hour or until thickened. Cool.
■ Preheat oven to 400 degrees.
■ Sift flour, 1 tablespoon sugar and 1 teaspoon salt into bowl. Cut in butter until crumbly.
■ Combine egg yolk with enough milk to measure ½ cup. Add to flour mixture; mix well. Roll on lightly floured surface. Cut into 2¼-inch rounds.
■ Spoon fruit mixture onto half the rounds. Top with remaining rounds. Seal edges; pierce tops. Place on cookie sheet. Brush with egg white.
■ Bake for 35 minutes or until golden brown. Cool on wire rack. Drizzle mixture of lemon juice and confectioners' sugar over pastries.
■ Yield: 6 dozen.

CUSTARD SAUCE

1½ cups milk	4 egg yolks
2 tablespoons sugar	½ teaspoon vanilla extract
¼ teaspoon salt	

■ Combine milk, sugar, salt and egg yolks in double boiler pan. Cook over hot water until mixture is slightly thickened and coats silver spoon, stirring frequently; do not boil.
■ Remove from heat. Blend in vanilla. Cool to serving temperature or chill in refrigerator.
■ Serve with Mincefruit Pastries.
■ Yield: 2 cups.

GROGG

½ cup raisins	⅔ cup sugar
½ teaspoon whole cloves	2 cups water
2 (3-inch) sticks cinnamon	4 cups nonalcoholic wine
Peel of ¼ orange	¼ cup whole almonds

■ Combine raisins, cloves, cinnamon, orange peel, sugar and water in saucepan.
■ Simmer for 15 minutes. Remove raisins; reserve raisins and liquid.
■ Combine liquid and nonalcoholic wine in saucepan. Heat to serving temperature. Pour into cups; garnish with raisins and almonds.
■ Yield: 10 cups.

PLUM PUDDING

1½ cups currants	2 cups all-purpose flour
2 cups seedless raisins	1 teaspoon soda
2 cups golden raisins	4 cups soft bread crumbs
¾ cup candied fruit peel	1 cup packed dark brown sugar
¾ cup chopped candied cherries	1 teaspoon salt
2 cups chopped walnuts	1 teaspoon cinnamon
1 tart apple, chopped	¼ teaspoon nutmeg
1 carrot, shredded	1 teaspoon allspice
2 tablespoons grated orange rind	6 eggs, beaten
2 teaspoons grated lemon rind	1 cup Brandy
1½ cups chopped suet	⅓ cup orange juice
	¼ cup lemon juice

■ Combine dried fruit, candied fruit, walnuts, apple, carrot, orange and lemon rind and suet in large bowl.
■ Mix flour, soda, bread crumbs, brown sugar and seasonings in bowl. Add to fruit; mix well.
■ Add mixture of eggs, Brandy and juices; mix well.
■ Spoon into 2 oiled 8-cup molds. Cover tightly with foil. Place on rack in stockpot. Add enough water to reach halfway up mold. Cover stockpot. Steam for 6 hours.
■ Unmold onto serving plate. Garnish with sprig of holly. Serve warm with Fluffy Hard Sauce
■ May store, tightly wrapped, in refrigerator. Reheat by steaming in original mold for 2 hours.
■ Yield: 16 servings.

"Oh, a wonderful pudding!"

FLUFFY HARD SAUCE

1 cup butter, softened	¼ cup whipping cream
2 cups sifted confectioners' sugar	2 teaspoons vanilla extract
1 egg yolk	

■ Combine all ingredients in mixer bowl. Beat until light and fluffy. Chill in refrigerator.
■ Yield: 1½ cups.

Children's Parties

Christmas is a magical time, especially when viewed through the eyes of a child. Suddenly, the world is a fairyland of enchantment where evergreen trees are transformed into glistening, shimmering spectacles; where cookies and candies abound; where mysterious boxes tied in bright ribbons multiply overnight; and where a jolly, fat man in a red suit pilots a reindeer-drawn sleigh through the sky!

The key to successful children's holiday parties is to have the youngsters do something tangible that contributes to Christmas. It is easier if the projects are simple and the results are immediate. Decorating Christmas cookies falls into this category. If you decide to have a cookie decorating party, have all your cookies baked, and be sure to have plenty of pastry tubes and icing on hand. Taking turns at a party is no fun.

Our choice for children of all ages is making a bird tree (see page 67). Even the littlest guest can participate, and it appeals equally to both boys and girls. The children love the idea of "playing Santa" to hungry little birds. They experience how nice it feels to share the Christmas spirit with even the smallest of God's creatures. When the birds feed from the tree, the children take delight in watching them, knowing they made it possible.

BIRDSEED PINE CONES

Materials:

Wire or string	Paper bag
Pine cones	Birdseed
Corn syrup	Waxed paper
Coffee can	

Directions:

■ Secure wire or string around base of pine cone to make loop for hanging.
■ Pour corn syrup into coffee can. Dip pine cone into syrup; drain over can.
■ Fill paper bag with birdseed. Place syrup-coated pine cone in bag; shake to coat.
■ Place pine cone on waxed paper until ready to hang on bird tree.

CHICKADEE BIRD CONES

Materials:

12 thick red 12-inch chenille pipe cleaners	½ cup peanut butter
	½ cup flour
12 flat-bottom ice cream cones	½ cup cornmeal
	½ cup oats
1½ cups ground suet, at room temperature	5 to 8 cups sunflower seed
¼ cup sugar	Sunflower seed

Directions:

■ Insert 1 end of pipe cleaner through thick edge of rim of each cone to inside of cone. Bend 1 inch of pipe cleaner upward. Repeat on opposite side.
■ Combine suet and next 6 ingredients in bowl; mix well.
■ Fill cones with suet mixture.
■ Move pipe cleaners to 1 side. Smooth top of suet. Dip in additional sunflower seed.
■ Place cones in muffin cups. Freeze until time to hang on bird tree.
■ Yield: 1 dozen.

DOUGHNUT ORNAMENTS

Materials:

2 dozen miniature powdered sugar doughnuts	24 (8-inch) lengths rug yarn

Directions:

■ Thread each doughnut with 1 length rug yarn. Tie ends into bow. Hang on bird tree.
■ Yield: 2 dozen.

ORANGE BASKETS

Materials:

1 dozen oranges	Popped popcorn
12 (8-inch) lengths 1-inch wide ribbon	Fresh cranberries

Directions:

■ Cut 2 wedges from top of orange, leaving 1-inch center strip for handle. Scoop out pulp carefully.
■ Fill with popcorn or cranberries.
■ Tie ribbon around handle. Hang on bird tree.
■ Yield: 1 dozen.

PEANUT BUTTER NIBBLES

Materials:

Soft drink bottle caps	½ cup peanut butter
1 (3 x 12-inch) branch	1 cup wild birdseed
Nails	2 (12-inch) pieces wire or heavy string
1 cup cornmeal	

Directions:

■ Attach bottle caps to branch with nails.
■ Fill bottle caps with mixture of cornmeal, peanut butter and birdseed.
■ Attach wire to branch; hang on bird tree.

POPCORN AND CRANBERRY GARLAND

Materials:

Dental floss	2 (12-ounce) packages fresh cranberries
Long thin needle	
2 quarts popped popcorn	

Directions:

■ Thread needle with floss.
■ String popcorn and cranberries alternately on floss until all ingredients are used.
■ Drape garland on bird tree.

PRETZEL CHAIN

Materials:

¼-inch wide red satin ribbon	2 (8-ounce) packages miniature pretzels

Directions:

■ Thread ribbon through holes in pretzels to make long chain.
■ Drape chain on bird tree.

Children's Christmas Party

Menu

Animal Cracker Sandwiches or Christmas Pizzas
Crispy Cheese Buttons or Holiday Snackers
Puppy Dogs or Tuna Hero
Stuffed Celery
Cranberry Flips
Peanut Butter Fondue
Jingle Popcorn Balls or Rudolph's Antlers
Santa's Cocoa Mix

ANIMAL CRACKER SANDWICHES

3 hard-boiled eggs
¾ cup ground ham
½ teaspoon prepared mustard
¼ cup mayonnaise
¼ teaspoon salt
¼ teaspoon pepper
24 thin slices bread
12 (1-ounce) slices American cheese
¼ cup butter, softened

■ Chop eggs finely. Combine eggs, ham, mustard, mayonnaise, salt and pepper in bowl; mix well. Chill in refrigerator.
■ Cut bread and cheese into animal shapes with cookie cutters. Spread egg filling on half the bread shapes; top with matching bread shape.
■ Spread tops of sandwiches with butter. Place matching cheese shape on each sandwich. Arrange on serving plate.
■ Yield: 12 servings.

CHRISTMAS PIZZAS

2 (10-count) cans refrigerator biscuits
1 (16-ounce) jar pizza sauce
1 (4-ounce) package sliced pepperoni
2 cups grated mozzarella cheese
½ cup chopped green pepper
½ cup sliced stuffed green olives

■ Preheat oven to 350 degrees.
■ Place biscuits on foil-lined baking sheet. Flatten into 4-inch circles. Spoon pizza sauce over biscuits. Sprinkle with cheese.
■ Arrange 3 slices pepperoni in triangle on each pizza. Sprinkle with green pepper and olives.
■ Bake for 10 to 15 minutes or until crust is brown and cheese bubbles.
■ Yield: 20 miniature pizzas.

CRISPY CHEESE BUTTONS

1 cup butter or margarine, softened
2 cups grated sharp Cheddar cheese
2 cups all-purpose flour
½ teaspoon garlic powder
2 cups crisp rice cereal
½ cup pecan halves

■ Preheat oven to 350 degrees.
■ Combine butter and cheese in bowl; mix well. Stir in flour and garlic powder. Fold in cereal.
■ Shape into 1-inch balls. Place on foil-lined baking sheet. Flatten with fork. Press pecan half into each.
■ Bake for 20 minutes or until very light brown. Cool on baking sheet. Store in airtight container.
■ Yield: 5 dozen.

HOLIDAY SNACKERS

2 cans date-nut bread
8 ounces cream cheese, softened
2 teaspoons sugar
1 (8-ounce) can crushed pineapple, drained
1 tablespoon maraschino cherry juice
¼ cup chopped maraschino cherries

■ Slice bread thinly.
■ Combine cream cheese, sugar, pineapple, cherry juice and cherries in bowl; mix well. Spread on bread. Cut into halves or quarters.
■ Arrange on serving plate. Chill, covered, until serving time.
■ Yield: 2 to 4 dozen.

PUPPY DOGS

2 (16-ounce) packages bacon
2 (8-count) packages hot dogs
2 cups packed light brown sugar
32 small dinner rolls

■ Cut hot dogs in half crosswise.
■ Wrap 1 slice bacon spiral-fashion around each hot dog. Secure with toothpicks.
■ Layer hot dogs and brown sugar in Crock•Pot.
■ Cook on Low for 10 to 12 hours or until bacon is brown. Drain.
■ Transfer hot dogs to baking dish; remove toothpicks. Keep warm in 250-degree oven until serving time. Serve on dinner rolls.
■ Yield: 32 servings.

TUNA HERO

2 (7-ounce) cans tuna, drained
½ cup mayonnaise
¼ cup chopped celery
2 tablespoons sweet pickle relish
1 loaf French bread
4 lettuce leaves
3 (1-ounce) slices cheese
6 stuffed green olives

■ Combine tuna, mayonnaise, celery and pickle relish in bowl; mix well.
■ Split French bread lengthwise. Spoon tuna mixture over bottom half of loaf. Arrange lettuce and cheese on top.
■ Place remaining bread on top. Secure with 6 toothpicks. Place 1 olive on each toothpick. Slice sandwich between toothpicks.
■ Yield: 6 servings.

STUFFED CELERY

3 ounces cream cheese, softened	2 tablespoons mayonnaise
¼ cup chopped green pepper	1 bunch celery
4 ounces dried beef, chopped	1 (4-ounce) jar pimento cheese
	½ cup peanut butter

■ Combine cream cheese, green pepper, dried beef and mayonnaise in bowl; mix well.
■ Trim celery; cut into 2-inch pieces.
■ Fill celery with pimento cheese, peanut butter or cream cheese mixture. Arrange on serving plate. Chill for several hours or until serving time.
■ Yield: 2 dozen.

CRANBERRY FLIPS

1 (16-ounce) can jellied cranberry sauce	1 cup finely chopped nuts
2 (3-ounce) packages raspberry gelatin	1 cup (about) sugar

■ Combine cranberry sauce and gelatin in sauce-pan. Bring to a boil, stirring constantly. Remove from heat. Stir in nuts.
■ Pour into greased 5 x 9-inch loaf pan. Chill, covered, overnight.
■ Cut into 1 x 1½-inch pieces. Roll in sugar. Chill for 24 hours. Reroll in sugar.
■ Store in refrigerator.
■ Yield: 2½ dozen.

PEANUT BUTTER FONDUE

2 apples	1 cup creamy peanut butter
2 pears	
2 bananas	1 cup half and half
2 tablespoons lemon juice	6 tablespoons honey
	2 cups flaked coconut

■ Cut apples and pears into wedges. Cut banana into chunks. Sprinkle with lemon juice.
■ Combine peanut butter, half and half and honey in fondue pot. Cook over low heat just until mixture comes to a boil, stirring constantly.
■ Arrange fruit and coconut in serving dishes around fondue. Dip fruit into fondue with fondue forks. Coat with coconut.
■ Yield: 8 servings.

JINGLE POPCORN BALLS

12 cups popped popcorn	1½ teaspoons vinegar
2 cups chopped gumdrops	¾ teaspoon salt
1 cup chopped nuts	1 tablespoon butter or margarine
1 cup light corn syrup	1½ teaspoons vanilla extract
½ cup honey	

■ Combine popcorn, gumdrops and nuts in bowl.
■ Mix corn syrup, honey, vinegar and salt in saucepan. Bring to a boil over medium heat. Cook to 260 to 265 degrees on candy thermometer, hard-ball stage.
■ Stir in butter and vanilla. Pour over popcorn mixture; mix well.
■ Shape into 2-inch balls. Place on waxed paper-lined surface. Let stand until firm. Wrap in plastic wrap; tie with ribbon.
■ Yield: 2½ dozen.

RUDOLPH'S ANTLERS

1 cup semisweet chocolate chips	1 (3-ounce) can chow mein noodles
½ cup butterscotch chips	12 maraschino cherries

■ Combine chocolate and butterscotch chips in double boiler pan. Heat over hot water until melted, stirring occasionally. Remove from heat.
■ Stir in noodles. Drop by rounded teaspoonfuls onto waxed paper-lined cookie sheet. Shape into 2-inch V-shaped cookies.
■ Cut cherries in half. Place 1 cherry half in center of each cookie. Chill for 1 hour.
■ Yield: 2 dozen.

SANTA'S COCOA MIX

8 cups nonfat dry milk powder	1½ cups confectioners' sugar
1 (10-ounce) jar instant nondairy creamer	1 (8-ounce) package marshmallows
1 (16-ounce) package instant cocoa mix	1 (6-ounce) package peppermint sticks

■ Combine dry milk powder, creamer, cocoa mix and confectioners' sugar in bowl; mix well. Store in airtight container.
■ Combine ⅓ to ½ cup cocoa mix with 1 cup boiling water in mug for each serving; mix well.
■ Top with marshmallows. Garnish with peppermint stick stirrers.
■ Yield: 24 to 36 servings.

SUGAR COOKIES

1½ cups butter or margarine, softened	**6 cups all-purpose flour**
3 cups sugar	**3½ teaspoons baking powder**
3 eggs, beaten	**1 teaspoon salt**
1 tablespoon vanilla extract	**3 tablespoons milk**

■ Preheat oven to 350 degrees.
■ Cream butter and sugar in mixer bowl until light and fluffy. Add eggs and vanilla; mix well.
■ Mix flour, baking powder and salt. Add to creamed mixture alternately with milk, mixing well after each addition.
■ Wrap with plastic wrap. Chill until firm.
■ Roll to ⅛-inch thickness on floured surface. Cut with cookie cutters. Place on greased baking sheet.
■ Bake for 10 minutes or until light golden brown. Remove to wire rack to cool completely.
■ Frost with Confectioners' Sugar Frosting or Royal Icing. Decorate as desired.
■ Yield: 5 dozen.

CONFECTIONERS' SUGAR FROSTING

2 tablespoons butter or margarine, softened	**2 cups confectioners' sugar**
1 teaspoon vanilla extract	**1 tablespoon milk**
	Food coloring

■ Combine first 4 ingredients in bowl; mix well. Add enough additional milk to make of spreading consistency. Tint with food coloring of choice.

GINGERBREAD PEOPLE

¼ cup butter or margarine, softened	**1 teaspoon soda**
	¼ teaspoon cloves
½ cup packed light brown sugar	**½ teaspoon cinnamon**
	2 teaspoons ginger
½ cup light molasses	**½ teaspoon salt**
3½ cups all-purpose flour, sifted	**¼ cup water**
	¼ cup raisins

■ Preheat oven to 350 degrees.
■ Cream first 3 ingredients in bowl until light.
■ Sift flour, soda, spices and salt together. Add to creamed mixture alternately with water, mixing well after each addition.
■ Roll on floured surface. Cut with cookie cutter. Place on greased cookie sheet.
■ Bake for 8 minutes. Cool on pan for 4 minutes. Remove to wire rack to cool completely. Decorate with Royal Icing and raisins for eyes and buttons.
■ Yield: 8 to 12 cookies.

ROYAL ICING

1¼ cups confectioners' sugar	**⅛ teaspoon cream of tartar**
1 egg white, beaten	**Food coloring**

■ Combine confectioners' sugar, egg white and cream of tartar in bowl; mix well.
■ Tint with food coloring of choice. Add enough water 1 drop at a time to make of spreading consistency, mixing well after each addition.

SUGARPLUM COOKIE TREE

2 recipes Sugar Cookies dough	**½ cup green M and M's chocolate candies**
9 graduated star patterns or cookie cutters	**1 jar silver dragées**
	1 (½ x 12-inch long) wooden dowel
8 recipes Royal Icing	**1 (10 x 1½-inch thick) wooden circle**
Green food coloring	

■ Preheat oven to 350 degrees.
■ Divide dough into 12 portions. Wrap in plastic wrap. Chill until firm and easy to handle.
■ Roll 1 portion at a time to ⅛-inch thickness on floured surface. Cut 2 cookies from each pattern or cookie cutter. Place on greased cookie sheet.
■ Roll remaining dough to ¼-inch thickness. Cut three 3-inch circles, eight 2-inch circles and eight 1½-inch circles. Place on greased cookie sheet.
■ Bake for 10 to 12 minutes or until pale golden brown. Cool large cookies on cookie sheet for 5 minutes. Cut out centers with ¾-inch doughnut hole cutter. Cut out centers of smaller cookies immediately. Leave two 1½-inch circles intact. Cool on wire rack.
■ Tint 6 batches Royal Icing pale green. Frost cookies. Drizzle white Royal Icing around edges. Decorate with green candies and silver dragées.
■ Secure dowel in center of wooden circle. Frost circle with remaining white Royal Icing. Let stand until frosting is firm.
■ Place stars and round cookies alternately on dowel, beginning with largest star and circle and ending with smallest circle and star. Attach solid circles to either side of dowel with frosting.
■ Note: Roll larger cookies on cookie sheet. Two recipes Sugar Cookies yields enough dough for one tree and extra cookies in case of breakage.

To help assemble the Sugarplum Cookie Tree, see the photograph on page 2 or gather a group of little helpers as we did on page 68.

Comfort & Joy

Christmas Greenery

Nothing is more festive in the dead of winter than a home decked out in greenery for the holidays—garlands of holly and wreaths of boxwood . . . branches of white pine and blue spruce adorning mirrors and mantles, tabletops, and doorways . . . a perfectly shaped balsam fir, sparkling with decorations that glow in the reflection of colorful lights.

Take a deep breath. Smell the clean, fresh fragrance of evergreen. It smells so alive, so Christmasy! It lifts our spirits, putting us in the mood for joyous holiday celebrations.

Since prehistoric times evergreens have played a large role in ritual and legend. Fir trees were holy to the ancient Druids. The Romans exchanged green tree branches for good luck on the first day of January. The English took this custom for Christmas as expressed in an old rhyme, "Holly and ivy, box and bay, put in the church on Christmas Day." In Scandinavia mistletoe was the plant of peace. Enemies who met under it declared a truce for the day. Now, the custom is to kiss any person who stands beneath a sprig of mistletoe.

From a practical standpoint, evergreens are the only attractive natural decorating material available at a time of year when flowering trees and most other plants are dormant. It is not surprising that evergreens have been used since antiquity to symbolize immortality.

The Christmas tree, as we know it today, came from German tradition. However, long before modern times there were legends about trees that miraculously blossomed at Christmastime in freezing weather. The most famous of these are the thorn trees at Glastonbury, England. The blossoming of these trees was associated with the birth of Christ, and all the villages wanted one. In order to simulate this tree, blossoms made of paper were attached to an evergreen. Thus the decorated Christmas tree was born in the 16th century.

Legend tells us that the first Christmas tree in America was set up in New Jersey in 1776 by mercenary German Hessian soldiers serving in the British Army. Aware of the German penchant for big Christmas celebrations, General George Washington chose that night to cross the Delaware and attack.

Whether or not Washington took the idea for a Christmas tree back to Mount Vernon is not known, but we do know that the custom slowly gained popularity in the years after the American Revolution.

By the middle of the 19th century, Christmas trees were a well-established custom. In 1877, the *Philadelphia Weekly Press* noted that "Americans might as well dance without music as to keep Christmas without a Christmas tree."

In that respect Christmas has changed little in American homes, for it is still true that no custom is more symbolic of the holiday season than the Christmas tree.

The Germans were the first to develop tree decorating to an art form. At first they made whimsically shaped candies and cookies which hung all over the *Christbaum*, or Christ tree.

Then came cardboard decorations. These were intricately layered with gold and silver and shaped into three-dimensional forms. By the 1870's these ornaments were being imported into the United States. Next came crystal icicles and glass balls. German glass blowers developed a formula that gave their blown glass an exceptional sheen. Also, a process for blowing glass into molds was perfected so that shiny glass trinkets shaped like animals, birds, and Santas could be created and mass-produced.

By the 1880's the Germans had created two additional tree decorations to delight the American market—spun-glass strands called angel's hair and silver foil icicles. With all these innovations, Christmas trees were truly transformed into magical visions for children of all ages.

History credits Martin Luther with being the first to think of "lighting" a tree. The bright stars in a clear sky one Christmas Eve inspired him to put candles on his tree as a symbol of the Christ child's light to the world. Candlelit trees were incredibly beautiful, and the custom caught on quickly. They were also dangerous, so a bucket of sand along with a bucket of water was always placed beneath the tree as a precaution against fire.

People continued to illuminate trees with candlelight long after Thomas Edison made the first electric Christmas lights in 1882, and it is no wonder. The average cost of electric lights for one tree was at that time over a thousand dollars! It was not until the 1920's that the typical American family could afford electric lights.

Styles and fashions in Christmas trees change from time to time, but the ritual of unpacking the ornaments and decorating the tree remains one of the high points of the Christmas season. For some the tradition is to decorate the tree on Christmas Eve and to leave it decorated until New Year's Day. Others like to decorate their tree several days or even weeks before Christmas so they can enjoy it longer.

In the past the type of tree and the greenery available for Christmas decorating depended entirely on the climate and the vegetation of an area. Now, trees are shipped in from all over the country, as well as from Canada, and florist shops carry a large variety of greenery. So much variety makes choosing a tree or greenery more difficult, of course, but the selection process is also much more exciting.

Selecting A Christmas Tree

The length of time you plan to leave your tree inside, the price of the tree, the size of your room, and the size, weight, and number of decorations you use are the major considerations in selecting a Christmas tree.

The most important factor in selecting your tree is its freshness. Feel the foliage to make sure it is pliable; shake the tree to check for dropping needles. A tree with brittle or shedding foliage is too dry. It will not remain pretty throughout the season and is a potential fire hazard.

If you plan to leave your tree inside for several weeks, select a fir. The Fraser and noble firs maintain their foliage for six to eight weeks after cutting. The balsam fir is the least expensive of the firs and should last for at least a month.

The Scotch pine is also long lasting. Unfortunately, the foliage tends to lose its color after a couple of weeks.

Spruces are popular and pretty but will not last more than a couple of weeks.

Red cedar, hemlock, Virginia pine, and white pine dry out quickly and should be selected only if you plan to leave your tree inside for less than a week.

Trees look smaller on the lot than they really are. Be sure to measure the height of your ceiling and the width of your tree area before you go shopping.

Your decorations are another consideration in selecting a tree. If you have only a few ornaments, select a tree with dense foliage, such as a Scotch pine. If you have a large collection of ornaments, select an open tree from the fir family.

All trees should be conditioned before being decorated. Cut two inches from the trunk, then place the tree in a container of water. Allow the tree to absorb the water, overnight if possible. The tree must have a source of water throughout the holidays. For best results purchase a good two-quart reservoir-type stand.

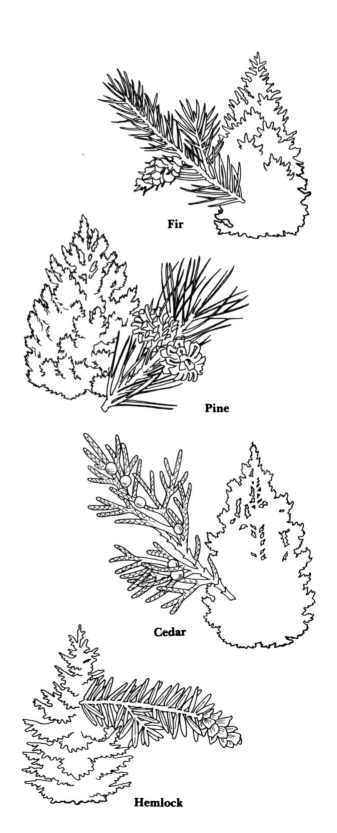

Fir

Pine

Cedar

Hemlock

A Living Christmas Tree

Many families like to buy a living tree to plant outdoors after Christmas. A row of trees across the back of the yard could represent many years of joyous holidays.

Living Christmas trees may be bought directly from a nursery or from Christmas tree lots. In the latter case, the tree will already be planted, most likely in a wooden tub. If you buy the tree at a nursery, its roots will be covered in a generous ball of dirt wrapped in burlap. At home the tree must be placed in a tub that will hold water so the roots can be kept moist. While indoors, extra watering is necessary. Otherwise, the heat will dry the tree and it might not survive. Also, the tree may become accustomed to the warmth if kept indoors too long after Christmas and may not be able to adjust to the outside quickly enough to survive the cold.

Prepare the ground for planting the Christmas tree before freezing weather arrives. Protect the planting area with several bushel baskets of leaves or straw, to serve as insulation to prevent freezing of the soil. In climates where the weather is severe after Christmas, the tree should be kept out-of-doors, roots well covered and protected, until spring.

Wreaths, Garlands And Tabletop Decorations

When it comes to the choice of Christmas greenery, there are a number of varieties that are best for large wreaths, among them boxwood, white pine, fir, blue spruce, Oregon holly-grape, English ivy, galax, mountain laurel, American holly, English holly, Southern evergreen, huckleberry, and ground pine. Spruce and hemlock shed their needles quickly indoors but are very satisfactory when used for outdoor decorations.

Add touches of color to wreaths and garlands with almost any fruit: small apples, small oranges, kumquats, cranberries, lemons, or limes. Small white onions, radishes, small gourds, and green, red, and yellow peppers can also be used for interesting color effect. Shiny Christmas ornaments, candy canes, and bright ribbons add delightful touches to boxwood, pine, or fir wreaths.

NATURE'S WINDOW SPRAY

Legend tells us that for a few hours on every Christmas Eve all the trees bloom, the animals speak, and fruit reaches perfection in honor of Jesus. Evergreens have always symbolized endless life through their evergreen leaves. We treasure these holiday decorations because nature's beauty is unsurpassed and man will always remain in awe of its glory.

Materials:

1 (3 x 4-inch) Oasis® block	Dark plastic wrap
Boxwood sprigs	Florist wire
Chicken wire	Apples
	Red berries

Directions:

- Saturate Oasis® block in water. Soak boxwood in water overnight.
- Wrap chicken wire around Oasis® block.
- Wrap block with dark plastic to retain moisture.
- Attach loop of florist wire for hanger.
- Insert boxwood sprigs into Oasis® block.
- Add apples and berries to the center.
- Hang spray from window lock.

CHRISTMAS APPLE TREE

Welcome! This is the season to celebrate love and friendship—the true meaning of the Christmas holiday. Fresh greenery, bright colors, and candle glow combine textures and aromas that remind our guests how welcome and treasured they are.

Materials:

1 truncated wooden pyramid:
11 inches tall,
6 inches square at base, 2 inches square at top (Local lumber yards will shape this block for you.)

1 (8 x 8-inch) square wood base
Nails with small heads
Green paint
Chicken wire
Florist wire
Boxwood branches
17 red apples

Directions:

■ Secure wooden pyramid to wood base with nails.
■ Paint pyramid and base with green paint.
■ Wrap chicken wire around pyramid, overlap edges and secure with florist wire.
■ Place first nail 2 inches above base. Place remaining nails at 2½-inch intervals above bottom nail. Repeat nail placement for remaining 3 sides of tree pyramid. Place one nail at the top of the tree.
■ Soak boxwood branches in water overnight to reduce wilting.
■ Cover tree with boxwood. Wedge stems into chicken wire.
■ Place 1 apple on each nail.
■ Entire apple tree may be sprayed with a florist leaf-shining spray.

FESTIVE MAGNOLIA FAN

Gather your magnolia leaves in the spring of the year. This will prevent any damage that might occur after the leaves have fallen to the ground. If magnolia leaves are unavailable in your geographic location, most commercial nurseries sell them at Christmas time. As the leaves dry, their color softens to an antique green mingled with soft brown. A coat of liquid wax will keep the magnolia leaves beautiful for years.

Materials:

Round tray	20 large magnolia
Candlestick	leaves
1 (12-inch) red candle	Sprigs of red berries
Glass hurricane	
chimney	

Directions:

■ Use a flat round tray as the base for your decoration. You may want to use this decoration in your entryway prior to the Christmas holidays and then move it to the center of your holiday dinner table for entertaining.
■ Place candlestick in the center of the tray. Insert candle.
■ Place glass chimney over candle.
■ Overlap magnolia leaves around the base of glass chimney, covering the base. Place stem ends of leaves against glass.
■ Cluster red berries around base of glass chimney.

THE SOUND OF CHRISTMAS

Holiday sights and sounds—we cannot have one without the other. Traditional music so old yet so familiar, this is the sound of the Christmas season. Our simple wreath enhanced with a gleaming brass instrument awakens the sound of carols in our hearts.

Materials:

Brass horn	Tape
1 fresh evergreen	Extra long twist ties
wreath (Choose the	Red ribbon
most textured	Berries
evergreen available	Pine cones
so it will contrast	Florist wire
with the smooth	
brass instrument.)	

Directions:

■ Select position for horn on wreath.
■ Tape the center portion of an extra long twist tie to each end of the back of the horn. Attach horn to wreath with twist ties.
■ Tie red ribbon into large bow. Attach bow to top of wreath.
■ Add berries and pine cones to the wreath.
■ Use a length of florist wire to make a loop to hang wreath.

BERIBBONED VINE WREATH

Red and green—the colors of Christmas—are vividly brilliant on our bleached vine wreath, mimicking nature's evergreens and berries in snowy winter settings and symbolizing everlasting life. Surrounded by glowing candles, it represents the radiant light of Bethlehem. We think this mantle is a shining tribute to the spirit of the Christmas season.

Materials:

Glue
Spanish moss
Red excelsior
Bleached vine wreath
5 yards (⅜-inch wide)
  Offray Fashion
  Plaid Ribbon,
  pattern #5301, C.16
2 yards (⁹⁄₁₆-inch wide)
  Offray Feather
  Edge Satin Ribbon,
  pattern #7102, 580
  Emerald

5 yards (2¼-inch
  wide) Offray Double
  Face Satin Ribbon,
  pattern #2201, 250
  Red
2 yards (1½-inch
  wide) Offray Fashion
  Plaid Ribbon,
  pattern #5301, C.15
Pods, pine cones, nuts,
  berries, bells and
  candy canes
Eucalyptus

Directions:

■ Glue Spanish moss and red excelsior to top half of wreath.

■ Glue ⅜-inch ribbon pattern #5301 in back and forth design to bottom half of wreath.

■ Make small bows from ⁹⁄₁₆-inch ribbon pattern #7102 and glue evenly to bottom half of wreath over first ribbon.

■ Make large bow from 2¼-inch ribbon pattern #2201 and glue to top center of wreath. Add loops of 1½-inch ribbon pattern #5301 evenly into large bow, gluing to secure.

■ Glue pods, pine cones, nuts, berries, bells, candy canes and eucalyptus evenly on both sides of large bow. Glue additional bells to the bottom of wreath over ribbons.

■ Make a loop from piece of leftover ribbon to hang wreath.

CHORUS OF ANGELS

A chorus of old world angels with violins, drums, trumpets, harps, and cymbals herald the Christmas season. Natural dried pine cones and seed pods form a muted wreath to enhance the pastel colors of the angels. This classic wreath will become a family heirloom for years to come.

Materials:

Florist wire	Wire wreath form
Large and small pine cones	Collection of angels
	Pastel and lace ribbons
Sweet gum balls	Baby's breath sprigs
Seed pods similar in color to pine cones	Red berry sprays
	Evergreen sprigs

Directions:

■ Wrap florist wire around stem ends of pine cones, sweet gum balls and seed pods. Attach to wreath form.
■ Wrap lengths of wire around angel wings and attach angels to wreath.
■ Weave pastel ribbon and lace ribbon around entire wreath. Insert sprigs of baby's breath, red berries and evergreens evenly around wreath.

COLONIAL WINDOW SWAG

Spice-scented lemons, limes, and persimmons will highlight this swag of boxwood and magnolia leaves. This traditional-style exterior decoration is an elegant Colonial American window treatment.

Materials:

Magnolia leaves	Florist picks
Boxwood branches	Lemons, limes and persimmons
Blocks of Oasis®	
Plastic wrap	Seed pods
1 (36 x 10-inch) piece chicken wire	Red berry bunches

Directions:

■ Soak magnolia leaves and boxwood branches in water for 24 hours.
■ Saturate Oasis® blocks in water. Drain; wrap in plastic to retain moisture.
■ Lay chicken wire on a flat surface. Place Oasis® blocks at frequent intervals lengthwise across center of wire. Bring loose edges of wire together around blocks to form 36-inch cylinder. Wire edges together. Fold the wire cylinder at the center to form a right angle.
■ Place wire cylinder on window ledge.
■ Push magnolia leaves and boxwood branches through wire into Oasis® blocks. Fill tightly to cover wire base.
■ Attach florist picks to fruit; place at intervals along window decoration.
■ Add seed pods and red berry bunches to finish window swag.

A GRAND GARLAND

A grand staircase deserves a grand garland. Fresh
evergreen boughs interlaced with iridescent
ribbons, shimmering pearlized strands, and
twinkling miniature lights combine to make a
memorable holiday decoration. The addition of
an elf who just slid the length of the staircase, Mr.
and Mrs. Claus taking a well-deserved rest, and a
beautiful antique sled filled to the brim with
elegant white poinsettias will be a welcome sight
for all your Christmas visitors.

Materials:

Evergreen branches,
    cut into uniform
    lengths
Clothesline rope
Candle wax or
    plastic wrap

Green florist wire
Miniature light strands
Pearlized strands
Iridescent ribbon

Directions:

■ Soak the evergreen branches in water for at
least 24 hours.
■ Measure the length of your garland by draping
a clothesline rope with appropriate swags from
the top to the bottom of the entire staircase.
■ Seal the stem ends of evergreen branches with
candle wax or wrap tightly with plastic wrap to
prevent resin stains on your staircase.
■ Secure evergreen branches to the length of rope
with green florist wire.
■ Wrap miniature lights, pearlized strands and
iridescent ribbon uniformly around garland.
■ Attach garland to handrail with remaining
iridescent ribbon. Tie ribbon into oversized
decorative bows.

Homemade Gifts And Greetings

There was a time when all Christmas gifts were homemade and getting ready for the holidays took eleven months of the year.

My grandmother told me once that as a young farm wife and mother back in the early 1900's she began making her Christmas gifts each year in January. She had five children, and, since she made everything she used (even her own soap), kept house, cooked three meals a day, sewed all their clothes by hand, took care of her chickens, and tended her flower garden, she had to get an early start in order to be ready for Christmas!

I remarked that she must have been sick of Christmas by the time it got there, and she said, "Oh, no. I enjoyed making gifts all year. It gave me something to look forward to and kept me in the Christmas spirit."

Today, it sometimes seems as though Christmas comes and goes before we have had a chance to relax and enjoy it. Yet, as my grandmother noted, by making Christmas presents throughout the year, it is possible to keep the spirit of the season alive.

There is no present on any occasion more meaningful than a gift made by hand. And, such a gift seems to be even more special at Christmas.

Those who have the talent to embroider, crochet, knit, or do woodworking know that any gift made is going to be joyously received. Others among us, like myself, with no proven talent for stitchery or crafts are hesitant about making Christmas presents. We are afraid the recipient will open it, snicker to himself, then put it away until the next yard sale. So, I was delighted to learn that in this chapter there are gifts even I can make. In fact, my place mats, package decorations, and children's toys turned out so well I am thinking of renting a booth at the next craft fair!

I love gifts presented in unusual wrappings, such as leftover fabric or wallpaper. There are some great ideas for making your own gift-wrap beginning on page 102.

One creative mother I knew wrapped all her Christmas presents in white laundry paper. She let her youngsters decorate them any way they wanted with red and green felt markers. The children were happily occupied for hours, and her gift-wraps were always unusual.

The important thing about homemade gifts or wrappings is not that they look perfect and professional but that the gifts represent a part of the person giving them.

MERRY BERRIE BEARS

Everyone loves teddy bears. We love our Merry Berrie pair, and so will you. We know this pair, dressed in their coordinated primitive prints, will delight the youngest to the oldest bear *afficianado*. Prewashing your fabrics before you begin cutting will ensure that your bears are machine washable.

Materials for Mrs. Berrie:

½ yard fake fur	⅔ yard crochet-type
Thread	lace edging
Polyester stuffing	¼ yard (¼-inch wide)
3 small black buttons	green ribbon
Black embroidery	2 (⅞-inch) buttons
floss	to cover
Green print remnant	Carpet twine or other
for dress and	strong thread
sleeves	Tapestry needle
Berry print remnant	See pattern pages
for smock	170-172.
Tan remnant for	
collar	

Materials for Mr. Berrie:

½ yard fake fur	½ yard (¼-inch wide)
Thread	green ribbon
Polyester stuffing	3 (½-inch) wooden
3 small black buttons	buttons
Black embroidery	2 (⅞-inch) buttons
floss	to cover
Berry print remnant	Carpet twine or other
for vest	strong thread
Tan remnant for shirt	Tapestry needle
collar and sleeves	See pattern pages
1 (¼-inch) shirt	170-172.
button	

Directions for Constructing Bears:

■ Cut out pattern pieces. Lay pattern pieces on wrong side of fake fur. Draw around the patterns. These lines will mark the SEAM line, not the cutting line. Cut out marked pieces leaving large seam allowances around the seam lines so you can easily handle the small pieces.
■ Pin arm pieces, right sides facing. Sew along marked line around arm, leaving opening for turning. Trim seams; clip curves. Turn right side out and stuff firmly. Sew opening closed.
■ Pin leg pieces, right sides facing. Sew along marked line around leg, leaving opening for turning. Trim seams; clip curves. Turn and stuff.
■ Pin ear pieces together, right sides facing. Sew along lines, leaving straight part of ear open. Trim seams; clip and turn.

■ Hand baste around edge of nose piece. Pull thread to gather slightly. Place a small amount of stuffing inside cupped nose. Position on head. Hand sew in place.
■ Pin head and body pieces together, right sides facing. Sew around, leaving flat bottom line open. Trim seams; clip curves. Turn and stuff firmly.
■ Turn under ½ inch along open edge of body. Slip open ends of legs into body; sew in place.
■ Turn under ½ inch along open ends of ears. Position on head; sew in place.
■ Determine placement for eyes and nose buttons. A slight movement closer together or farther apart will give a totally different facial expression. Sew in place. Use all 6 strands of embroidery floss to stitch mouth.

Directions for Mrs. Berrie's Clothes:

■ Note: We mixed prints from V.I.P. Very Important Prints and Granny's Trunk collections.
■ Cut out pattern pieces for dress, sleeves and smock. Lay patterns on wrong side of fabric and draw around them. These lines are SEAM lines, not cutting lines. Cut out fabric, leaving wide seam allowances around seam lines.
■ Pin sleeves, right sides facing. Sew around, leaving only lower edge open. Trim seam; clip curves. Turn. Press under to seam line on open end; hem. Slide bear arms into sleeves. Set aside.
■ Pin dress pieces, right sides facing. Sew side seams. Turn. Turn under ½-inch hem along bottom. Sew. Gather neck edge. Press. Slip dress onto bear. Adjust neck gathers to fit. Sew in place.
■ Repeat dress directions for smock.
■ Cut 4x24-inch collar. Turn under ½ inch on all edges; hem. Sew lace along one long edge. Run gathering thread 1 inch from opposite long edge. Adjust gathers to fit bear's neck. Sew in place. Tie ribbon over gathering thread.
■ Cover two ⅞-inch buttons in fabric to match sleeves. Sew on arms with heavy thread and tapestry needle. See diagram page 172.

Directions for Mr. Berrie's Clothes:

■ Cut out pattern pieces for vest, vest lining, pockets, shirt collar and sleeves. Lay pattern pieces on wrong side of fabric and draw around them. These lines are SEAM lines, not cutting lines. Cut out fabric leaving wide seam allowances around seam lines.

■ Repeat sleeve directions as for Mrs. Berrie.

■ Pin collar, right sides facing. Sew around collar leaving opening in lower edge for turning. Trim seams; clip curves. Turn. Close opening. Press. Put collar on bear's neck, adjust to fit, then secure by sewing on a ¼-inch shirt button at front extensions. Tie ribbon bow around neck.

■ Sew darts on shoulders of vest and vest lining. Pin vest and lining, right sides facing. Sew around, leaving opening for turning. Trim seams; clip curves. Turn. Close opening. Press.

■ Press under ¼ inch on top edges of pockets. Stay stitch ¼-inch seam around curved edges of pockets. Press seam allowance toward wrong side of pocket. Pin pockets to vest. Sew in place.

■ Put vest on Mr. Berrie. Close front by sewing 3 wooden buttons through all thicknesses.

■ Attach arms to body as for Mrs. Berrie.

STAINED GLASS ANGEL

Looking up to the tiptop of your tree will reveal this beautiful angel reminiscent of stained glass angels seen in cathedrals. The shimmering fabrics and threads used for this angel will reflect the textures of ornaments, tinsel, and lights hung lovingly on your tree.

Materials:

Tracing paper	Susan Bates Anchor®
⅓ yard off-white satin	Embroidery Floss =
Dressmaker's carbon	8m skeins
paper	(2 skeins each):
⅓ yard polyfleece	#111 Lavender,
batting	#130 Cobalt Blue,
1 (10-inch)	#944 Wheat,
embroidery hoop	#326 Apricot,
1 (No. 6) embroidery	#47 Carmine,
needle	#923 Emerald,
Susan Bates Anchor®	#6 Salmon,
Metallic Thread =	#403 Black
50m spool	See pattern pages
(1 spool each):	167-168.
Gold, Silver	

Directions:

■ Trace pattern onto tracing paper.

■ Transfer design onto fabric, using dressmaker's carbon. DO NOT CUT FABRIC. Use pattern to cut 2 pieces polyfleece batting for lining.

■ Secure fabric tautly in embroidery hoop.

■ Complete designs, following color key and stitch guide. Use 2 strands embroidery floss and 3 strands metallic thread throughout.

■ Add ½-inch seam allowance to sides and top of angel and 1-inch seam allowance to hem. Cut fabric along seam allowance.

■ Baste polyfleece batting pieces to angel front and back. Pin front and back, right sides facing; matching bottom edges, hands, wing tips and halo edges. Use zipper foot to sew pieces together, stitching next to, but not in, black chain stitching.

■ Trim seam allowances to scant ¼ inch with pinking shears to reduce excessive fraying. Clip seam allowances near hands and neck. Turn right side out.

■ Use black thread to whip together black chain stitching if any white satin shows through in seams.

■ Turn under ¼ inch along bottom to hem. Turn hem to inside along lower row of chain stitching; whip in place.

HEIRLOOM QUILT

Decades of use will sooner or later reduce a family's heirloom quilt to an unusable item. We were thrilled to resurrect the usable parts of our quilt and to share them at Christmas with the whole family. What a thoughtful, loving gift to give to family members. We created an all-American Christmas theme with our quilted angel, table runner, napkin rings, trivet, and matching towel holder (pages 88 and 89). We framed individual quilt squares (page 88), and we also fashioned a quilted stocking (pages 91 and 95). Each is a fitting tribute to our heirloom quilt.

Heirloom Art

We think a framed individual square of our antique quilt will have a treasured spot in each family member's home. By adding great-grandmother's name and the year she made her quilt, you can treat her design as a work of art. All family members can now have a part of her quilt in their homes and also a heartwarming appreciation of your thoughtfulness.

Heirloom Angel

We love this centerpiece angel, so new and pretty yet wearing the fabric quilted so long ago. Her lacy wings are made from an antique collar our quilter wore for special holiday occasions. We are reminded, when we look at our angel, of all the good and loving members that were part of our special and unique family.

Materials:

Antique quilt	Medallion-type lace
1 yard (1¼-inch	for neckline,
wide) cotton lace	about 4 inches
for bottom of robe	Ribbon, about 7
1 yard (½-inch	inches of narrow
wide) cotton lace	ribbon
for sleeves	Off-white felt #4214
Small pieces of felt:	4½ x 4½-inch card
#186 Pink for hands,	stock
3 coordinated colors	Glue
for halo detail	Starched lace collar
10 or 12-inch	for wings
styrofoam cone	See pattern pages
Size #7 doll head	176-177.

Directions:

■ Note: Cut pattern from waxed paper or heavy plastic so your quilt fabric can be seen through it.
■ Cut 2 robe pieces from old quilt. Zigzag around sleeves and bottom of robe to prevent fraying.

■ Pin robe pieces, right sides facing. Sew underarm, side and shoulder seams, leaving ¼-inch seam allowance. Clip seams at underarm; turn.
■ Sew wide lace around bottom of robe. Sew 2 rows of narrow lace around edge of each sleeve.
■ Cut hands from felt. Sew one inside each sleeve; stitch sleeve closed. Hand sew sleeves on insides to hold hands in praying position.
■ Trim top of cone to fit through neck of robe and into doll's head. For 12-inch cone, cut enough from top of cone so robe lace just touches table when slipped over cone.
■ Hand stitch a few pleats in the medallion lace to make collar for robe. Sew one 3½-inch piece of ribbon to each end; tie around neck of angel.
■ Cut circles of off-white felt and card stock as shown on pattern for halo. Glue circles together with card stock sandwiched between felt. Glue felt pieces on circles as indicated on page 177. Secure halo to back of head with a pin.
■ Hand stitch collar center to robe back at neck, outer edges for shoulders, ends for tips of wings.
■ Note: We used felt from the Felters Company because they have a very extensive color range.

Heirloom Accessories

Bits of our quilt are repeated on our towel holder and our holiday table in the table runner, napkin rings, and hot pot trivet.

Materials for Towel Holder:

Antique quilt	Velcro closure
Bias tape	See pattern pages
⅓ yard cotton lace	176-177.
Hand towel	

Directions:

■ Cut 2 patterns "A." Cut 1 pattern "B."
■ Zigzag bottom of each "A" to prevent fraying. Sew folded bias tape over top of each "A."
■ Pin "A" pieces, right sides facing. Sew side seams. Turn right sides out.
■ Sew folded bias tape around 3 sides of "B." Insert raw edge of "B" ½ inch into top of "A." Sew across all thicknesses, ¼ inch down from top of "A." Sew lace around bottom of "A."
■ Cut towel 10 inches long excluding fringe. Fold towel in thirds lengthwise; zigzag across top of folded towel to prevent fraying.
■ Insert raw edge of folded towel into bottom of "A." Sew across all thicknesses. Hand stitch Velcro to back of "B" and top back of "A."

Materials for Table Runner:

Antique quilt	3½ yards (3-inch wide) pleated cotton lace

Directions:

■ Cut quilt piece 10 inches wide and 42 inches on the sides; ends may be pointed or rounded to fit the design of the quilt. Stitch around quilt piece with tightly spaced medium-width zigzag stitch.
■ Pin lace around runner, hiding cut edges. Overlap ends of lace, folding under raw edge. Stitch lace to table runner.

Materials for Napkin Rings:

Antique quilt Wide bias tape	Cotton lace, 14 inches for each ring

Directions:

■ Cut 7 x 2-inch strips from quilt.
■ Sew folded bias tape around both 7-inch sides. Sew lace over bias tape.
■ Fold strip in two, right sides facing. Sew raw ends together, leaving 1-inch seam allowance.
■ Slip stitch seam allowances open. Turn.

Materials for Trivet:

Antique quilt 1 (9½ x 9½-inch) piece of prewashed muslin	1⅛ yards cotton lace 7 x 7-inch stove and counter mat

Directions:

■ Cut 8½ x 9½-inch piece from quilt. Cut with one 9½-inch edge along bound edge of quilt or else bind 1 long side with bias tape.
■ Turn under one side of muslin ½ inch; turn under ½ inch again. Press and sew.
■ Pin quilt and muslin together, right sides facing. Sew the 3 unfinished edges, leaving a ½-inch seam allowance. Clip corners; turn right side out.
■ Pin lace along edges of quilted top. Stitch, leaving pocket open. Insert mat.

COLONIAL BABY DOLL

Our all-cloth baby doll features a loveable cross-stitched face. She reminds us of the dolls played with by the daughters of the Colonists long before toys were mass-produced look alikes. She is soft, cuddly, and machine washable and dryable.

Materials:

2 (16 x 20-inch) pieces prewashed evenweave fabric, weave equaling approximately 14 stitches per inch	1 small safety pin
Embroidery hoop	½ yard white batiste
C.J. Bates embroidery floss: #0892, #0857, #0882, #010, #0352, #148, #145 and white	5 yards (½-inch wide) flat lace trim
Cross-stitch needle	3¼ yards (½-inch wide) pink satin ribbon
Polyester stuffing	¾ yard light blue batiste
1 (12-inch) square white flannel	1⅔ yard (¼-inch wide) pink satin ribbon
	See pattern pages 172-174.

Directions for Doll Body:

■ Trace pattern for doll onto paper. Cut out pattern. Pin this pattern on wrong side of one piece of evenweave fabric. DO NOT CUT. Draw around pattern onto fabric. This line will be the stitching line.
■ Hand baste a horizontal and vertical line on center of face area.
■ Place fabric right side up in embroidery hoop with basted lines centered. Refer to face chart on page 172 to work cross-stitch details.
■ Pin cross-stitched fabric to remaining blank fabric, right sides facing. It is not necessary to trace around pattern on blank fabric. Machine stitch along drawn lines through both thicknesses, leaving 3-inch opening for turning. Trim seam allowance to ¼ inch. Clip curves and turn right side out.
■ Stuff firmly with polyester stuffing. Sew 3-inch opening closed.
■ Cut several 5-inch lengths of brown embroidery floss. Fold in half. Sew to doll's head for bangs at the seam line above eyes.

Directions for Diaper:

■ Fold flannel square in half to form a triangle. Lay doll on triangle with folded edge to back.
■ Fold points of triangle around doll and secure with safety pin.

Directions for Gown:

■ Transfer pattern to paper. Cut out pattern; pin to white batiste. Cut out. Cut one 2 x 11-inch bias strip.
■ Pin back facing lengthwise over center back, right sides facing. Sew along lines shown on pattern. Slash through both thicknesses to point. Turn facing to wrong side. Press.
■ Sew sleeves to back and front pieces with right sides facing.
■ Gather neck edge. Adjust to fit bias strip, leaving a 1-inch extension on both ends of strip. Pin bias strip over gathers, right sides facing; sew in place. Fold strip to inside. Fold under extensions on each end. Sew in place.
■ Fold gown, right sides facing; sew underarm and side seams. Turn and press.
■ Press under ½-inch hems on sleeves and gown.
■ Sew lace in place to secure hems. Sew 2 more rows of lace around bottom.
■ Place gown on doll. Tack neck opening together or sew on a snap. Cut two 12-inch lengths of ½-inch ribbon. Tie one to each wrist to hold sleeves.

Directions for Bonnet:

■ Cut two 7 x 25-inch pieces blue batiste.
■ Pin pieces, right sides facing. Stitch, leaving ½-inch seams and an opening for turning. Trim seams. Turn; sew opening closed. Press.
■ Stitch close to one long edge. Stitch again ⅜ inch from edge to form casing. Cut threads between rows of stitching on each end so that a ribbon can be run through.
■ Stitch another casing 1½ inches from opposite long edge.
■ Sew 2 rows of lace and 1 row of ½-inch ribbon to brim area between last casing and outside edge. This will be the bonnet brim.
■ Cut one piece ¼-inch ribbon 24 inches long. Run through the back casing. Gather tightly and tie bow.
■ Cut one piece ¼-inch ribbon 36 inches long. Run through front casing. Adjust gathers to fit doll's head; tie bow under chin.

Directions for Bed Jacket:

■ Transfer pattern to paper. Cut out pattern; pin to blue batiste.

■ Pin 2 pieces, right sides facing. Stitch, leaving opening to turn. Clip curves. Turn; sew opening closed. Press.

■ Cut 8 pieces of ½-inch ribbon 8 inches long. Sew a pair under each arm opening to tie. Sew 2 pairs at front opening.

CURLY RIBBON BONNET

Ribbons are everywhere this time of the year. We love ribbons curled garland-style across our baby bonnet. These ribbons could as easily be antique ribbons from an older relative's collection of laces and ribbons or the bonnet itself from a treasured fabric heirloom. Let sentiment and imagination dictate the style of your Christmas bonnet.

Materials:

1 (9 x 16-inch) piece white fine-wale corduroy
1 (9 x 16-inch) piece lining fabric
1¼ yards (⅜-inch wide) blue satin ribbon
3 yards (¾-inch wide) red satin ribbon
1¼ yard (⅛-inch wide) green satin ribbon

Directions:

■ Pin corduroy and lining fabric, right sides facing. Sew ½-inch seam around, leaving an opening for turning. Trim seams and corners. Turn right side out; sew opening closed. Press.

■ Stitch close to one long edge. Stitch again ½ inch from edge to form casing. Cut threads between rows of stitching on each end so that a ribbon can be run through.

■ Cut ¾-yard length of ⅜-inch blue ribbon. Insert ribbon through casing. Draw ribbon tight to gather back of bonnet back. Tie ribbon to hold gathers in place.

■ Cut three 1-yard lengths of ¾-inch red ribbon. Two lengths are sewn into satin ribbon "curls."

■ To make ribbon curls, hand baste across ribbon in zigzag pattern the full length of the ribbon. Pull basting thread to gather ribbon.

■ Hand sew curled ribbon about 2 inches apart on bonnet front edge. Sew remaining lengths of ⅜-inch blue and ⅛-inch green ribbon between these rows. The remaining yard of ¾-inch red ribbon is used for ties.

■ Note: Directions for Heirloom Quilt Stocking (pictured above) are on page 95.

SANTA'S SWEAT SHIRT

Fusible felt lets you create wonderful crafts very quickly since you no longer have to stitch or glue your designs. You could choose any seasonal design to decorate your sweat shirt—Santa Claus or reindeer, Christmas trees, or elves. Even the smallest design can be enlarged inexpensively at your local copier shop. Gift-wrap and last year's Christmas cards are good sources for design inspiration. Let your imagination and fusible felt work together to "seasonalize" clothing, gifts, and home decorations!

Materials:

Stacy's Fusible Felt®: white, pink, red and black	Scissors Colored or white pencil
Tissue paper	Iron
Dressmaker's carbon paper	Red sweat shirt
Cardboard or heavy paper	See pattern page 169.

Directions:

■ Note: Always test-fuse scraps of Fusible Felt® with background material to ensure a good bond.
■ Draw pattern pieces on tissue paper.
■ Place dressmaker's carbon paper under tissue pattern, and trace shapes onto cardboard or heavy paper. Cut out pieces.
■ Draw around pieces needed for parts of Santa's face on felt, using colored pencil. White felt—eyebrows, mustache, hair, beard, hat band and ball on hat. Pink felt—face and nose. Red felt—hat and mouth. Black felt—eyes.
■ Set iron at "wool" temperature setting.
■ Place resin-coated side of felt against surface being decorated (red sweat shirt). Start with face first; add hair, hat, beard and facial features.
■ Place iron on felt; apply steam and light pressure for 15 seconds. DO NOT SLIDE IRON. Check bond by allowing felt to cool then gently try to separate pieces. If not completely bonded, increase fusing time.

VERY IMPORTANT BEAR BUNTING

Charming bears and alphabet blocks make this darling baby bunting to swaddle your newcomer snugly. In future years you may want to rework this bunting into a very special, personalized Christmas stocking.

Materials:

1½ yards quilted V.I.P. Very Important Bear screen print for bunting	2 (12-inch) neck-opening zippers to match background color
½ yard quilted V.I.P. Very Important Bear screen print for strips of bears and applique	4 (size 4) snaps 1 yard silk-covered cording See pattern page 175.
1½ yards V.I.P. Very Important Bear all-over alphabet print for lining	

Directions for Cutting:

■ **Quilted Fabric**—Place front and back pattern pieces on fold; cut 1 of each. Cut 2 each of hood and front shoulder overlay; do not place overlay on fold. Cut two 3½ x 15⅜-inch strips of bears. Cut out 3 bears separately, leaving ¹⁄₁₆-inch seam allowance for appliqueing.

■ **Lining Fabric**—Follow the same instructions as for the Quilted Fabric for hood, front shoulder overlay, front and back, adding 3¼ inches to the length of front and back.

Directions for Assembling:

■ Note: Leave ⅝-inch seam allowance unless otherwise indicated.

■ Stitch bear strips to bottom of front and back of quilted fabric with right sides facing, leaving ⅜-inch seam allowance.

■ Stitch center seam of hood and lining. Trim seams to ¼ inch. Stitch hood to hood lining around face opening with right sides facing.

■ Stitch quilted shoulder overlay pieces to bunting back at shoulder and side seams with right sides facing. Repeat for lining.

■ Stitch bunting shoulder overlay pieces to lining shoulder overlay pieces at center front and bottom edges with right sides facing, leaving a ¼-inch seam allowance. Clip corners. Turn; press.

■ Stitch quilted hood to bunting at neck edge formed by back and shoulder overlay with right sides facing. Center back of hood should match center back of bunting. Front of hood will extend ½ inch beyond shoulder overlay. Trim seam allowance to ¼ inch on back neck edge only. Repeat process for lining.

■ Turn lining to inside. Tack lining to bunting at neck and shoulder. Stitch around face opening of hood ½ inch from edge to form casing.

■ Applique small bears to front of bunting.

■ Stitch front lining to front bunting across top and 3½ inches down sides with right sides facing.

■ Stitch back lining to front lining across bottom edge and 4 inches up sides with right sides facing. Repeat process for bunting leaving ⅜-inch seam allowance with right sides facing; hold lining out of way.

■ Baste and stitch 1 zipper to bunting only in side seam, holding lining out of way. Repeat process with other zipper. Press under ⅝-inch seam allowance on lining sides. Hand-stitch lining along zippers.

■ Sew snap tops to underside of bunting front across top. Sew snap bottoms on shoulder overlay to secure front to overlay.

■ Attach safety pin to 1 end of cording. Slip pin and cording through casing around hood face opening to form drawstring; knot ends.

FIRESIDE AFGHAN

Warm, rich shades of peach and rust combine to make an afghan that glows like a toasty fire. The light-weight yarn makes this afghan a portable project. Our Delicata Kid mohair is the premium first wool cutting from young kids combined with 10% nylon for extremely strong yarn. If Lanas Margarita yarn in not available locally, write to P.O. Box R, Island Heights, N.J. 08732 for the appropriate retailer in your area.

Materials:

Lanas Margarita	**1 75-inch piece**
Delicata Kid:	**smooth lightweight**
#88 Peach - 10 balls,	**yarn in contrasting**
#30 Rust - 13 balls	**color**

Size: About 40 x 72 inches, without fringe.
Needles: #11 circular needle or size
required for correct gauge, 1 small straight needle,
1 tapestry needle, 1 crochet hook.
Gauge: 2.75 stitches = 1 inch (11 st = 4 in)
Note: Afghan is worked in double strand yarn
throughout, 1 strand each color except as noted.
Select method you wish to follow before starting.
Cast on 160 stitches using 1 strand #88 Peach and
1 strand #30 Rust. **Method I** is done on circular
needle in rounds, not joining ends, but leaving 12
inches yarn free before starting next row. Lengths
will be cut in half to form fringe. All knitting is
from front side only. **Method II** is done on circular
needle, working back and forth, as for straight
needles. Fringe will be added.

Directions:

■ **I**—Garter stitch: Knit (K) 1 row, Pearl (P) 1 row.
Stockinet stitch: K all rows. Leave 12-inch length
yarn between rounds throughout. Maintain
4-stitch garter stitch edges throughout.
■ **II**—Garter stitch: K all rows. Stockinet stitch: K
1 row, P 1 row. Maintain 4-stitch garter stitch
edges throughout.
■ **I and II**—Work 6 rows garter stitch and 4 inches
stockinet. Work 5 Pleats and 4 Lace Patterns
alternately, beginning and ending with Pleats.
Work 2 inches stockinet between Pleats and Lace.
End with 4 inches stockinet with garter stitch
edges and 6 rows garter stitch. Bind off loosely.
■ **Fringe I**—End with 4 inches stockinet and 6
rows garter stitch. Bind off loosely. Cut 12-inch
fringe lengths in half. Knot 4 fringe lengths at a
time. Trim. May add additional fringe as for II.
■ **Fringe II**—Cut remaining yarn into 12-inch
lengths. Place afghan, right side up, with garter
stitch edge facing. Hold desired number of fringe
strands together; fold in half, forming loop. Insert
crochet hook through loop on outer edge of
afghan. Place fringe loop on hook; draw fringe
loop through edge loop. Pull loose ends through
fringe loop; pull tightly to secure. Repeat at
desired intervals. Trim fringe evenly.
■ **Pleats I and II**—** (Maintain garter stitch
edges.) Thread tapestry needle with smooth yarn.
Thread through each stitch on needle to mark
row. Work 6 rows stockinet. Using small knitting
needle, pick up first stitch from marked row; slip
onto left hand needle. K first stitch on needle and
first stitch from marked row together. Repeat
with remaining stitches. Remove marker yarn.
Work 3 rows stockinet. Drop 1 strand Peach;
attach additional strand Rust. Repeat from ** to
make second pleat of Rust only. Drop second
strand Rust; attach strand Peach.
■ **Lace Pattern** (Maintain garter stitch edges.)
I—Row 1: P. Row 2: K. Row 3: *K 2 tog, YO,
repeat from *. Row 4: K. Row 5: *YO, K 2 tog,
repeat from *. Row 6: K. Row 7: *K 2 tog, YO,
repeat from *. Row 8: K. Row 9: P.
II—Row 1: P. Row 2: P. Row 3: *K 2 tog, YO,
repeat from *. Row 4: P. Row 5: *YO, K 2 tog,
repeat from *. Row 6: P. Row 7: *K 2 tog, YO,
repeat from *. Row 8: P. Row 9: P.

REBECCA'S FIRST CHRISTMAS

The love and joy that celebrate the birth of Rebecca are symbolized by the hearts twinkling in the sky over the Nativity. There is a good deal of symbolism in this stocking which helps convey the depth of meaning of this special holiday season. References to the symbols on the stocking are found in the following scriptures:

Lamb—John 1:29   "The next day he saw Jesus coming to him and said, 'Behold, the Lamb of God who takes away the sin of the world!' "

Shepherd—John 10:11   Jesus said, "I am the good shepherd; the good shepherd lays down his life for the sheep."

Tree—I Peter 2:24 (of Jesus)   "Who His own self bare our sins in His own body on the tree, that we, being dead to sins, should live unto righteousness: by whose stripes ye were healed."

Snow—Isaiah 1:18   " 'Come now, and let us reason together,' says the Lord. 'Though your sins are as scarlet, they will be white as snow; though they are red like crimson, they will be like wool.' "

Alpha and Omega—Revelation 21:6   "And He said to me, 'It is done. I am the Alpha and the Omega, the beginning and the end. I will give to the one who thirsts from the spring of the water of life without cost.' "

Materials:

Susan Bates Anchor® embroidery floss #'s 70, 76, 160, 214, 291, 366, 369, 397, 375, 880, 401	⅝ yard ruffled white eyelet lace
19 x 13-inch 14-count Aida cloth	6-inch strip linen bias tape for hanging loop (Or, make your own loop by triple folding a ¾ x 6-inch length of linen and stitching the length.)
½ yard linen-look suiting fabric	
½ yard bleached permapress muslin	See pattern pages 178 and 179.

Directions:

■ Use ⅜-inch seam allowance.

■ Complete cross-stitch design following pattern.

■ Cut out one stocking from cross-stitched fabric, one from linen, and two from muslin for lining.

■ Cut two 3 x 14¾-inch cuff pieces from linen.

■ Pin muslin stocking, right sides facing. Stitch stocking, leaving top open. Repeat with cross-stitch stocking. Clip curves. Turn cross-stitch stocking. Insert lining into stocking, wrong sides facing.

■ Baste lace to bottom edge of cuff piece, matching raw edges, right sides facing. Pin cuff pieces together, right sides facing. Sew bottom and 2 sides. Lace should be between cuffs. Turn cuff.

■ Fold bias tape in half to make loop. Stitch loop to top back of stocking, matching raw edges. It will be turned up later.

■ Pin cuff to the top of the stocking with cuff inside stocking, matching raw edges.

■ Sew around top of stocking through all 4 layers. Turn cuff to outside of stocking. The seams will now be hidden under cuff.

Heirloom Quilt Stocking

■ Cut stocking front and back from quilt using pattern for Rebecca's First Christmas stocking. Zigzag around pieces to prevent fraying. Line with matching print material. Assemble and finish using directions above.

■ Note: Matching heirloom crafts are on pages 88 and 89. Photograph of stocking is on page 91.

HOLIDAY TABLE COVER

Solve that extra diner seating problem with a
tailored felt table cover and chair backs to match.
With your card table and our table cover, you can
expand your guest list with confidence. Our
tailored chair back covers will let you unify your
table grouping even if your extra chairs are an
eclectic mix.

Materials:

Card table	Scissors
5 yards (72-inch wide)	Yardstick
green felt	¼-inch thick plywood
Green thread	table top (opt.—Use
Dressmaker's	if card table is
carbon paper	old and tends to
37 yards (2¾-inch	sag in center.)
wide) Offray plaid	See cutting diagram
craft ribbon	page 166.

Directions for Table Cover:

■ Measure table top carefully. Our table measured
30¼-inches square. Add ½-inch seam allowance
to table top measurement.
■ Cut your table cover top to fit your table. Ours
measured 31¼ x 31¼-inches.
■ Measure from table top to floor. Our table
height was 26½ inches. We added ½ inch for a
seam allowance, making our skirt length 27 inches.
■ Refer to cutting diagram for cutting chair backs
and table cover top and skirt with pleats. Cut felt.
■ Stay stitch ½ inch from cut edge around 4 sides
of top.
■ Mark corner and pleat placement lines on skirt
using dressmaker's carbon paper.

■ Stitch 2 sections of skirt together, using ½-inch
seam allowances. Press seams open.
■ Pin pleats in place at 4 corners.
■ Pin skirt to top, clipping top corners as needed.
Stitch carefully.
■ Cut four 1½-yard lengths of ribbon. Fold in
half; stitch folded edges to corners for streamers.
■ Tack end of remaining ribbon to one corner.
Twist ribbon over and over. Tack to next corner
to make swag. Cut. Repeat on remaining 3 sides.
■ Make large decorative bows with at least 10
loops per bow. Place large bow at each corner;
baste in place.

Directions for 4 Chair Backs:

■ Measure width and length of your chair backs.
Ours measured 25 inches tall by 19 inches wide.
Our chair back measurement, including ½-inch
seam allowances, measured 50 x 20 inches.
■ Cut fabric. Mark center line for chair top on
each chair back, using dressmaker's carbon paper.
■ Cut 25-inch length of ribbon for each chair back
swag. Twist ribbon once, gathering ends, and pin
in place on right side of fabric.
■ Mark 19 inches down both sides of chair back
for side bow placement.
■ Cut sixteen 1-yard lengths of ribbon for side
bows. Gather one cut edge of ribbon. Turn under
raw edge; stitch in place on right sides of fabric.
Stitch 2 tiebacks to each side of chair back.
■ Stitch side seams, right sides facing, keeping
tiebacks out of the way.
■ Clip corners. Turn right sides out. Fold up any
excess felt at chair seat. Tie side bows.

GOOD TIDINGS MAILBOX COVER

Simple to do and inexpensive to construct, this is a holiday craft for everyone. Our mailbox cover was made for a standard single-sized rural mailbox. You may want to make a pattern of newspaper so your cover will be tailor-made for your mailbox. Prewash your quilted fabric so moisture will not effect the size of your cover.

Materials: ½-inch seam allowances are included.

3 yards (¾ to 1-inch wide) fabric ribbon
1 (20 x 22½-inch) piece prequilted fabric (Scotchguard fabric is ideal.)

1 piece matching lining fabric
½ yard (1-inch wide) black elastic

Directions:

■ Lay fabric ribbon on right half of right side of mailbox cover fabric, simulating a wrapped package. Straight stitch in place. Repeat for left half of mailbox cover.
■ Stitch lining to cover, right sides facing, leaving a space for turning. Clip corners. Turn and press. Straight stitch opening closed.
■ Safety pin elastic to cover where suitable to secure to mailbox.

HOLIDAY PATCHWORK FLAGS

Our patchwork flags are echoes of our ancestors' simpler Christmas celebrations. Treasured scraps of fabric fashioned into a star symbolize the journey to Bethlehem. Stars in a forest of greenery remind your visitors of that long-ago journey.

Materials for Each Flag:

Cardboard or plastic for quilt templates
Fabric remnants in light and dark colors
Remnant of quilt batting

Embroidery floss
1 (⅜ x 14-inch) wooden dowel
Wood stain
See quilt pattern pages 166 and 167.

Directions:

■ Transfer pattern pieces to cardboard or plastic to make templates. Cut out pattern templates.
■ Draw around templates on wrong side of fabric. Refer to photo and pattern for the correct colors and number of pieces for each template.
■ Cut out pieces, leaving ¼-inch seam allowance. Piece flag as shown in pattern diagram.
■ Cut a piece of batting and coordinated fabric for lining.
■ Pin pieced star and lining, right sides facing. Pin batting over lining. Sew around all sides, leaving 3-inch opening on one side for turning. Clip corners. Turn right side out. Press.
■ Cut two 2 x 8-inch strips of fabric. Fold in thirds lengthwise to make string ties. Turn in raw edge; stitch close to folded edge. Sew ties to one edge of flag.
■ Tack around star at several places, using 6 strands of embroidery floss.
■ Stain dowel with wood stain.
■ Tie flag to dowel.

EVERBLOOMING POINSETTIA SET

Poinsettias have been synonymous with Christmas ever since the Franciscan Friars adorned their nativity scenes with this tropical plant. Dr. Joel Robert Poinsett, our first ambassador to Mexico, discovered the "Flower of the Holy Night" in 1828. Credit for the development of the Poinsettia in America goes to Paul Ecke. He was a Swiss farmer who grew vegetables and flowers in the Ventura area, north of Los Angeles, California. This area has become California's "Poinsettia Belt" where these flowers grow well outdoors. Paul Ecke Jr. donated the poinsettias for our book. Our poinsettia place mats and napkins will joyously bloom on Christmas tables for many years to come.

Materials for Set of 6:

3½ yards white linen fabric
Tracing paper
Washable marking pen
Dressmaker's carbon paper
1 (6-inch) embroidery hoop
Susan Bates Anchor® Embroidery Floss = 8m skeins (3 skeins each):
#19 Deep Burgundy,
#46 Crimson,
#246 Grass Green,
#257 Parrot Green,
1 skein #891 Brass

Susan Bates Anchor®
1 spool (950m) Silver Metallic thread
1 (No. 6) embroidery needle
See pattern page 169.
Finished measurements:
Place mats—
11½ x 17½ inches
Napkins—
15 x 15 inches

Directions:

■ Cut 6 pieces of fabric 15 x 20 inches for place mats, and 6 pieces 18 x 18 inches for napkins.
■ Trace patterns from diagram onto tracing paper. Transfer larger poinsettia motif onto left hand corner of place mats approximately 3 inches up from bottom edge and 3 inches from left hand edge with dressmaker's carbon paper. Repeat for napkins with smaller motif.
■ Stretch fabric tautly in hoop. Following key to diagram, embroider design using 3 strands of floss throughout for large motif and 2 strands of floss throughout for small motif. All parts similar to numbered parts on diagram are worked in same color and stitch.

■ Launder place mats and napkins carefully if necessary. Press on wrong side of needlework.
■ Trim place mats to 12½ x 18½ inches, cutting fabric to within 2 inches of embroidery on 2 sides. Turn under ¼-inch hems twice on all 4 sides, mitering corners. Stitch in place.
■ Trim napkins to 16 x 16 inches and finish as for place mats.

WOVEN PRINT PLACE MATS

Simple to make and simply smashing to see. We were delighted with our place mats that are cut strips of scrap fabric woven through latch hook canvas. We mixed several coordinated print strips in each place mat, two matching prints for our napkins. Use the colors in your prints when selecting flowers, candles, baskets, and tableware to coordinate your table setting.

Materials:

1 yard (3 squares per inch) latch hook canvas
Scissors
V.I.P. Museum Chintz Prints
2 yards–4 place mats
1 yard–4 napkins

Pinking shears
Tapestry needle
Embroidery floss and thread to match fabric

Directions for Place Mats:

■ Note: Create stripes by using 2 or more contrasting fabrics.
■ Cut latch hook canvas into 11½ x 18-inch rectangles with scissors.
■ Cut print fabric into ½ x 24-inch strips with pinking shears.
■ Thread tapestry needle with fabric strips. Weave into canvas, going over and under each square.
■ Pink ends to make 1½-inch fringe.

Directions for Napkins:

■ Cut fabric squares 16½ x 16½ inches using 2 or more V.I.P. prints.
■ Select floss to match background color of print. Do not separate strands.

■ Lay floss on cut edge of napkin. Set your sewing machine for a close zigzag satin stitch. Satin stitch over floss and edge of napkin.

■ Stop stitching at corner. Have machine needle on outside of napkin. Insert a pin from edge of fabric (catching ½ inch of fabric), pointing back toward edge just stitched.

■ Lift presser foot and turn fabric. Holding head of pin will enable you to make a clean sharp corner and keep your fabric feeding under the presser foot as you stitch around each corner.

■ Stitch all sides of napkin with satin stitch. When you reach the starting point, cut off floss and continue stitching to enclose cut end.

STRAW AND RIBBON GARLAND

The smallest of Santa's helpers can easily make a vivid garland to decorate the family Christmas tree. Soda straws and scraps of ribbon are readily available and inexpensive materials. Your garland could be even more colorful if you use a wide variety of ribbon colors. This garland could grow longer each year as the children save ribbons from their presents to be added to the project before it is stored for next year's holiday.

Materials:

Red and white drinking straws	Tapestry needle
Red and green ribbon	String
	Scissors

Directions:

- Cut straws into thirds.
- Cut ribbon into 10-inch strips.
- Thread tapestry needle with length of string desired. Knot string.
- Loop ribbon back and forth to make 2-inch bow.
- Pierce center of folded ribbon with needle and push ribbon to end of string.
- Thread a straw piece onto string.
- Repeat until string is filled, ending with a ribbon section. Knot end of string.

GRAND GARLAND TREE SKIRT

At last, a sturdy tree skirt that is both elegant and substantial. We chose our golden tassel and fleur-de-lis stencil because it coordinated with our traditional room setting. Stencil Ease® produces a wide variety of stencils that are exclusively styled for Christmas. With fabric and fabric paint, you will want to add holiday stencils to wall hangings, place mats and napkins, and tablecloths or runners.

Materials:

1¼ yards (45-inch wide) white chintz fabric	Stencil-Ease® White Bristle Brushes: Size 12, one for each color used
Equal amount of fusible interfacing (May have to be pieced to obtain 45-inch width.)	Stencil-Ease® Design: HV-14 Grand Garland
Water erasable pen	5 yards metallic trim for skirt edge
Fab-Tex® Paint: Dark Green, Bright Red and Gold Lustre (optional colors: Pilgrim Green and Barn Red for shading)	Craft glue or hot glue gun
	Iron, masking tape, yardstick, thumbtack, string and paper towel
	See diagram page 169.

Directions: Read through entire directions before beginning to work.

- Prewash and iron chintz. (Do not prewash fusible interfacing).
- Carefully fuse interfacing to wrong side of chintz, following manufacturer's directions. To piece interfacing, lay pieces side by side; DO NOT OVERLAP.
- Tape prepared fabric right side up to flat area.
- Locate center of fabric with yardstick and use thumbtack to secure one end of string to center of fabric.
- Attach erasable pen to other end of string 22½ inches from thumbtack. Position pen at edge of fabric.
- Keeping the string taut, swing pen around to mark a circle 45 inches in diameter.
- Shorten the string to 2½ inches and mark a 5-inch diameter hole in center of skirt.
- Cut out the Christmas tree skirt along lines you have marked.
- Fold skirt into quarters, then fold once again. Crease on these fold lines to mark skirt into 8 sections. See diagram A. These 8 creases will aid in placement of the stencils.

Directions for Applying Paint:

- Use Fab-Tex™ as it comes out of the jar. Do not dilute.
- Place about ½ teaspoon of each color on paper palette or saucer.
- Dampen a paper towel or soft cloth. Wipe your brush across the damp towel, picking up a slight amount of moisture in bristles. Wipe across a dry towel to remove excess moisture. Bristles should be moist enough to ensure that paint penetrates fibers, but if bristles are too wet, paint will "bleed" into fabric.
- Dip bristles into paint. Wipe off excess paint on paper towel until your brush is free of globs of paint and is fairly dry.
- Hold brush perpendicular to surface. Using a clockwise motion (about 3 inches in diameter), work around edge of cut-out area of stencil and gradually build up color.
- Now switch to a counterclockwise motion, building up paint to desired color. Properly stenciled, a design area is dark around the edges and light toward the center.
- Complete all areas of the design in this manner.
- For clean-up, wash brushes with warm soapy water; wipe stencil gently with a damp paper towel.

Stencil Instructions for Skirt:

- Be sure skirt is flat on smooth surface.
- Place the fleur-de-lis design of Print 1 over one of the creases you have made. The guideline on the stencil should be 2½ inches from edge of skirt. Stencil fleur-de-lis, using Dark Green paint.
- Repeat over each crease. You will have stenciled the fleur-de-lis 8 times.
- Reposition Print 1 so the flower garland is centered between 2 fleur-de-lis. Stencil leaves Dark Green.
- Repeat 7 more times.
- Position Print 2 over one set of leaves; use register marks to aid placement. Stencil flowers, using Bright Red paint.
- Repeat 7 more times.
- Reposition Print 2 and stencil a tassel under each fleur-de-lis, using Gold Luster paint.
- Return to Print 1. Position stencil with aid of register marks and stencil flower centers, using Gold Luster paint.

- Stencil a flower over each of the 8 creases of center of skirt. The top of the flower should be 2 inches from center hole of skirt.
- Stencil leaves for alternate flowers (4 sets of leaves). Stencil the flower centers.
- Repeat each step of your stenciling, using a second color to shade and give design more depth. Stencil lightly around all green areas, using Pilgrim Green. Stencil lightly around all red areas, using Barn Red.

Directions for Finishing:

- Allow paint to "cure" overnight. Heat set by ironing with a dry iron at low cotton setting. Iron directly over each stenciled area for 30 seconds.
- Cut an opening from edge of skirt to center.
- Glue metallic trim in place around edge of skirt and around center hole.

NET-WRAPPED GIFTS

Simple and inexpensive yet smashing Christmas gift-wrapping is done with nylon net. We love the lacy texture that makes these gifts so feminine.

Materials:

Wrapping paper	Nylon net fabric
Tape	Greenery or berry
Scissors	sprigs

Directions:

■ Wrap packages with wrapping paper.
■ Create bows, bags or ribbon to decorate packages using netting.
■ Add greenery sprigs or berry sprigs for a more traditional Christmas look.

PLAID CHRISTMAS BASKET

Baskets are important decorative accessories in most homes today. Our special Christmas basket festooned with moss, berries, nuts, flowers, and ribbons deserves a treasured spot in your seasonal decorating. Or, arrive in style at Christmas parties with your basket filled to the brim with presents.

Materials:

Glue	5 yards (2¼-inch
Spanish moss	wide) Offray Double
Wicker basket	Face Satin Ribbon
4 yards (⅞-inch wide)	#2201, 250 Red
Offray Fashion	1 yard (⅝-inch wide)
Plaid Ribbon	Offray Feather Edge
#5301, C.16	Satin Ribbon
1 yard (⅜-inch wide)	#7102, 580 Emerald
Offray Taffeta	1 yard (⅝-inch wide)
Tartan Ribbon	Offray Feather Edge
#5291, C.4	Satin Ribbon
1 yard (⅜-inch wide)	#7102, 250 Red
Offray Fashion	Berries, nuts, dried
Plaid Ribbon	flowers and cones
#5301, C.16	
5 yards (2¼-inch	
wide) Offray Double	
Face Satin Ribbon	
#2201, 580 Emerald	

Directions:

■ Glue Spanish moss to edge of basket.
■ Glue ⅞-inch ribbon (pattern #5301) in back and forth design over moss.
■ Wrap handle with ⅜-inch ribbons (patterns #5291 and #5301), gluing ends to secure.
■ Make 2 large bows with 2¼-inch ribbons (pattern #2201, Emerald and Red). Make 2 smaller bows with ⅝-inch ribbons (pattern #7102, Emerald and Red). Glue to center of large bows (red with green and green with red). Glue large bows to sides of handle of basket.
■ Glue berries and nuts to Spanish moss. Glue dried flowers evenly around basket.
■ Glue cones to basket behind bows at the end of each side of handle.

ROUND RIBBONED CHRISTMAS BOX

Red plaid ribbon gives our modest wooden box a traditional Colonial air. Use the box as a holiday decoration or for a very special gift. If tying bows has been a disaster for you, seek help from the designers at your local floral supply store. There are some simple "magic" tricks to tying bows that they will be happy to show you.

Materials:

Round wooden box
1 yard (⅞-inch wide)
  Offray Taffeta
  Tartan Ribbon
  #5291, C.4
2 yards (¼-inch wide)
  Offray Woven
  Metallic Ribbon
  #5721, C.1
1 yard (⅞-inch wide)
  Offray Fashion
  Plaid Ribbon
  #5301, C.17
White glue

1 yard (⅜-inch wide)
  Offray Taffeta
  Tartan Ribbon
  #5291, C.4
4 yards (1½-inch
  wide) Offray
  Fashion Plaid
  Ribbon #5301, C.15
2 yards (⅝-inch wide)
  Offray Feather Edge
  Satin Ribbon
  #7102, 250 Red
Berries
Dried baby's breath

Directions:

■ Wrap box sides with ⅞-inch ribbon (pattern #5291), ¼-inch ribbon (pattern #5721) and ⅞-inch ribbon (pattern #5301), gluing in place. Wrap side of top with ⅜-inch ribbon (pattern #5291), gluing in place.

■ Cut 2 pieces of 1½-inch ribbon (pattern #5301) the diameter of box top. Cut ends in "V" shape. Glue to top of box, crossing middles. Cut 2 pieces of ⅝-inch ribbon (pattern #7102) slightly larger than diameter of box top. Cut ends in "V" shape. Glue to top, crossing middles and centering between 1½-inch ribbons.

■ Make bow with 1½-inch ribbon (pattern #5301); glue to top of box. Make 4 small bows with ⅝-inch ribbon (pattern #7102) and 3 small bows from ¼-inch ribbon (pattern #5721). Glue small bows evenly around center of large bow. Glue berries and baby's breath evenly in and around bow.

PERMANENT GIFT-TAG

Never run out of gift-tags again! Design your own rubber stamp and your local office supply company will make it. Add a red stamp pad and a red stamp pad inker, and you are ready for any gift-giving occasion all year long. You can eliminate the tag and stamp your "tag" directly onto your gift. Best of all, our gift-tag is large enough that the names can be read easily.

MAGNETIC JUGGLING CLOWN

Center stage in his own circus ring is our juggling magnetic clown. His circus ring is a transformed cookie tin with a lid that will hold all those small treasures children collect. Metal knickknacks are held high over his head. This clown looks like fun for everyone!

Materials:

> Cookie tin with lid,
> at least 8½ inches
> in diameter
> Yellow and red
> spray paint
> Ceramacoat paints:
> Palace Flesh,
> Sunbright Yellow,
> Ultra Blue,
> Crimson, White
> Squeeze nozzle to
> fit these bottles
> Paper grocery bag
>
> Clear self-adhesive
> vinyl
> 1 (6 x 6-inch) block
> of 1¼-inch pine
> Band saw or scroll saw
> Sandpaper
> Clear acrylic spray
> 5 magnetic cabinet
> locks with ¾ x 1-inch
> magnets
> Clear epoxy glue
> See pattern page 180.

Directions:

■ Remove lid from tin. Spray paint lid yellow; let dry. Turn tin upside down. Spray paint side red; let dry. Replace lid. Measure height of can below lid; cut a strip of paper this wide to fit exactly around tin.

■ Place ends together; crease in half. Fold in half again; continue folding in half to 1 inch or less. Stretch paper pattern around tin; secure with tape.

■ Put a pencil mark on tin at top of every other crease and a mark at the bottom of alternating creases. Remove pattern. Turn tin on its side. Squeeze yellow Ceramacoat paint to connect marks forming a zigzag. Do only a small section at a time, allowing paint to dry before doing next section.

■ Paint 1 dot of blue paint at the top of each point on rim of lid. Cut circle of clear self-adhesive vinyl to fit the top of the tin and apply. This will prevent magnets from scratching paint.

■ Cut clown from wood block with a band or scroll saw. See pattern page 180. Sand smooth. Paint clown according to pattern directions. Spray with clear acrylic.

■ Remove metal rectangles and magnets from cabinet locks. Glue metal rectangles to bottom of the feet and top of hat and hands of the clown. Press magnets to metal pieces. Place clown on top of painted tin. Place paper clips or magnets on hands to resemble juggling.

DINOSAUR PUZZLE

Puzzles and dinosaurs, what a combination! What little boy could resist this dinosaur on the prowl! Large simple sections let very young children easily solve this puzzle.

Materials:

> Wood (2 x 10 x 20-inch)
> Band saw or jigsaw
> Sandpaper
> Paint brushes
>
> Acrylic or enamel
> paint: green, yellow,
> red, black and white
> See pattern page 181.

Directions:

■ Transfer cutting lines from pattern to wood. Cut along lines.

■ Take puzzle apart to sand each piece.

■ Reassemble puzzle. Transfer painting lines from pattern onto puzzle.

■ Paint, referring to pattern for color placement.

■ Note: Graduated shades of green may be achieved by adding small amounts of yellow paint to the green. May paint row of heavy black dots along painting line beneath bony plate from neck to tail.

MINI VINE WREATH
SWEET GUM BALL WREATH

We love these miniature wreaths of natural vine and sweet gum balls. Their circular shape is symbolic of the neverending love of God for mankind. Each wreath is a gift in itself that will trim the trees of your friends for years to come.

Materials for Mini Vine Wreath:

> Lengths of small vines
> (We used wild
> muscadine, but other
> grape or honey-
> suckle vines would
> also work well.)
>
> Assorted trims:
> metallic soutache
> braid, narrow red
> ribbon, white and
> metallic silver trim
> Twist ties for bows

Directions:

■ Hold vine tightly in your hand. Begin wrapping in a circle, starting with the thickest end of the vine. After a few loops are made into a circle, begin wrapping the vine around itself as you add more vine to the wreath.

■ End each piece of vine by tucking in the loose end and add new vines by tucking the end under some of the vine already in the wreath.

■ Continue until wreath is the desired thickness.

■ Wrap trim around wreath and secure at top with a knot, leaving approximately 6 inches of trim on each end. Tie a simple bow with ends. Or, make 9-loop bow as below and attach with twist tie.

Materials for Sweet Gum Ball Wreath:

6 or 7 sweet gum balls
Hot glue gun and glue
  stick
Gold or white spray
  paint

1¼ yards (⅛-inch
  wide) red ribbon
Twist tie

Directions:

■ Arrange 6 or 7 sweet gum balls in circle. Place dab of hot glue between each to join.
■ Spray paint wreath if desired.
■ Tie a 4-inch piece of ribbon around the wreath as a hanging loop.
■ Make bow with nine 1-inch loops of ribbon on each side; secure bow in middle with a twist tie. Use ends of the twist tie to secure bow to wreath at the same spot as the hanging loop.

NATURE'S GREETING CARDS

Children will enjoy collecting leaves all fall. They can search their backyards and the routes they walk to and from school looking for unusual shapes and sizes. Flatten the leaves in a book to prevent curling. A little spray paint and "Voila!" greetings from nature saying "Happy Holidays!"

Materials:

Newspaper
Plain white cards
  and envelopes
Cardboard

Assorted leaves and
  ferns
Spray paint

Directions:

■ Protect your work surface with newspaper.
■ Open card on work surface. Cover back of card with a piece of cardboard.
■ Place leaves and ferns in a random pattern on front of card.
■ Spray lightly with paint.
■ Wait a few minutes before removing leaves and ferns. Dry cards thoroughly.

Christmas At Home

Christmas at home means the comfort and joy of being with family. Whether 'home' is a humble cabin isolated by miles of open country, a high-rise apartment in a bustling city, or an imposing mansion in the suburbs, something magical happens when loving families gather together to celebrate this most cherished of holidays.

The family has been called the nucleus of civilization, but it is much more—our continuity, our identity, our mirror, our bond to life. From this inner circle of love and security, we learn to relate to the outside world. Each of our families is unique, just as we as individuals are one-of-a-kind. Together, we make up the miracle of civilization, the family of mankind.

Family holiday gatherings are important as they bring together loved ones who live too far apart to see one another regularly. Coming together for Christmas reestablishes family ties and reinforces love and support in a more meaningful way than is possible by letter or by telephone.

I know a couple whose five children had never been able to enjoy Christmas together from the time they married and left home to start families of their own. They longed to spend Christmas together, but most of them could not afford the trip back home every year. So, they devised a plan. They created a family tradition by starting a Christmas fund, appointing one of the sisters as the family's treasurer. They each sent a monthly $25.00 contribution to the fund. By Christmas they had $1,500.00 to be divided among those who needed traveling money.

Each year their Christmas get-together was held at the home of a different family member. They each had a turn hosting the Christmas celebration, as well as the opportunity to visit one another's homes. Their children had the fun of getting to know cousins and grandparents, and the brothers and sisters shared the joy of remaining close.

We cherish our personal family traditions just as we respect the customs of others because these holiday rituals reflect our individuality. The gifts we receive as children are often forgotten, but the memories of family Christmases remain with us all our lives. We treasure these memories so much that we want to recreate them for our own children—the excitement of choosing and decorating the tree, hanging stockings by a crackling fire, awakening at dawn on Christmas morning in giddy anticipation, and savoring those mouth-watering holiday aromas wafting from the kitchen.

And so every year we do our best to relive past Christmases, always striving to regain the wonderful sense of security that enveloped us as children when the family was gathered close for the holidays. In this way our family customs and traditions are passed along to each generation so that many of us are unknowingly celebrating Christmas in a manner much like our ancestors of a hundred or more years ago.

In the early years of American history, Christmas celebrations varied more from family to family than in today's world. Whether there was an exchange of gifts, a Christmas tree, a gift-bearer, or a special feast on Christmas day depended primarily on one's religion and national origins.

By the time Victoria ascended the throne of England in 1837, the Christmas customs brought to America from Europe had begun to blend together, and Americans were well on their way to developing a set of Christmas traditions all their own. Holiday celebrations were influenced by the marriage of Victoria to Prince Albert, a German, who decorated the first royal Christmas tree for Buckingham Palace. The small tree was pictured in magazines on both sides of the Atlantic, and overnight, the Christmas tree became as fashionable for adults as it was delightful for children.

In the mid-1800's American villages, towns, and cities bustled with special Christmas events, from concerts to shooting matches. There were masked balls, taffy pulls, ice skating and sledding parties, Christmas fairs and exhibitions. And, nearly every community had a life-sized Nativity scene where parents brought their children to see baby Jesus in the manger.

Holiday planning was done weeks and even months in advance. There were gifts and decorations to make, Christmas goodies to bake, and parties to plan. Guests were invited weeks ahead of time because they often had to travel for days to get there. Guests were expected to spend several nights before returning home, and special parties were planned for each evening of their visit.

Samuel Clemens, better known as Mark Twain, wrote with affection of the holiday parties held at his Hartford, Connecticut home.

His wife, Olivia, was famous for her festive holiday parties and lavish banquets. She had a secret wrapping room for the scores of gifts she gave family and friends. On Christmas afternoon, Clemens would fill the sleigh with gifts and toys for the poor. Then, his daughters would climb in beside him and off they would go down the snow-covered streets, 'sleigh bells-a-ringing', delivering joy to the needy.

In contrast to the extravagant holiday celebrations which were in vogue at that time in Eastern cities, Christmas on the frontier was simple and homespun, but this did not make it any less joyous. Even though pioneer families were isolated from one another by miles of prairie and forest, they clung tenaciously to their sentimental customs, determined with what little they had to make Christmas a time of celebration.

The traditional tree, covered with handmade decorations and strings of red berries and popped popcorn, added a colorful touch to an otherwise drab cabin. A simple gift was made for each child from those materials which were available. Most often, the girls received rag dolls; the boys, wagons. If a neighbor lived close enough to share a special holiday meal, there was a celebration indeed. Usually wild game—deer, boar, turkey, or goose—was served along with vegetables from the root cellar.

Stockings were hung by the fire on Christmas Eve, then the family sat together to read the story of the birth of Jesus from the Bible. Many sparsely settled frontier areas had no church, so a family's home became their 'house of worship'.

Children went to bed hoping to hear reindeer hooves on the snow-covered roof before the morning. At dawn they were up again, filling the small cabin with squeals of excitement as they discovered Santa's gifts under the tree.

Most of us share the childhood memory of trying to stay awake all night to listen for Santa's reindeer on the roof.

My parents told me that I must never get out of bed to peek even if I heard Santa, because if I saw him, he would leave, taking my gifts along with him. On Christmas Eve, before I went to bed, I always left Santa Claus a snack. This had been a custom in my mother's home when she was a child. She would help me set out a slice of fruitcake and a glass of milk. Then, I would go up to bed and lie awake for what seemed like hours, straining to hear the sound of hoofbeats.

One year, I began to worry. It occurred to me that if children all over the world were leaving Santa Claus cake and cookies, he might get too sick to continue his journey and not make it to my house. Judging by his size, he had a hearty appetite for sweets, and besides, he would not want to hurt anyone's feelings by not eating what they left out for him.

I decided to leave nothing to chance. I slipped downstairs with a bottle of Pepto-Bismol, terrified that Santa was going to come down the chimney, catch me, and take back all my gifts. I put the bottle next to the cake and quickly scribbled a note in third-grade cursive telling him to take two tablespoonfuls if his tummy hurt. Then, I hurried back to bed.

The next morning, the Pepto-Bismol bottle was still there. The cake was gone, and on the back of the note I had left Santa, there was a message from him. He said that he had taken some of the medicine and that it had made him feel much better. He thanked me for caring and for being thoughtful, pointing out that I had acted in the true spirit of Christmas.

I knew I had been thinking more about whether Santa would make it to my house with presents than I had about his health. I was ashamed, and I prayed that Santa would never find out the truth.

For the first time, I was beginning to understand what my parents had always told me—that Christmas is not just parties and presents to celebrate the birth of Jesus. Christmas is the spirit of loving and giving, of sharing and caring.

I treasured that note long after I was too old to leave refreshments out for Santa. At first I kept it because I was the only kid on the block (or in the entire city of Atlanta for all I knew) who had a handwritten note from Santa Claus. As I grew older, I kept it to serve as a reminder of the real meaning of Christmas and of the unexpected ways in which parental messages are delivered.

Although it might not seem like Christmas without a tree and Santa, we are the most sentimental about the personal holiday traditions within our immediate families.

Members of one family I know always exchange handmade gifts. Even the youngest child contributes with a finger painting, a clay handprint, or a crayon drawing. These gifts are treasured for a lifetime, long after the 'store-bought' presents are gone and forgotten.

Another family's tradition began three generations ago with a young mother's desire to commemorate Christmas dinner in a special way. She asked her children to write their names on her white linen holiday table cloth. She embroidered over their letters in bright Christmas colors. When the children grew up and married, the signatures of their husbands and wives were added, then those of the grandchildren, and now great-grandchildren. The tablecloth has become a family heirloom of names and dates, a Christmas history for all to share.

Some families add a new Christmas ornament to the tree for each year or for important events such as weddings, a new family member, memorable vacations, even a new job. These precious decorations are packed away carefully after Christmas (in a box marked *irreplaceable* at my house) then brought out the next year to adorn the new Christmas tree with memories.

A number of years ago, a fire destroyed my home, along with all my possessions. A few months later when Christmas rolled around, I was still so depressed I vowed not to put up a tree. My children were grown and living away from home, and I no longer had the cherished ornaments collected over the years. The thought of buying new decorations that would hold no memories for me was much more depressing than the thought of having no tree at all.

Then a few days before Christmas, my son called to say he was coming over that evening to "show me something." He arrived, carrying a six-foot tree and several boxes of lights— things I did not want.

Just then my door swung open to reveal a large group of friends, carrying food, wine, and little packages. Inside the small boxes were wonderful ornaments of every type imaginable. Some were hand-sewn, some hand-crocheted, and others cut from wood and hand-painted. These had all been made especially for me. Then there were those from their own family collections— antique balls, miniature toys, and carved wooden characters.

Imagine my surprise! More than the new collection of Christmas memories I had suddenly inherited, the expression of love that filled my small apartment filled me with joy, driving away my Christmas blues in no time.

Some families seem to have a special knack for creating their own holiday customs.

One Christmas Eve, a grandfather of my acquaintance was asked to model a red flannel nightshirt he had just been given. He made a great show of parading around the Christmas tree in his new sleeping attire while his giggling grandchildren snapped pictures.

When the family gathered the following year on Christmas Eve to open presents, Grandpa gave them each an identical package. Inside each was a red flannel nightshirt. This time, *they* had to model as *he* snapped the camera. Now, they all don red flannel nightshirts each Christmas Eve before gathering around the tree to exchange gifts. Someone even got the idea of making one for the family pooch, who wore it with resigned reluctance.

I have never seen a more memorable Christmas "family portrait" than the one I received from them showing all eleven, including the Beagle, dressed in red flannel nightshirts. The pup was staring forlornly at the camera above a caption that read: "You may think this is funny, but I think it's a dog-gone shame!"

Family photos are always among the most treasured remembrances of the holiday season. Often, families will keep these photographs in separate albums containing nothing but Christmas pictures. It is fun to bring the albums out each year to relive Christmases past, to see how the children have grown, to share the wonderful memories, to laugh at old hairstyles and fashions, or to wonder if we were ever really that young and slim.

I remember a friend who used photographs to make a very special Christmas memory book for his daughter. The book contained pictures he had taken of her each year, along with a description of what she was like at that age. He recalled her first Christmas as a baby, a toddler, then as a student in school, high school, and college. He did not tell his daughter about the book until she was married and about to give birth to her first child. He then presented the album to her for Christmas, with the wish that she keep a similar record for each of her children from Christmas to Christmas until they were grown.

My favorite story of a unique family tradition was shared with me by a close friend, the youngest daughter in a family of five.

When she was very small, her grandmother died just a few weeks before Christmas.

The grandmother left seven children and twenty-six grandchildren, all of whom adored her. A sadness hung over the family's Christmas gathering, the first one without Grandma. Just as they were about to open the last gifts, a letter in a big red envelope was delivered to their door. It was addressed simply: "To My Children and Grandchildren."

My friend's father opened the letter and read it aloud:

"I have asked my dear friend and attorney Harold Matthews to see that this is delivered to you on Christmas day, for I know I won't be there to give it to you.

"As you celebrate the birth of Christ and look forward to a

New Year, I want to tell each of you how much I love you and how special you are to me.

"In the existence that we call life, I have learned two things: that each of us is unique in the universe and that love is the most powerful force in our lives.

"The greatest contribution you can make to your world is to love yourselves, to love one another, and to love your neighbors everywhere. Through love, each of you has the power to enhance the universe. This was the message Jesus came to tell us, and it is the message I want to leave you to pass on to our future generations.

"Always remember how blessed we are as a family and how strong the bonds of love we share. Remember, too, how blessed we are as human beings. What a beautiful, abundant planet we share! Cherish and protect it as you do one another.

"Remember that happiness is your birthright. It is already within you, waiting to be acknowledged. All you have to do to find it is to recognize that it is there. God created you to be happy. He intended it. You are perfect in His eyes—and in mine as well.

"Many joyous Christmases will follow this one. The children will grow up and have children of their own, and sooner or later, each of you will be ready to move on to another spiritual plane, as I am ready now. Do not mourn my passing. It is only that—a passing. I have had a beautiful life. And I leave behind a beautiful legacy. If you want proof of that, look around at one another.

"Celebrate this season with all the love in your heart. Let it last all year. It's the best Christmas gift I could wish for you.

"I love you all very much.

"Grandma"

Understandably, the reading of this letter was the most moving Christmas experience this family had ever shared. Not wanting to forget this feeling, they have continued to read the letter aloud each year.

As members of the family grow up and go out on their own, they are given a framed copy of the letter. My friend keeps hers on the wall in her bedroom, a year-round reminder of the loving message her grandmother left behind.

More than any other holiday, Christmas inspires us to forget our problems and to remember things more abiding. It is a time when we are clearly aware of our uniqueness and, at the same time, of our bond to the universal family. It is the season that blends personal family traditions with world-wide holiday customs, linking us to our past heritage, to our future promise, and to one another. It is that promise of comfort and joy that binds all mankind, especially at Christmastime.

God Rest You Merry, Gentlemen

Traditional

Traditional English
Arranged by Sir John Stainer

1. God rest you mer-ry, gen-tle-men, Let noth-ing you dis - may, Re-
2. From God our Heav'n-ly Fa - ther, A bless-ed An-gel came; And
3. "Fear not then," said the An - gel, "Let noth-ing you af-fright, This
4. The shep-herds at those ti - dings Re - joic-ed much in mind, And
5. And when they came to Beth-le-hem Where our dear Sav-iour lay, They

mem - ber Christ our Sav - iour Was born on Christ-mas Day, To
un - to cer - tain Shep-herds Bro't ti - dings of the same: How
day is born a Sav - iour Of a pure Vir - gin bright, To
left their flocks a - feed - ing, In tem-pest, storm, and wind: And
found Him in a man - ger, Where ox - en feed on hay; His

save us all from Sa - tan's pow'r When we were gone a - stray;
that in Beth - le - hem was born The Son of God by Name.
free all those who trust in Him From Sa - tan's pow'r and might."
went to Beth - le - hem straight way, The Son of God to find.
Moth - er Ma - ry kneel - ing down, Un - to the Lord did pray.

ff *(after each verse)*

O— ti-dings of com-fort and joy, com-fort and joy, O— ti-dings of com-fort and joy.

Christmas Planning

The day before Christmas Eve is the same every year at my house. I look around at piles of presents still to be wrapped, stacks of cards yet to be addressed, lists of last-minute gifts to be bought, and a schedule of errands to be run. There is a full day's work ahead preparing Christmas dinner, and I say, "Never again! Next year I am *not* going to let Christmas slip up on me. Next year I am going to *plan ahead*!"

I've made this vow dozens of times and have done nothing so far but break it. *Planning* to plan ahead is not enough. One actually has to *do it* in order to reap the benefits of a relaxed, hassle-free, and fun-filled Christmas season.

I know only one person who always has Christmas under control year after year. She is the mother of a close friend. I spent a lot of time at her house during my high school years and always marveled at her proficiency as a homemaker. The house was always clean and neat, ironing always caught up, and kitchen never in disarray, even in the midst of preparing a meal! She made all this seem effortless, remaining calm, cheerful, and relaxed in the midst of our teen-age turmoil.

It was not until I married and moved across the street from her that I realized her secret was the ability to organize and plan ahead. This was especially evident when it came to planning for Christmas. My first inkling of the extent of her preparations came one day in the middle of summer when I helped unload her car after a shopping trip. A stack of gift boxes prompted me to ask if it were someone's birthday.

"Oh, those are Christmas presents," she explained. "I do my Christmas shopping throughout the year so I can take advantage of sales and also have time to find just the right gift for everyone."

That night when I visited my neighbor, I found her husband wrapping packages in Christmas paper. He laughed at my shock at seeing Christmas presents being wrapped in July.

"She wouldn't have it any other way," he smiled. "She does all her Christmas baking well ahead, too. And she usually has the cards addressed before Thanksgiving. When our girls were small, we wanted to be free to have fun with them when the holidays began. Now, we enjoy a bit of Christmas all year, and we're never too rushed to appreciate the season."

For years I have promised myself a Christmas just like my friend's, and now with the help of this section, such a Christmas is possible. All you have to do is fill in the blanks and follow the suggestions! The organization has been done for you.

Think of being finished with Christmas preparations in time to be free to give your family and friends your undivided attention and joyous enthusiasm for the holidays. What a unique gift that will be!

The Twelve Months Of Christmas

A little planning can take the hassle out of the merriest holiday of them all. Here is an easy month-by-month plan that will make next year's Christmas the happiest, easiest, best one ever. And the planning starts early— as early as Christmas Day of 1987.

December

Christmas Day

Take a family portrait in front of the Christmas tree to use on next year's Christmas cards.

The Week After Christmas

Begin "stocking up" for next year at the after-Christmas sales. A list makes shopping a snap. Use the chart on page 140.

Gather those holiday cards, and list names and addresses for next year. Add any new names or addresses to last year's list. Delete names as necessary. Use the lists on pages 164 and 165.

To avoid crowds, shop early or around lunch and dinner time. Make a list to divide with an older son or daughter. Make a mental note of special items you saw before Christmas.

Wrap and store your bargains carefully, double-sacking them in a large plastic bag to prevent exposure to light, dust, and dampness. Refer to your list of purchases before you begin shopping next fall so that you do not duplicate purchases. Use the chart on page 141 to keep track of your purchases made during the year.

A Grateful Heart

Some of the nicest times at Christmas can be the quiet moments of reflection after the hustle and bustle are over. Take a moment to make a list of all those who remembered you and to write them a brief note of thanks. Most of your addresses may be found on your Christmas card list on pages 164 and 165.

January

Begin Gift-Making Early

Long January evenings are a great time to begin making long-term Christmas presents, especially cold weather gifts like quilts, afghans, and sweaters. And if you wait much longer, the materials you need may not be available.

Don't Forget January White Sales

February

Curing The Christmas Budget Blues

Nothing dampens the Christmas spirit faster than an empty pocketbook. Now's the time to gather all those Christmas bills for review so that your Christmas budget can be worked out well in advance. Add a monthly amount to your budget. Use the chart on page 139.

As special gift-buying opportunities come along during the year, use your Christmas account. If the purchase exceeds your savings to date, make a note and reimburse yourself out of the savings you set aside for the next month or so. This is quite likely to be what happens as you take advantage of those January and February sales. This simple plan will not only make next year's Christmas shopping worry free, it will help you stretch your Christmas budget 25% to 50% further.

March

Keep Up With The Family News All Year

Bad weather? What nicer time to curl up in your favorite chair and plan a Christmas newsletter from your family to all your relatives and friends? A lot of newsy items you would like to share will be forgotten if you wait until next December to start your newsletter. So, we've divided the year into the four seasons to make it easy for you to jot down a few choice moments your family shared over the year. You'll be amazed at how much better—and easier—your next year's letter will be. Use "Planning A Christmas Newsletter" on pages 142 and 143.

April

"He who sees things grow from the beginning will have the best view of them."—Aristotle

Plan A Summer Garden With Christmas Giving In Mind

A few good choices include:

Herbs For Drying

Bay	Savory
Basil	Marjoram
Parsley	Oregano
Rosemary	Tarragon
Sage	Dill

Flowers For Pressing

Ferns	Forget-Me-Nots
Pansies	Acacia
Violets	Roses
Geraniums	

Flowers For Sachets And Potpourri

Roses	Lavender
Magnolia	Sweet Peas
Honeysuckle	Violets
Jasmine	Stock

Consult your local library or county extension agent if planting instructions are needed.

Keep An Eye Out For Garage Sales And Flea Markets For Gifts That Can Be Recycled.

May

Plan Your Holiday Vacation Now

If you plan to take a special vacation for the holidays, now is the time to talk with your travel agent, choose your destination, and make your reservations. Holiday resorts fill up fast!

- Double check holiday vacation dates for all students and working family members.

- Make a list of possible destinations. Then visit your travel agent, and bring home materials about each destination.

- After you have selected your destination, talk with your travel agent again, and make all reservations necessary.

Putting Down Holiday Roots

Propagate house plants now for Christmas giving. There are three common ways of propagating house plants: division of a mature plant into two or more parts, making a stem cutting and rooting the stem, or making a leaf cutting and rooting the leaf. For more detailed instructions, consult your favorite gardening book, or try your local library. The following are a few examples of the types of plants which may be propagated by each of the three methods:

Propagation By Division
African violet, airplane plant, asparagus fern, Chinese evergreen, sansevieria

Propagation By Stem Cuttings
Dieffenbachia, dracaena, English ivy, fiddleleaf fig, Norfolk Island pine (makes a beautiful miniature Christmas tree), peperomia, philodendron, rubber plant, schefflera

Propagation By Leaf Cuttings
African violet, begonia, jade plant, peperomia, philodendron, sansevieria

Willow Work

Spring is the time to cut young willow shoots while they are at their most flexible stage. Vines or young willow shoots can be used to make attractive wreaths. (See pages 81, 104, and 105.)

June

"Gather Ye Rosebuds While Ye May"
—Robert Herrick

Preserve Summer's Bounty

Preserving summer's bounty for winter's cold months is like saving sunshine for a rainy day.

Microwave-Dried Flowers

Trim your favorite flowers while they are at their peak, leaving ½-inch stems. Pour a layer of silica gel into a microwave-proof dish. Place the flowers in the dish, and cover evenly with silica gel, making certain the spaces between the petals are filled. Leave no part of the blossoms exposed to the air.

Place a small dish or cup of water in one corner of the microwave. Place the flowers in their dish in the microwave, and heat for 2 to 3 minutes. Allow them to cool for 15 to 20 minutes. Then remove the flowers carefully, one at a time, and carefully brush all silica gel away with a soft brush. After the flowers are completely dry, attach to a stem of florist's wire, and wrap the stem in florist's green tape. Arrange them in an attractive bowl or basket, or store carefully until ready to use.

Potpourri

No gift is a sweeter reminder of your caring than homemade potpourri. Although there are an almost infinite number of potpourri recipes, all are basically a mixture of fragrant flowers or spices, a fixative to preserve the fragrance, and oils to intensify the fragrance. The crowning touch is an interesting jar, dish, or sachet bag to hold your fragrant gift. To make your potpourri, either consult a craft book for recipes or use a simple combination of rose petals, honeysuckle, sweet peas, or violets. Dry slowly over a period of several days or until completely dry. Use 6 cups fresh flower petals. After they are dry, mix with ¼ cup each whole cloves, cinnamon sticks broken into pieces, whole allspice, 1 teaspoon salt, 1 cup orrisroot, and a mixture of ⅛ ounce

each cinnamon oil, lemon oil, rose oil, and ¼ ounce musk oil. Let stand, covered, for 3 to 4 weeks. Divide into containers, and seal tightly until ready to gift-wrap.

Update Your Christmas Newsletter

Jot down a few notes about items of interest that have happened to family members during April, May, and June. Use the space provided on page 142.

July

Be A Crafty Shopper

If do-it-yourself projects are just not your thing, remember that many of the best craft fairs and festivals are held during the month of July. And for the really "crafty" shopper, these events provide a great opportunity to find unique gifts that are homemade or handcrafted and just right for someone on your Christmas shopping list. Most craftspeople have cards you can keep if you do not decide to buy on the spot. (Be sure to list any purchases on your gift list on page 141 so they aren't forgotten in December.)

Order special handmade gifts from talented people in your own hometown. Ordering them in July will allow the craftsmen plenty of time to complete the crafts before Christmas.

Begin Your One-Of-A-Kind Gifts Now

The lazy days of summer are also a good time to begin work on one-of-a-kind presents that will take thought and time to find or complete:

- An out-of-print favorite book, a hard-to-find old record or movie
- A photo album with pictures of the family over the years
- A needlepoint or painted family tree
- A special old toy or doll refurbished for a younger family member
- A family cookbook, including the favorite recipes of all the different cooks in the family with credit properly given and, if you have artistic ability, illustrations provided.

Not only are such personal projects great fun to work on, they bring back the true spirit of Christmas which is sometimes lost in the hectic days of pre-Christmas shopping. And . . . they are guaranteed to please the recipient!

Watch For Unusual Gifts While On Your Summer Vacation

August

Harvest Your Summer Garden Now

Use summer's bounty—from your garden or a friend's, or from your local farmer's market—in gifts to delight the senses on a cold winter day.

Harvesting And Drying Herbs

Cut leafy herbs like basil, savory, and marjoram just before the blossoms form. Cut herbs late in the morning. Wash them quickly, and dry them in a shady spot. Or if you're the impatient type, spread herbs evenly on a baking sheet, and dry them in a slow oven (temperature less than 150 degrees) with the door left open. It takes only minutes, so watch the process carefully.

Thyme, parsley, and rosemary can be dried on trays in a dry, shady spot.

Sage, oregano, marjoram, basil, and savory dry well, hanging in bunches, in a warm place for two days.

Dry the seed herbs like dill, caraway, and fennel, tied in bunches, in a closed paper sack.

Storing Dried Herbs

Crumble or break into the desired size, and store in clean, dry glass containers with airtight covers. Label carefully and, for a nice touch, add your name and the date.

Preserving Fruits And Vegetables

Modern freezing and canning techniques and innovative, simple recipes make it easy to capture the best of summer's delicious fruits and vegetables.

Some easy projects include no-cook jams, mixed vegetable relishes, apple butter, spiced fruit, and chutneys. (See pages 18 through 20.)

Be sure to include any younger children in these projects as the best part of Christmas is still the sharing.

September

Update Your Christmas Newsletter

Your notes should cover all the interesting news items about the family that happened during July, August, and September.

Update And Complete Your Christmas Card List

Use the lists on pages 164 and 165. Delete or correct names and addresses, adding new names and addresses as needed. Get out the cards you selected at the after-Christmas sale and address the envelopes. Signing the cards, writing a brief note, and inserting your Christmas newsletter can come later when you're more in the Christmas spirit.

Shop By Mail

The first of the mail-order catalogs will find their way to your mailbox this month. Keep an eye out for special gifts, and turn down these pages. If a certain gift seems just right, go ahead and order—it's not too soon!

Give Puppy Love

If there is a puppy or perhaps a kitten in a loved one's future this Christmas, inquire now for the perfect pet. You may need to allow several months for the pet to be ready to leave its mother for a new home at Christmas time.

Share Instant Pleasure

September is a good month to mix up several batches of instant hot chocolate or spiced tea mix for friends who love a cup of something hot on cold nights.

Shop For Gifts For The Younger Set

Take in a few back-to-school sales to look for gifts for the younger set. Be sure to take your size chart along. Don't forget to save all receipts just in case something has to be exchanged.

October

Decorate Naturally

Take several walks through the countryside to gather dried materials, nuts, and cones that can be used for winter decorations.

Some good choices would include pine cones of several different sizes, bittersweet with its bright orange berries, and kudzu, grape, or other vines to be used to make wreaths.

Make a harvest wreath with autumn colors to be used from now until your Christmas wreath goes up. Make an extra one for a friend.

Update Your Shopping Progress

Take a quick inventory of gifts to date to determine your shopping progress. Make a special note of items that need to be taken care of immediately. If necessary, contribute additional funds to your Christmas savings account to carry out the rest of your plans.

Schedule Your Christmas Photograph Now

If you didn't take a family photo by last year's tree and you've decided you'd like to include one in this year's cards, make plans to get everyone together for a formal or informal photography session.

Knit, Pearl, Knit, Pearl

Now is the time to press forward on the finishing touches of all projects begun last winter such as sweaters, afghans, or other handmade craft items. In November, you'll be too busy.

Sweets To Eat

Spend an evening going through your cookbook and recipe files to select the cookies, candies, and other treats you want to bake for your family, for entertaining, or for gifts. Assemble these recipes so that they can be found quickly when you're ready to cook. Use the chart on page 127.

November

Plan Your Christmas Wish List

Post a Christmas Wish List for the members of the family in a prominent place, such as the refrigerator door, and attach a pencil on a string. You may want to limit the number of items and watch the list change as favorite requests come and go.

Christmas Is For Children

Help your children make decorations for the house and tree or to give as gifts.

Have your children list their special friends and discuss ideas for exchanging gifts.

Set aside a Saturday or two to shop with young children before the crowds make shopping difficult. Shopping for friends and family members is a nice way to include the children in the joy of giving as well as receiving.

While shopping for gifts for your children's friends, buy one or two "generic" gifts that would be appropriate for a boy or a girl. Wrap them to have on hand for the unexpected.

Getting An Early Start

If your family draws names for exchanging gifts at Christmas, your Thanksgiving gathering may be the best time for this.

The week after Thanksgiving is a perfect time to begin baking the candies, cookies, and any other items which can be frozen or kept fresh in tins. Use chart on page 127.

Use your Holiday Calendar to begin blocking out all holiday plans and activities. Place it within easy view of everyone and encourage them to use it. If you plan to travel during the holidays, early November is the time to finalize all plans and to make reservations that haven't already been made.

Order all magazine subscriptions and mail-order gifts *before* December 1st.

Spend an evening putting the final touches on your Christmas newsletter. Let other family members read what you've said, adding their own note if they wish. Have enough copies made for everyone on your Christmas card list. Once this is done, it's time to get out the cards, sign them, insert the newsletter or write any notes you want to, and have them on hand ready to mail by December 8th.

December

It's Finally Here!

Set aside one evening for all last-minute wrapping and another for putting the final touches on the Christmas decorations.

If you plan to have a party during the holidays, now is the time to complete your plans. See pages 130 and 131.

Mail your Christmas cards and packages by the 8th to ensure Christmas delivery. Use the chart on page 138.

Discuss in advance any new Christmas tradition you'd like to introduce to your family. Giving everyone notice and getting their reaction will make it truly a "family" tradition.

Early in the month is a good time to make final plans with all interested relatives. Discuss where and when the traditional holiday gathering will be held and who will be responsible for what. Early planning reduces confusion and the chance for misunderstanding.

Note on your holiday calendar the day and time for going to get the tree. Make a special event of the decorating, and serve cookies and hot chocolate to all.

Consider an "old-fashioned" caroling party as a fun and easy way to get together with your neighbors during the holidays.

Begin preparation of your traditional family Christmas dinner early. Check the information on pages 128 and 129 to make certain nothing is overlooked.

Now just sit back and relax. You're ready for your merriest, easiest Christmas ever!

Holiday Calendar
1987

Be at the right place—at the right time

Saturday, November 28

Thursday, December 3

Sunday, November 29

Friday, December 4

Monday, November 30

Saturday, December 5

Tuesday, December 1

Sunday, December 6

Wednesday, December 2

Monday, December 7

Holiday Calendar
1987

Tuesday, December 8

Sunday, December 13

Wednesday, December 9

Monday, December 14

Thursday, December 10

Tuesday, December 15

Friday, December 11

Wednesday, December 16

Saturday, December 12

Thursday, December 17

Holiday Calendar
1987

Friday, December 18

Wednesday, December 23

Saturday, December 19

Thursday, December 24

Sunday, December 20

Friday, December 25

Monday, December 21

Saturday, December 26

Tuesday, December 22

Sunday, December 27

Holiday Calendar
1987

Monday, December 28

Saturday, January 2

Tuesday, December 29

Sunday, January 3

Wednesday, December 30

Monday, January 4

Thursday, December 31

Tuesday, January 5

Friday, January 1

Wednesday, January 6

Trimming Your Tree Safely

Safety first during the holidays

It's hard to believe, but that beautiful twinkling tree can be a fire hazard. In addition, it may be a source of other safety problems, especially for children and pets.

Take a moment to make your Christmas tree as safe as it is beautiful.

Make certain you choose a fresh tree or a flame-resistant artificial tree to reduce the chance of fire.

Store the tree outside in a bucket of water until time to bring it indoors. This will prevent drying out.

Mist the tree occasionally once it's brought indoors to keep branches fresh.

Clean the tree stand with a weak mixture of household bleach and water to kill microorganisms that can reduce the tree's water intake. Set the tree up away from all heat sources.

Fill the tree stand with enough lukewarm water to cover the cut end of the trunk, and check frequently to keep water at this level.

Use decorations that are noncombustible or flame-resistant.

Buy only lights that have the Underwriters Laboratories label. Discard any lights that have frayed or exposed wires. Fasten bulbs securely, and don't let hot bulbs touch needles or branches. Put no more than three sets of lights on a single extension cord. Keep all lights and wires away from the water supply.

Keep all fragile ornaments and ornaments of glass beyond the reach of small children and pets.

Use lead-free tinsel.

Turn off tree lights and other electrically-lighted decorations whenever you leave the house or go to bed.

Dispose of the tree as soon as it starts dropping lots of needles.

Christmas Baking

Plan a Christmas cooking spree

Timesaving Recipe File

Item	Occasion	Cookbook With Recipe	Page
_____	_____	_____	___
_____	_____	_____	___
_____	_____	_____	___
_____	_____	_____	___
_____	_____	_____	___
_____	_____	_____	___
_____	_____	_____	___

Shopping List

_____	_____
_____	_____
_____	_____
_____	_____
_____	_____
_____	_____
_____	_____

Containers Needed For Storage

Item To Be Stored	Type Container	Quantity
_____	_____	_____
_____	_____	_____
_____	_____	_____
_____	_____	_____
_____	_____	_____

Christmas Dinner

To satisfy our hearts as well as our hunger

Date _____   Place _____

Menu

Recipe Title	Cookbook	Page
_____	_____	_____
_____	_____	_____
_____	_____	_____
_____	_____	_____
_____	_____	_____
_____	_____	_____
_____	_____	_____
_____	_____	_____

Shopping List

Non-Food Items	Food Items
_____	_____
_____	_____
_____	_____
_____	_____
_____	_____
_____	_____

Christmas Dinner Agenda

Countdown to delicious food and cherished memories

2 Weeks Before

Notify guests   _____

Plan menu   _____

Order flowers   _____

1 Week Before

Shop for non-food items   _____

Check on availability of items
such as:

extra tables and chairs   _____

utensils   _____

serving dishes   _____

table decorations   _____

candles   _____

tablecloth   _____

napkins   _____

silverware   _____

cookware   _____

glasses   _____

china   _____

place cards   _____

other

_____   _____

3 Days Before

Complete heavy cleaning   _____

Remind everyone to decide
what to wear, and make certain
everything is ready   _____

2 Days Before

Plan very simple meals to
serve between now and the dinner   _____

Buy all perishable food items   _____

Wash and trim vegetables   _____

Prepare any dishes that can be
made in advance and stored   _____

1 Day Before

Prepare all dishes that can be
assembled a day ahead to be
served cold or cooked the
next day   _____

Make extra ice   _____

Pick up flowers, meat, ice, and
other last-minute items   _____

Day Of Dinner

Arrange the centerpiece   _____

Make one last check of the house   _____

Set the table for buffet service   _____

Prepare and cook all
remaining dishes   _____

Party Planning

What's A Holiday Without A Party!

If the thought of being hostess at a holiday party dampens your holiday spirit—take heart. The guide below will help you take it one step at a time.

The first step is to make your general plans without worrying about the details. Then, fill out the chart on page 131.

List the people you'd like to invite, and note the number.

List the food you'd like to serve—everything from soup to nuts.

List the beverages—coffee, tea, soda, juice, liquor, and mixers.

List other necessary items such as cocktail napkins, plastic glasses, dripless candles, ice, flowers, holiday plates, napkins, ashtrays, and records or tapes.

One Week Before Party Time

Shop for canned goods and other nonperishable items. Order now any items that can be reserved for pick-up later.

Four Days Before Party Time

Check to see if you have all the serving dishes, trays, and silverware you'll need. If necessary, borrow additional items from a friend. Decide on seating arrangements, and rent or borrow additional tables and chairs. Wash and iron table linens.

Three Days Before Party Time

Do all heavy cleaning. Get the family to lend a hand.

Two Days Before Party Time

Buy all perishable grocery items. Wash and trim vegetables. Prepare candies, cookies, and similar treats, and store them in airtight containers.

One Day Before Party Time

Prepare all dishes that can be served cold or cooked the day of the party. Make extra ice if needed. Plan any meals other than the party meal so that they are simple and easy to clean up, or plan to have the family eat out.

Party Time

Pick up flowers, meat, ice, and any other last-minute items. Put the finishing touches on the house, and check all bathrooms to make certain they are company ready. Set the table and arrange the centerpiece. Set up buffet and drink areas if needed. Prepare and cook all remaining dishes. Have a great time!

Party Planner

Occasion _____ **Theme** _____

Number Of People _____ **Date/Time** _____

Guest List (Mail invitations or call 2 weeks prior to the date of the dinner.)

_____	_____
_____	_____
_____	_____
_____	_____
_____	_____
_____	_____

Table Service

Tables _____	Chairs _____
Tablecloth _____	Napkins _____
Buffet runner _____	Napkin rings _____
Centerpiece _____	Candles _____
China _____	Silver _____
Glassware _____	Favors _____

Menu

Recipe Title	Cookbook	Page
_____	_____	_____
_____	_____	_____
_____	_____	_____
_____	_____	_____
_____	_____	_____

Holiday Party Styles

For holiday festivities we need to add a special touch to our usual party attire. All it takes is a little forethought, and you can look sensational from top to toe.

Hairstyles

Now's the time to consider a slightly, not extremely, different look. If you usually wear your hair down, consider putting it up, or vice versa. Add a few random curls at the temples or neck. Dust a little glitter through your hair. Tuck a sprig of holly or, if you're feeling adventurous, a sprig of mistletoe in your hair. Ribbons will add a colorful touch.

Clothes

Perhaps buying two or three new party dresses is out of the question, but you definitely need a different look. Take a classic black or cream skirt you already own and buy a glamorous new sweater— of angora, or with a plunging neckline worn front or back, or perhaps with sequins or pearls. If you sew, make a simple long skirt with elastic waistband in a bright red and green plaid taffeta. And you can make a matching stole of the same material.

Accessories

If your dress is simple, more glittering accessories are called for. If your dress glitters, keep the accessories to a minimum. Try adding a lace or ruffled collar to a dress or sweater, a touch of gold with belt or jewelry, glamorous satin or jeweled evening pumps, or hosiery in patterns or with rhinestone appliques.

Makeup

Chances are that the shades of makeup you find most flattering are the ones you should continue to use during the holidays. However, you might want to try a face powder with a touch of shimmer for your face and the tops of your shoulders. Use lipstick in your favorite shade, but in a shimmering version. Be a little more daring with eye shadow and eye liner as well, or try a mascara in a color. And don't forget a touch of your favorite scent. Treat your nails to a clear bright color or a color with glitter added.

Pre-Party Countdown

One of the most helpful things you can do to look your best for any holiday party is to give yourself an extra hour to get ready. Start with ten minutes R & R, lying down with a cool cloth over your eyes. Then, take a nice long soak in a warm tub. Shampoo your hair, and do your nails at your leisure. Before you dress for the party, take a minute and have a high energy snack so that you don't arrive at the party ravenous—and blow your diet for the week.

Our Christmas Party
1987

Making merry with friends and family

a photograph memory

Gift Idea Generator

Gifts that money can't buy

All of us have had the sinking feeling that *this year* we won't ever be able to come up with gifts for some of the more challenging people on our lists. Or perhaps it's just that some people are very dear to us, and we want our appreciation to be reflected in especially thoughtful gifts.

We've gathered together several categories of gifts for you to consider. They will surely spark ideas for truly thoughtful gifts for these special people.

The Gift Of Our Time

What's more precious at Christmas time than a few extra hours to do with as we please. Consider sending a friend a "gift certificate" for an hour or two of your time to run a few errands, baby-sit a child, or address cards. The options are almost limitless, and the gift is sure to be appreciated. But, put a little extra thought into this offer to be sure it is something truly needed by that particular friend.

The Gift Of Our Talents

Each of us has special talents which someone else may not share. Perhaps you are adept at arranging flowers or decorating. Perhaps you play an instrument, have an artistic flair, or bake delicious cookies. Chances are that you like doing what you do best. So why not offer to share your special talent, no matter how large or small, with a friend whose talents lie in a different area. Perhaps you can have a talent exchange! Your offer might take the form of a "gift certificate" to be used whenever it's needed, or you can make the offer for a specific time or place.

The Gift Of Our Love

A note to say how much you appreciate a friend all year round, a quiet visit to a shut-in, a handmade card—these and many more simple messages that say we care are especially appreciated at the holidays. This is the time of year more than any other when it is appropriate to "let our feelings show."

If you're still undecided, choosing just the right gift may be as easy as looking on the next page.

Gifts Of Your Time

Breakfast in bed
Car wash
Day of maid service
Night of baby-sitting
Limo service for an evening
Addressing Christmas cards
Running some errands
Washing dishes after a party
Taking an outing with a shut-in
Taking children to shop for presents for their parents
Wrapping gifts

Gifts Of Entertainment And Relaxation

Tickets to a sporting event, concert or play
Trip to a health spa
Lesson(s) for a special interest such as
  cooking class or hobby class
Subscription to a magazine in a special area of interest

Gifts Of Special Personal Meaning

Handmade family tree or coat of arms
Special photo, certificate or award framed for hanging
Poem you wrote for someone special
Record of music with special meaning for you both
Gift of a favorite flower or plant

Gifts Of A Unique Nature

Picnic basket outfitted for an indoor winter picnic
Colorful planter with a bag of soil and several packets of seeds
Bird feeder and bird guidebook
Stamp album and several starter packets of stamps
Old family photos enlarged and framed
Tarot cards with instruction book
Computer horoscope
Handwriting analysis or fun trip to the fortune teller
Tape of the voices of the children in the family or relatives who
  live far away, or a special message from you if you can't be home for Christmas
Gift of live entertainment for the family Christmas dinner, perhaps a
  joint effort by the talented members of the family
Stationery package with paper, envelopes, stamps and address book complete with the
  names and addresses of family and friends
Telephone gift certificates
Your own unique ideas:

_____

_____

_____

Family Favorites

It's the little things, the thoughtful things, that you do that make a gift really special. One of the best ways to make finding that special gift a little easier is to make a note of some favorite things of your favorite people. Let everyone on your gift list fill out the chart below to help you decide what to give them. You might be surprised at what you learn!

Names						
Favorite Color						
Favorite Music						
Favorite Scent						
Favorite Hobby						
Favorite Toy Or Gadget						
Favorite Sport						
Favorite Food						
Favorite Flower						
Favorite Type Book						
Favorite "Night Out"						
What I'd Really Like						

The "fitting" gift for everyone

One of the first (and best) things you can do to make giving for any occasion easy, and still keep your gift idea a surprise, is to have friends and family fill out a size chart. Be sure to include "types" of sizes such as petite, misses, junior, half-sizes, small, medium, large, extra-large, slim, or chubby. Now you'll never have to wonder if your gift will be "fitting," and you'll eliminate the need to return a treasured gift.

Name		Name		Name	
Height	Weight	Height	Weight	Height	Weight
Coat	Slacks	Coat	Slacks	Coat	Slacks
Dress	Pajamas	Dress	Pajamas	Dress	Pajamas
Suit	Bathrobe	Suit	Bathrobe	Suit	Bathrobe
Sweater	Shoes	Sweater	Shoes	Sweater	Shoes
Shirt	Hat	Shirt	Hat	Shirt	Hat
Blouse	Gloves	Blouse	Gloves	Blouse	Gloves
Skirt	Ring	Skirt	Ring	Skirt	Ring

Name		Name		Name	
Height	Weight	Height	Weight	Height	Weight
Coat	Slacks	Coat	Slacks	Coat	Slacks
Dress	Pajamas	Dress	Pajamas	Dress	Pajamas
Suit	Bathrobe	Suit	Bathrobe	Suit	Bathrobe
Sweater	Shoes	Sweater	Shoes	Sweater	Shoes
Shirt	Hat	Shirt	Hat	Shirt	Hat
Blouse	Gloves	Blouse	Gloves	Blouse	Gloves
Skirt	Ring	Skirt	Ring	Skirt	Ring

Name		Name		Name	
Height	Weight	Height	Weight	Height	Weight
Coat	Slacks	Coat	Slacks	Coat	Slacks
Dress	Pajamas	Dress	Pajamas	Dress	Pajamas
Suit	Bathrobe	Suit	Bathrobe	Suit	Bathrobe
Sweater	Shoes	Sweater	Shoes	Sweater	Shoes
Shirt	Hat	Shirt	Hat	Shirt	Hat
Blouse	Gloves	Blouse	Gloves	Blouse	Gloves
Skirt	Ring	Skirt	Ring	Skirt	Ring

Holiday Mailing Tips

Christmas Cards

U.S. Postal Regulations state that envelopes should be rectangular and no smaller than 3½ x 5 inches. Envelopes which are larger than 6⅛ x 11½ inches will require extra postage. Be sure to mail by December 8th to ensure delivery by Christmas.

Packages

Make certain that all packages are wrapped in a sturdy box with additional cushioning for fragile items. Close and secure all packages with tape designed for mailing. It is a good idea to include your name, return address, and the address of the recipient on the inside of the box in case the packaging is damaged. Make certain that the return address and address of the recipient are printed clearly on the outside of the package. Don't forget the zip code.

Packages may be sent by U.S. Postal Service parcel post in weights of 70 pounds or less and measurements of 108 inches in combined length and girth.

Check with the post office concerning mailing date for overseas packages for Christmas delivery.

If sending packages by any other delivery service, be sure to check with them for their regulations and delivery schedule during the holiday season.

Category	Examples	Container	Cushioning	Closure
Soft Goods	Shirt, towel	Strong cardboard-padded mailing envelope		Sealed with reinforced tape
Liquids	Perfume, food gifts	Waterproof interior containers	Absorbent	Sealed with filament tape
Powders	Dusting powder, spices	Airtight interior container		Sealed with filament tape
Perishables	Cheese, fruit	Airtight interior container	Absorbent	Sealed with filament tape
Fragile items	Glass, camera	Fiberboard (minimum 175-pound test container)	Foamed plastic or padding	Sealed and reinforced with filament tape
Awkward items	Globe, shears	Fiberboard tubes or boxes	Molded plastic foam or fiberboard shapes	Sealed with tube ends equal to side wall strength

A Holiday Budget
1988

Avoid Christmas budget blues

A. Gather November and December's cancelled checks and all charge card receipts. Make a note of any cash purchases.

B. Total last year's expenses:

Gifts, including cards, postage, etc.	$ _____
Entertainment expenses	$ _____
Special food purchases	$ _____
Decorations and tree	$ _____
Travel	$ _____
Special holiday clothes expenses	$ _____
Charitable contributions	$ _____
Other	$ _____
Total:	$ _____

C. Divide total by 12 $ _____

This is approximately the amount you will need to set aside each month to make next Christmas the most carefree ever. And just think, if you place these savings in a savings account, your money will even earn interest!

Budget Worksheet

"Stocking Up"
Shopping The After-Christmas Sales

Note special items as you find them for
smart buying later

Item	Quantity	Source/Store
Cards	_____	_____
Gift-wrap	_____	_____
Ribbon	_____	_____
Bows	_____	_____
Ornaments	_____	_____
Tree lights	_____	_____
Tinsel	_____	_____
Gift boxes and containers	_____	_____
Artificial wreath	_____	_____
Home decorations	_____	_____
Table decorations	_____	_____
Party items	_____	_____
Plates	_____	_____
Glasses	_____	_____
Candles	_____	_____
Napkins	_____	_____
Gifts with Christmas motifs	_____	_____
Guest towels	_____	_____
Mugs	_____	_____
Aprons	_____	_____
Stocking stuffers	_____	_____
Holiday cooking items	_____	_____
_____	_____	_____
_____	_____	_____
_____	_____	_____
_____	_____	_____
Holiday craft materials	_____	_____
_____	_____	_____
_____	_____	_____
_____	_____	_____
Other	_____	_____
_____	_____	_____
_____	_____	_____
_____	_____	_____
_____	_____	_____
_____	_____	_____

"Stocking Up"
Gifts Bought Throughout The Year
Making a list and checking it twice

Name Of Recipient	Item	Where I Stored It

A Christmas Newsletter

Notes And News Of Our Family

Keep up with the news all year long

Winter

Spring

Notes And News Of Our Family

Summer

Fall

Comfort & Joy

Christmas Memories

*"God gave us memory that we
might have roses in December"*

—James M. Barrie

Roses in December and Christmas all year long. Memory calls forth past joys to be savored over and over again, giving us a haven to get in touch with ourselves and a place to lift our spirits.

Christmas memories are cherished because Christmas is the time of the year when families are gathered in one place. It is a time to catch up on the events of the past year, marvel at how fast our children are growing up, share family jokes that make us laugh at ourselves, and feel the comfort and joy of being with loved ones.

As the new generations of our family mature and have families of their own, memories become even more meaningful. To a great extent, we *are* our memories. And for this reason, we want to keep the good ones with us forever. This chapter is brimming with ways to do just that, both from a practical and a sentimental standpoint.

It's nice *not* to have to rely on memory for the practical side of Christmas. There is a place in this chapter to record those who made holiday visits and to list others who sent cards or letters or who called.

It is also comforting to know you won't be giving the same present for the second or third time if you use the special gifts list and the page for "Gifts to Remember." And, no gifts will be forgotten at thank-you time if you note them on the 1987 Gift Record.

There are pages where you can record, both in pictures and in words, every wonderful moment of Christmas. Fill in an account of the holiday parties you attend on page 149. With the help of "Our Christmas Eve," recapture the night before Christmas, even filling the stockings once again—in writing.

Create your Christmas story on page 153, and remember special moments that reflect "The True Spirit Of Christmas," even favorite scents, sights, tastes, and sounds! And, there is a page for the reflections of your children of any age.

Most of us will never outgrow the childhood pleasure of making our own personal scrapbooks. This section will bring back those wonderful memories.

There are pages for photograph memories of your home, tree, and wreath as well as of family and friends together. Other pages will keep your Christmas card and Christmas church bulletin. The 'doing' provides as much fun as the recalling of memories during Christmases to come.

For us, the joys of today are the memories of tomorrow. Our memories become family history for future generations, a heritage experienced in the pages of this memory book.

The Christmas "Family Tree" includes a place for the names of all family members who were present for Christmas 1987, a place for special friends, and a place for those who could not be there but were remembered. There is a place under the tree for the family pet.

Our Home At Christmas

It is Christmas in the mansion,
Yule-log fires and silken frocks;
It is Christmas in the cottage,
Mother's filling little socks.

It is Christmas on the highway,
In the thronging, busy mart;
But the dearest, truest Christmas
Is the Christmas in the heart.
—Author Unknown

a photograph memory

Our Christmas Tree

"How lovely are thy branches"

This year we had a _____ tree, chosen by _____

with help and lots of advice from _____ .

When we got it home, _____

helped decorate it.

Our Christmas Wreath

So remember while December
Brings the only Christmas day,
In the year let there be Christmas
In the things you do and say;
Wouldn't life be worth the living
Wouldn't dreams be coming true
If we kept the Christmas spirit
All the whole year through?
                    —Anonymous

a photograph memory

Our Holiday Parties

"Tis the season to be jolly...."

On _____ I attended a party given by _____ .
We had _____ and _____ to eat. Games
we played were _____ . The party decorations included
_____ . The thing I liked most about the
party was _____ .
Several of my favorite people were there including _____
_____ and _____ .

On _____ I attended a party given by _____ .
We had _____ and _____ to eat. Games
we played were _____ . The party decorations included
_____ . The thing I liked most about the
party was _____ .
Several of my favorite people were there including _____
_____ and _____ .

On _____ I attended a party given by _____ .
We had _____ and _____ to eat. Games
we played were _____ . The party decorations included
_____ . The thing I liked most about the
party was _____ .
Several of my favorite people were there including _____
_____ and _____ .

On _____ I attended a party given by _____ .
We had _____ and _____ to eat. Games
we played were _____ . The party decorations included
_____ . The thing I liked most about the
party was _____ .
Several of my favorite people were there including _____
_____ and _____ .

Our Christmas Eve

"Twas the night before Christmas when all through the house...."

This year we shared
Christmas Eve with . . .

_____

_____

_____

_____

_____ .

As part of our tradition, we . . .

_____

_____

_____

_____

_____ .

For dinner we had . . .

_____

_____

_____

_____ .

The highlight of the evening
came when . . .

_____

_____

_____

_____ .

Special Christmas Eve
presents included . . .

_____

_____

_____

_____ .

We left these snacks for
Santa Claus . . .

_____

_____

_____

_____ .

The last one to bed was . . .

_____ .

The last one to sleep was . . .

_____ .

When the clock is striking twelve,
   When I'm fast asleep,
Down the chimney broad and black,
   With your pack you'll creep;
All the stockings you will find
   Hanging in a row;
Mine will be the shortest one,
   You'll be sure to know.

Johnny wants a pair of skates;
   Susy wants a sled;
Nellie wants a picture book;
   Yellow, blue and red;
Now I think I'll leave to you
   What to give the rest;
Choose for me, dear Santa Claus,
   You will know the best.

—Old Song

_____'s Stocking Gifts

_____

_____

_____'s Stocking Gifts

_____

_____

_____'s Stocking Gifts

_____

_____

_____'s Stocking Gifts

_____

_____

_____'s Stocking Gifts

_____

_____

_____'s Stocking Gifts

_____

_____

_____'s Stocking Gifts

_____

_____

Our Christmas Church Bulletin

"O come, let us adore Him. . . . "

Our Christmas Story
1987

For Christmas breakfast we had _____
_____
_____ .

Those present were _____
_____
_____ .

We dressed in _____
_____
_____ .

The Christmas feast:

The cook was _____ .

Family members present were _____
_____ .

The guests were _____
_____
_____ .

The table decorations included _____
_____ .

The menu this year was _____
_____ .

We wore _____
_____
_____ .

Those especially dear to us who could not be with us this year were _____
_____
_____ .

The highlight of the day was _____
_____
_____ .

The True Spirit Of Christmas

"Love and joy come to you...."

Sometimes it's easy to forget the true spirit of Christmas. This year, our family took a few moments to celebrate the real meaning of Christmas.

A special moment shared with someone in need of comfort _____

_____

_____

A special gift for someone less fortunate _____

_____

_____

A special quiet moment shared with someone in our family _____

_____

_____

_____

The Scents, Sights, Tastes, and Sounds of Christmas

Long after the gifts have been opened, memories of Christmas linger. All we have to do is shut our eyes, and in our mind we can hear, smell, and taste the joys of Christmas.

Favorite Scents (Spices, perfumes, aromas . . .)   **Favorite Tastes** (Sweets, treats, goodies to eat . . .)

_____ _____   _____ _____

_____ _____   _____ _____

_____ _____   _____ _____

Favorite Sights (Lights, smiles, movies . . .)   **Favorite Sounds** (Carols, music, laughter . . .)

_____ _____   _____ _____

_____ _____   _____ _____

_____ _____   _____ _____

What Christmas Means To Me

A keepsake of my children's thoughts

My children's Christmas thoughts _____

_____

_____

_____

_____

_____

_____

_____

_____

_____

_____

_____

_____

_____

_____

_____

_____

_____

_____

Our Favorite Christmas Moments

When the rush is over and all the packages have disappeared from beneath the tree, take a moment to sit quietly before the twinkling lights, reflecting on all the activities of the season and recalling those special times which will become treasured memories.

This year's special memories will include:

_____

_____

_____

_____

_____

_____

_____

_____

_____

_____

Family members' favorite moments:

Name _____

Favorite Moment

_____

_____

_____

Name _____

Favorite Moment

_____

_____

_____

Name _____

Favorite Moment

_____

_____

_____

Name _____

Favorite Moment

_____

_____

_____

Name _____

Favorite Moment

_____

_____

_____

Name _____

Favorite Moment

_____

_____

_____

Our Holiday Visitors

Remembering those who made the holiday a special one

Name _____   **Day of Visit** _____

_____   _____

_____   _____

_____   _____

_____   _____

_____   _____

_____   _____

_____   _____

_____   _____

_____   _____

_____   _____

_____   _____

_____   _____

_____   _____

_____   _____

Our Christmas Photographs
1987

Picture-perfect memories

More Picture-Perfect Memories

The Joy Of Giving

Somehow not only for Christmas
But all the long year through,
The joy that you give to others
Is the joy that comes back to you.

And the more you spend in blessing
The poor and lonely and sad,
The more of your heart's possessing
Returns to make you glad.
—John Greenleaf Whittier

Special Gifts	Recipient	Giver

Gifts To Remember

What Christmas would be complete without opening the presents we have selected for each other—all those well-kept secrets, all those mysterious packages we've been eyeing for days?

Presents that seemed to bring special joy to the recipient:

Name _____   Name _____

Gift _____   Gift _____

Name _____   Name _____

Gift _____   Gift _____

Name _____   Name _____

Gift _____   Gift _____

Our funniest gift amused us by _____ .

The biggest gift was _____ .

We were most surprised by _____ .

Our tiniest present was no larger than _____ .

The most special handmade gift was crafted by _____ .

A most unexpected gift was _____ .

The most exotic gift came from _____ .

The most creatively wrapped present looked like _____ .

We were touched by the most thoughtful gift of _____ .

The most delicious gift tasted like _____ .

Our Christmas Gift Record
1987

Well, it finally came . . . Christmas Day. All the shopping was done and the presents wrapped. A sense of anticipation was shared by all. The first one awake was _____ ; however, _____ soon followed. _____ was our sleepy head. To our surprise, we found that Santa Claus had come during the night and left a sack full of goodies for everyone.

Name	Gift	From
_____	_____	_____
_____	_____	_____
_____	_____	_____
_____	_____	_____
_____	_____	_____
_____	_____	_____
_____	_____	_____
_____	_____	_____
_____	_____	_____
_____	_____	_____
_____	_____	_____
_____	_____	_____
_____	_____	_____
_____	_____	_____

Our Christmas Card
1987

"Glad tidings we bring . . . . "

Special Holiday Greetings

Best wishes from our house to yours

Name	Address	Called	Sent A Card	Sent A Letter

Special Holiday Greetings

Best wishes from near and far

Name	Address	Called	Sent A Card	Sent A Letter
_____	_____	___	___	___
	_____			
_____	_____	___	___	___
	_____			
_____	_____	___	___	___
	_____			
_____	_____	___	___	___
	_____			
_____	_____	___	___	___
	_____			
_____	_____	___	___	___
	_____			

Patterns

HOLIDAY TABLE COVER

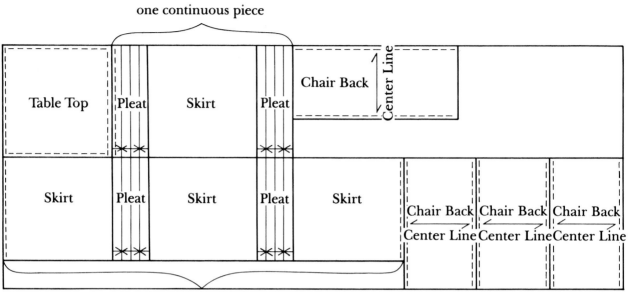

one continuous piece

Table Top	Pleat	Skirt	Pleat	Chair Back

Center Line

Skirt	Pleat	Skirt	Pleat	Skirt

Chair Back Center Line Chair Back Center Line Chair Back Center Line

one continuous piece

HOLIDAY PATCHWORK FLAGS

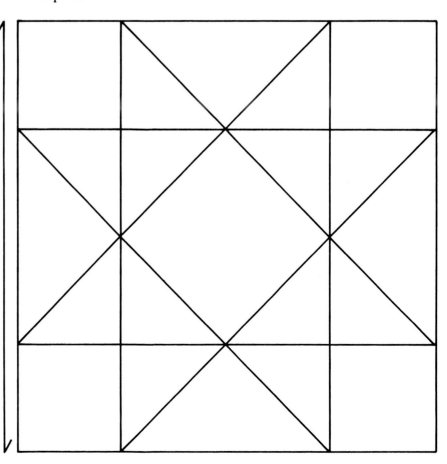

Enlarge to 6" square

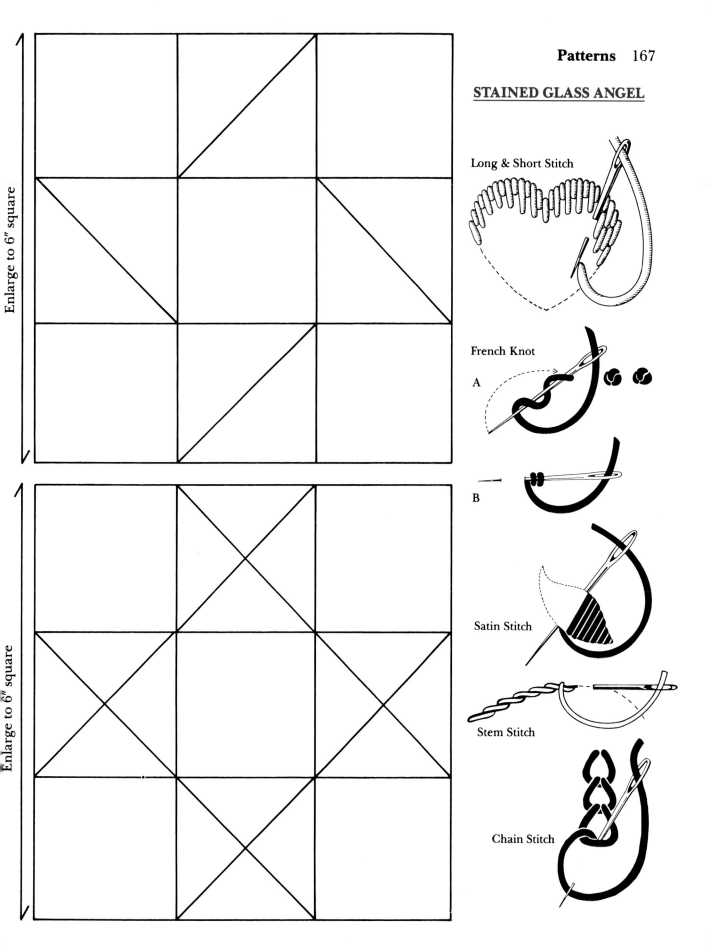

Enlarge to 6" square

Enlarge to 6" square

STAINED GLASS ANGEL

Long & Short Stitch

French Knot

A

B

Satin Stitch

Stem Stitch

Chain Stitch

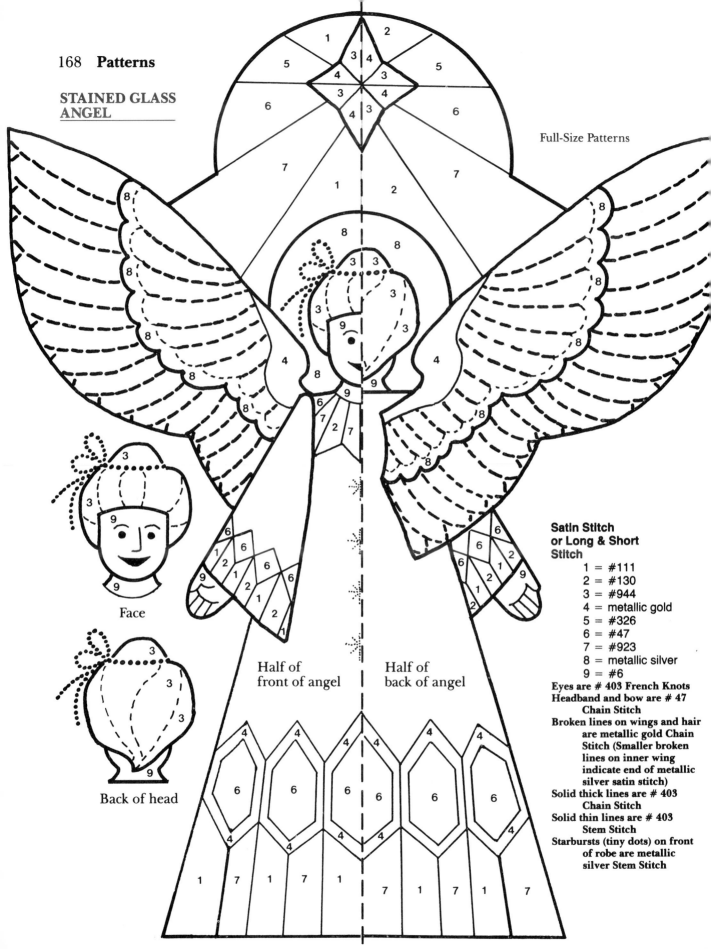

**STAINED GLASS
ANGEL**

Full-Size Patterns

Face

Back of head

Half of
front of angel

Half of
back of angel

**Satin Stitch
or Long & Short
Stitch**

1 = #111
2 = #130
3 = #944
4 = metallic gold
5 = #326
6 = #47
7 = #923
8 = metallic silver
9 = #6

Eyes are # 403 French Knots
**Headband and bow are # 47
Chain Stitch**
**Broken lines on wings and hair
are metallic gold Chain
Stitch (Smaller broken
lines on inner wing
indicate end of metallic
silver satin stitch)**
**Solid thick lines are # 403
Chain Stitch**
**Solid thin lines are # 403
Stem Stitch**
**Starbursts (tiny dots) on front
of robe are metallic
silver Stem Stitch**

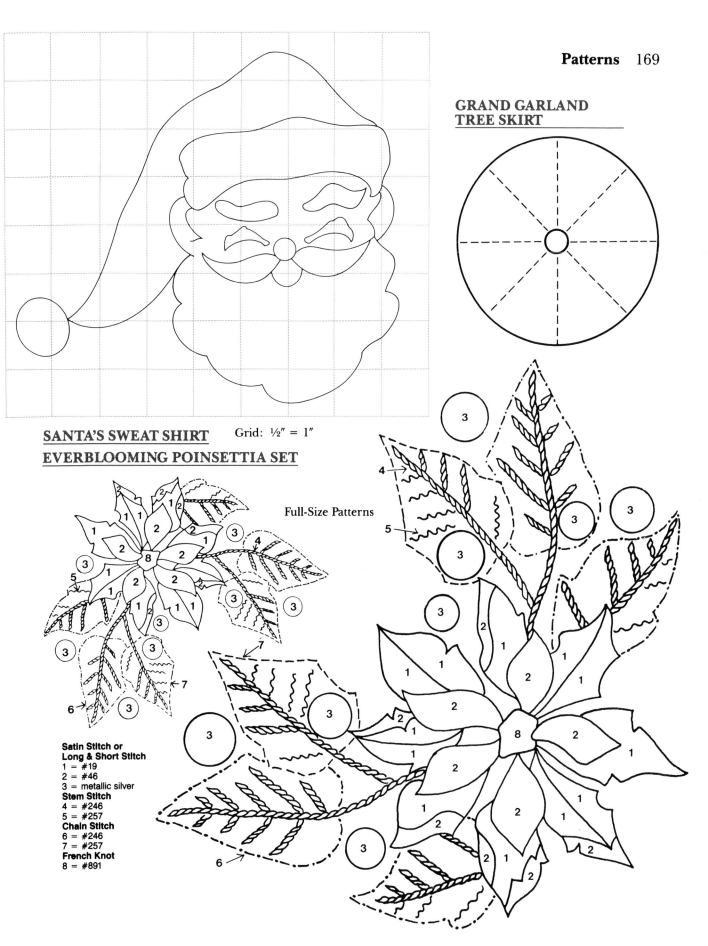

GRAND GARLAND TREE SKIRT

SANTA'S SWEAT SHIRT
EVERBLOOMING POINSETTIA SET

Grid: ½″ = 1″

Full-Size Patterns

**Satin Stitch or
Long & Short Stitch**
1 = #19
2 = #46
3 = metallic silver
Stem Stitch
4 = #246
5 = #257
Chain Stitch
6 = #246
7 = #257
French Knot
8 = #891

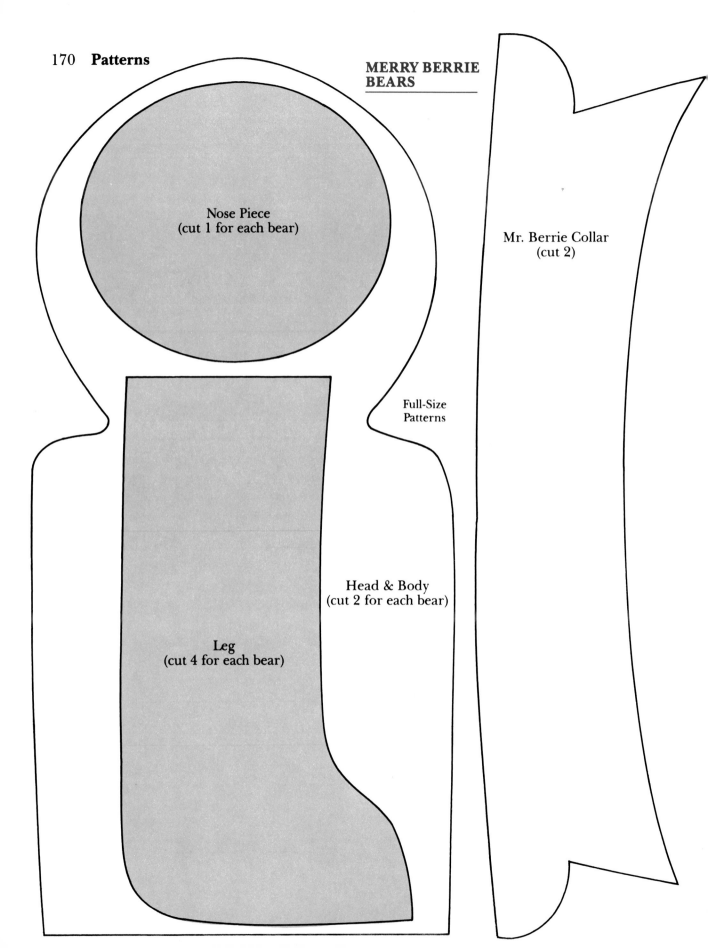

Nose Piece
(cut 1 for each bear)

Mr. Berrie Collar
(cut 2)

Full-Size
Patterns

Head & Body
(cut 2 for each bear)

Leg
(cut 4 for each bear)

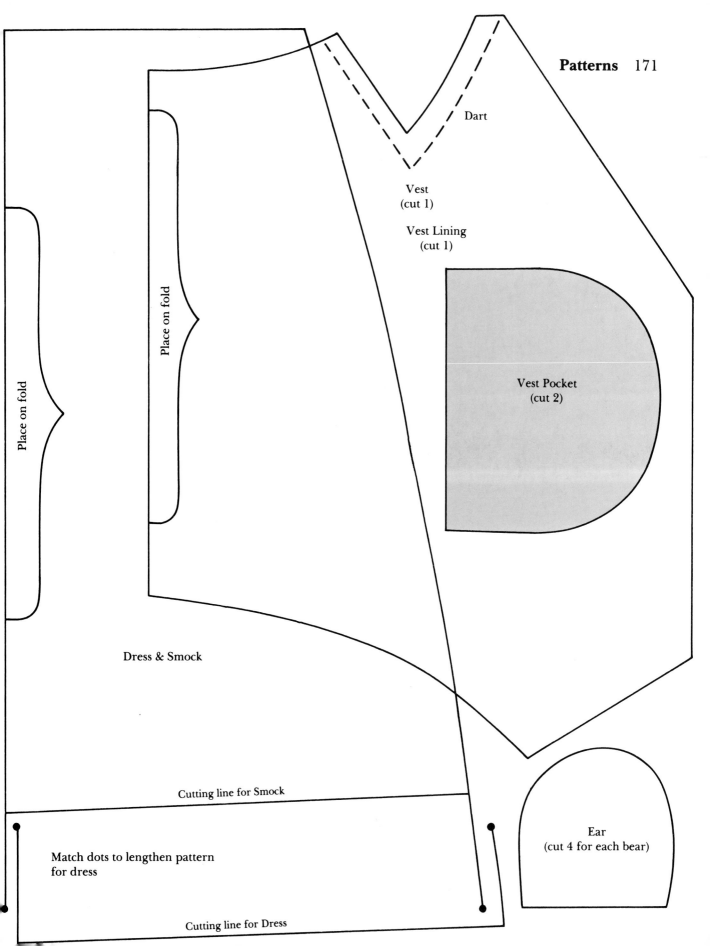

Dart

Vest
(cut 1)

Vest Lining
(cut 1)

Vest Pocket
(cut 2)

Place on fold

Place on fold

Dress & Smock

Cutting line for Smock

Match dots to lengthen pattern
for dress

Cutting line for Dress

Ear
(cut 4 for each bear)

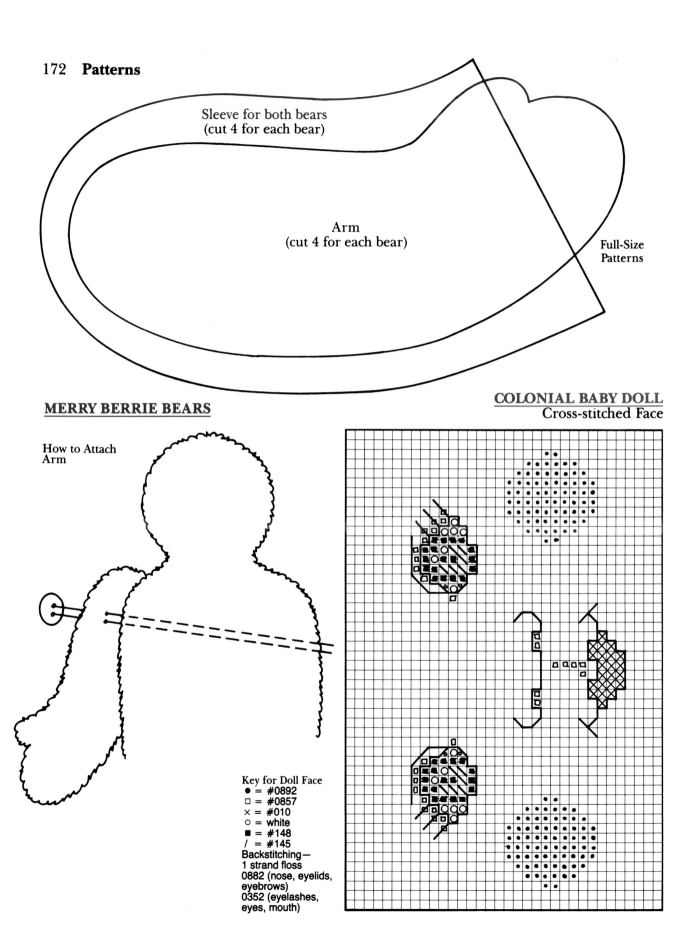

Sleeve for both bears
(cut 4 for each bear)

Arm
(cut 4 for each bear)

Full-Size
Patterns

MERRY BERRIE BEARS

How to Attach
Arm

COLONIAL BABY DOLL
Cross-stitched Face

Key for Doll Face
● = #0892
□ = #0857
× = #010
○ = white
■ = #148
/ = #145
Backstitching—
1 strand floss
0882 (nose, eyelids,
eyebrows)
0352 (eyelashes,
eyes, mouth)

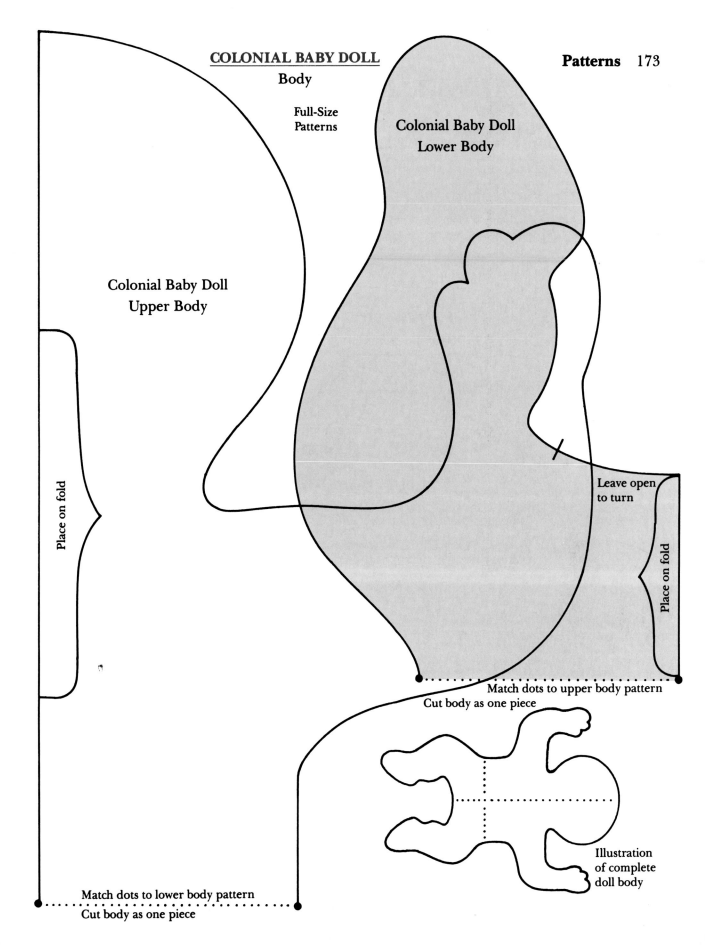

COLONIAL BABY DOLL
Body

Full-Size
Patterns

Colonial Baby Doll
Lower Body

Colonial Baby Doll
Upper Body

Place on fold

Leave open
to turn

Place on fold

Match dots to upper body pattern
Cut body as one piece

Illustration
of complete
doll body

Match dots to lower body pattern
Cut body as one piece

COLONIAL BABY DOLL
Clothes: Each square = 1″

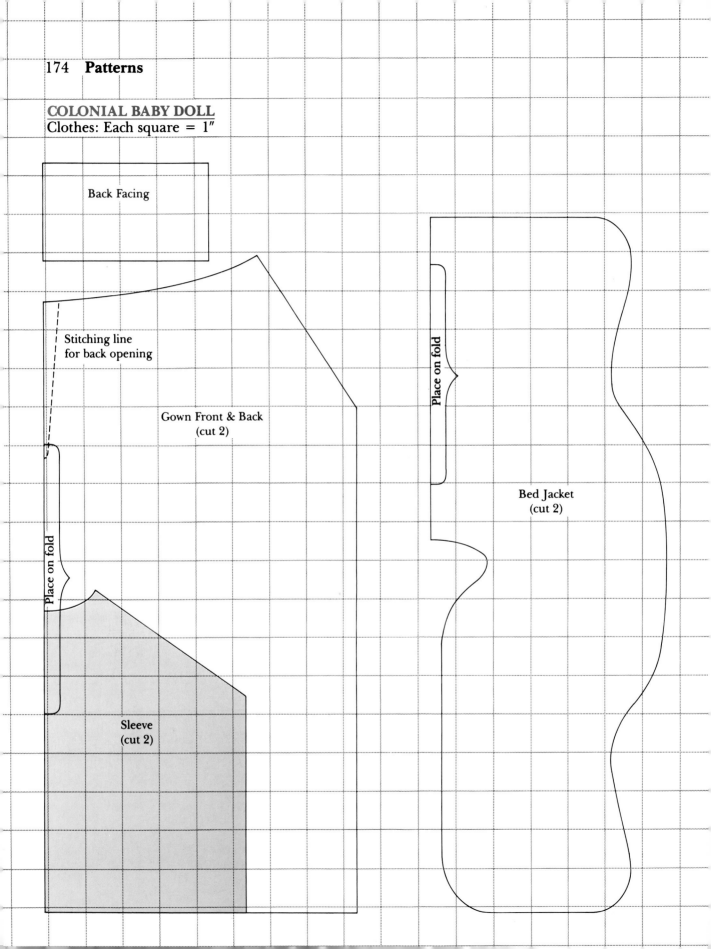

Back Facing

Stitching line
for back opening

Gown Front & Back
(cut 2)

Place on fold

Place on fold

Sleeve
(cut 2)

Bed Jacket
(cut 2)

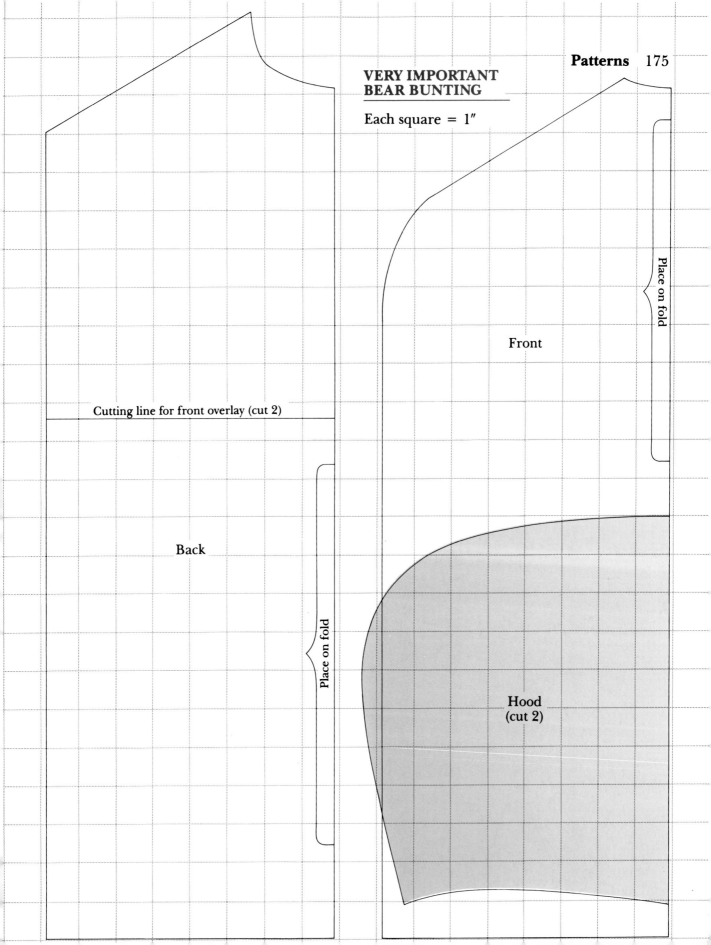

**VERY IMPORTANT
BEAR BUNTING**

Each square = 1″

Place on fold

Front

Cutting line for front overlay (cut 2)

Back

Place on fold

Place on fold

Hood
(cut 2)

Place on fold

HEIRLOOM QUILT

Angel Robe

Match dots of upper robe and lower robe

Cut robe as one piece

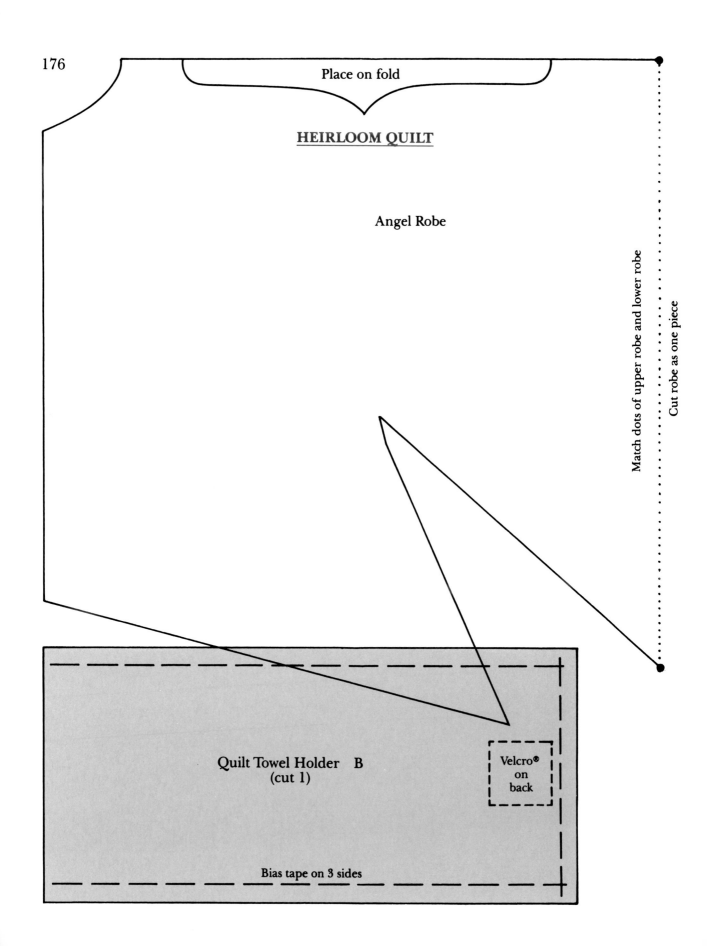

Quilt Towel Holder   B
(cut 1)

Velcro®
on
back

Bias tape on 3 sides

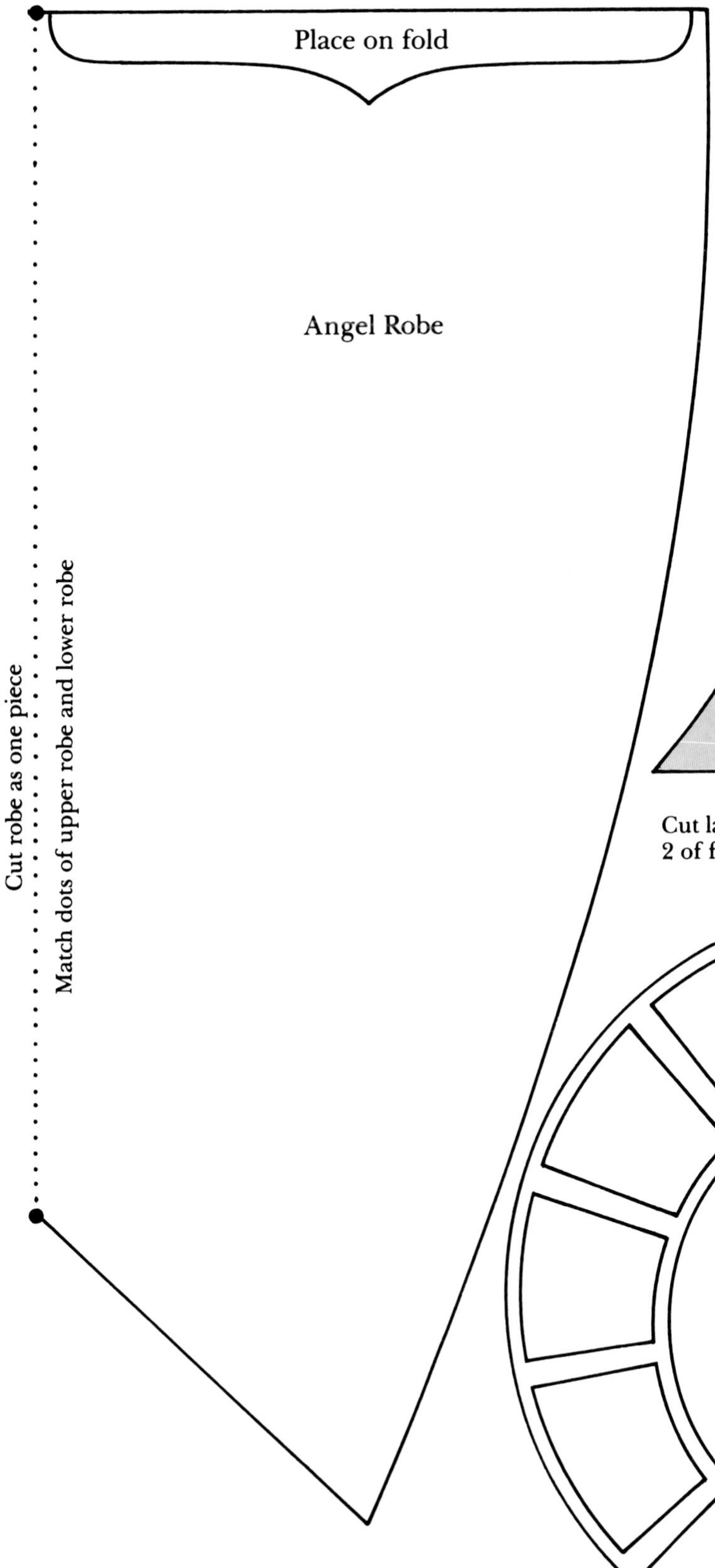

Place on fold

Angel Robe

Cut robe as one piece

Match dots of upper robe and lower robe

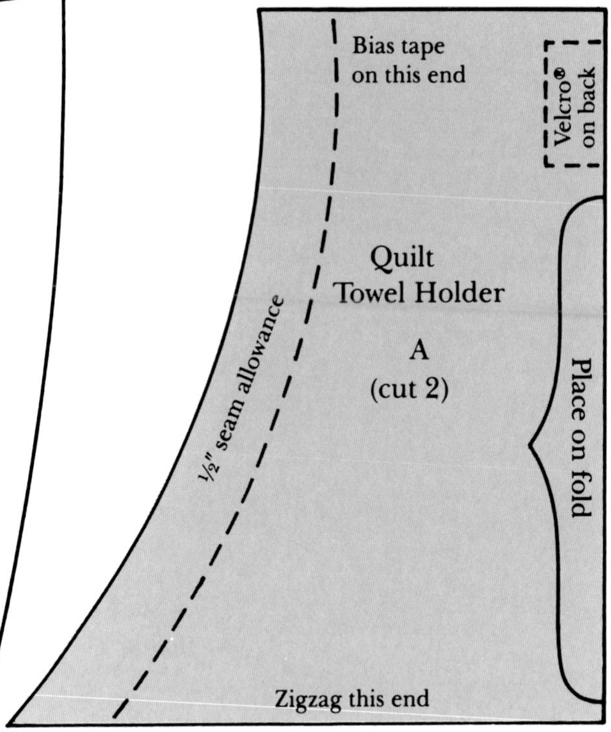

Bias tape
on this end

Velcro® on back

Quilt
Towel Holder

A
(cut 2)

½" seam allowance

Place on fold

Zigzag this end

Cut large circles: 1 of card stock,
2 of felt

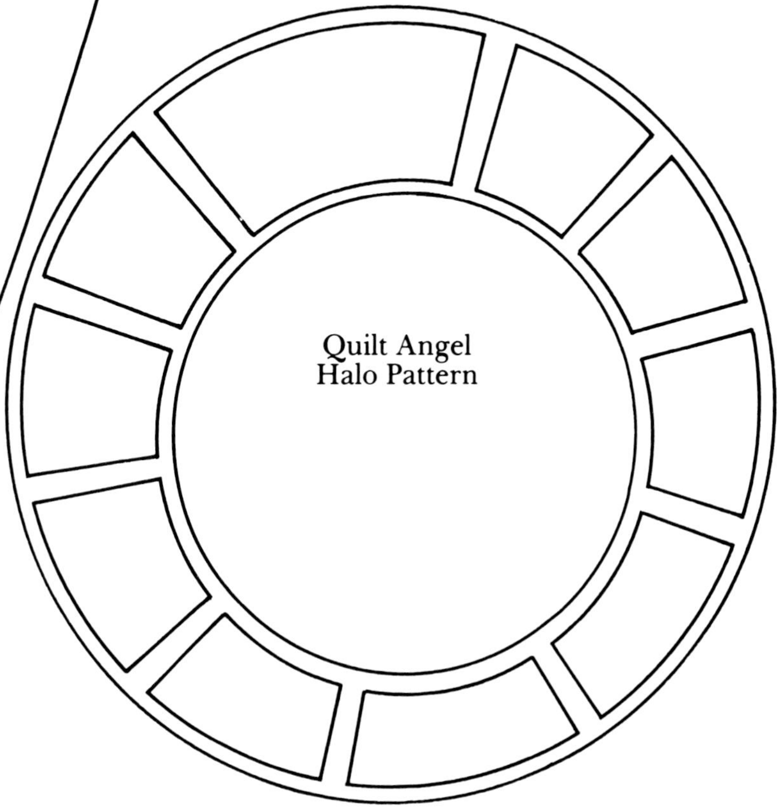

Quilt Angel
Halo Pattern

ABCDEFGHIJK
LMNOPQRSTU
VWXYZ

REBECCA'S FIRST CHRISTMAS

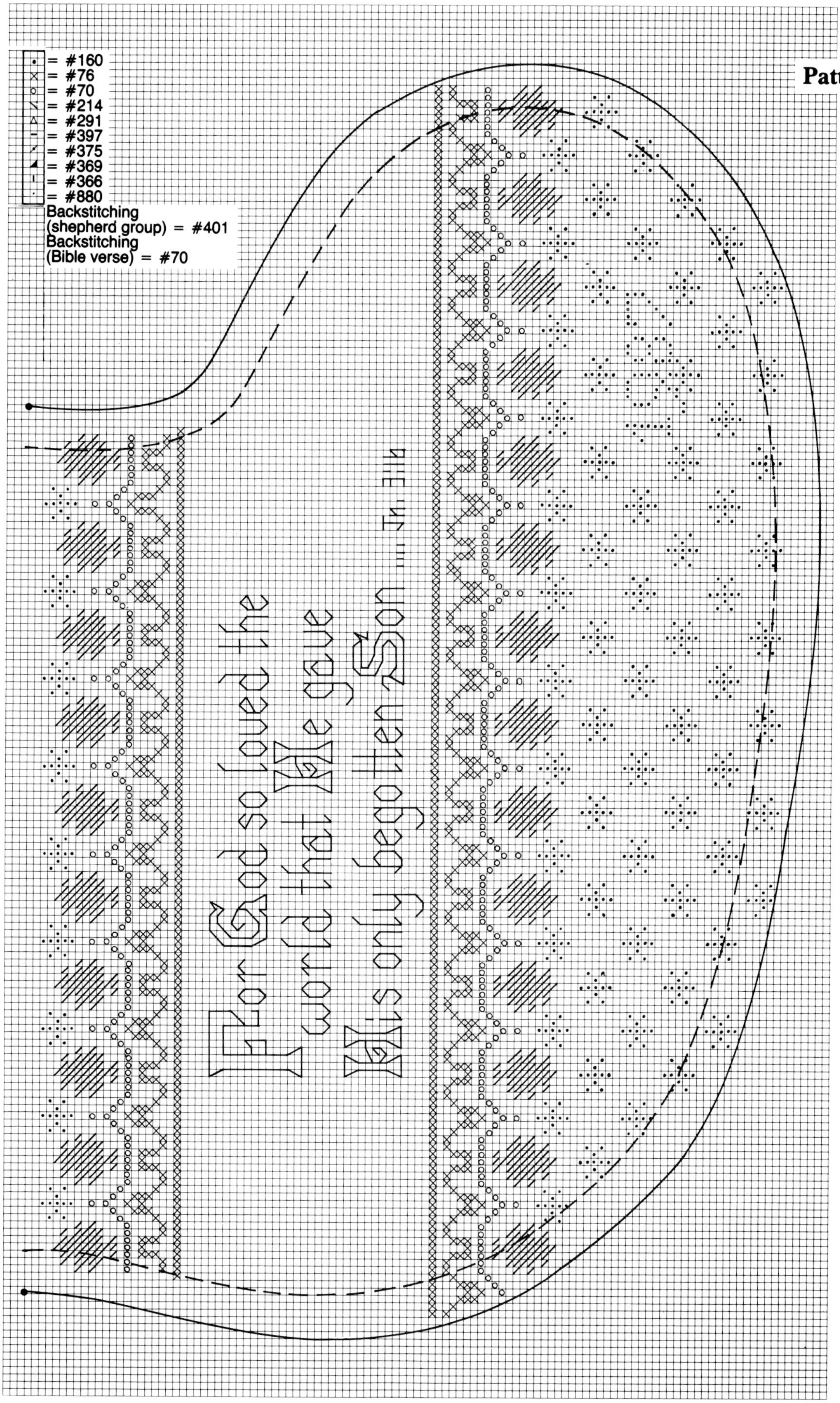

Legend:
- · = #160
- × = #76
- ○ = #70
- ＼ = #214
- △ = #291
- — = #397
- ／ = #375
- ◢ = #369
- ‖ = #366
- ‖ = #880

Backstitching (shepherd group) = #401
Backstitching (Bible verse) = #70

For God so loved the world that He gave His only begotten Son ... Jn. 3:16

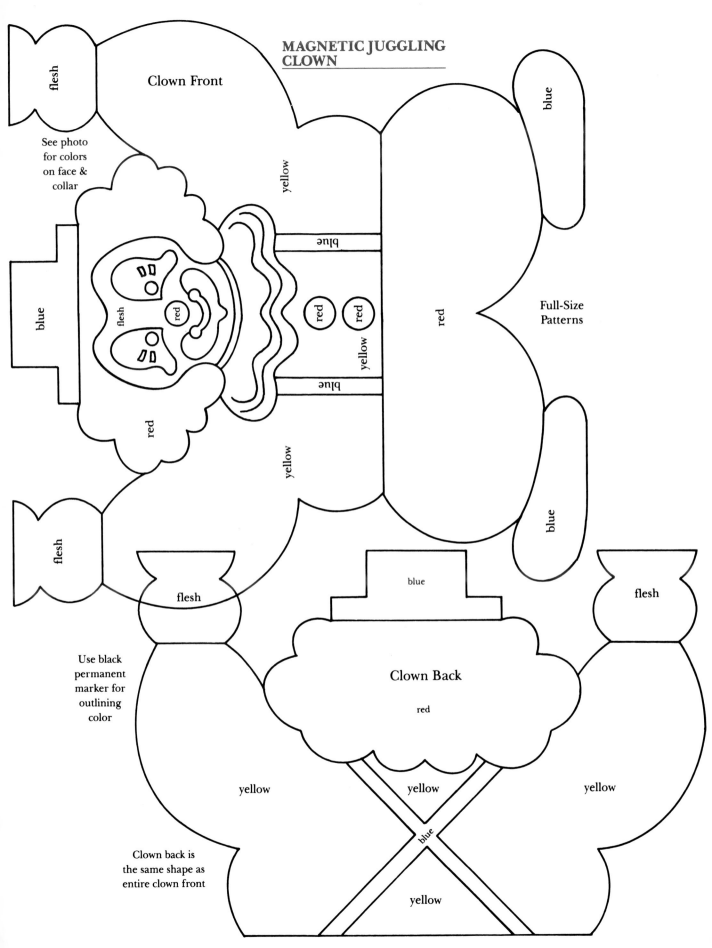

MAGNETIC JUGGLING CLOWN

Clown Front

flesh

See photo
for colors
on face &
collar

yellow

blue

blue

blue

red

red

Full-Size
Patterns

blue

red

flesh

red

yellow

flesh

yellow

flesh

yellow

flesh

Use black
permanent
marker for
outlining
color

flesh

blue

Clown Back

red

yellow

yellow

blue

yellow

yellow

Clown back is
the same shape as
entire clown front

yellow

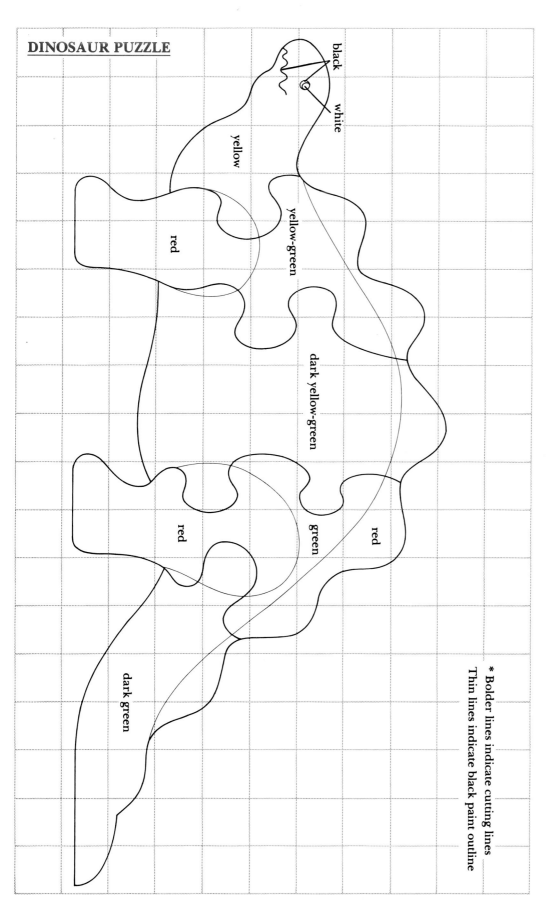

DINOSAUR PUZZLE

black

white

yellow

yellow-green

red

dark yellow-green

red

green

red

dark green

Each ½″ = 1″

Bolder lines
indicate
cutting lines

* Bolder lines indicate cutting lines
Thin lines indicate black paint outline

Recipe Index

184

Photograph Index

Recipes in this index are listed clockwise from top of each photograph.

Contributor Index

HERITAGE HOUSE, INC., a division of The Southwestern Company, offers a varied selection of porcelain collectibles. For details on ordering, please write: Heritage House, Inc., P.O. Box 1408, Nashville, TN 37202-1408